From Resurrection to Return:

Perspectives from Theology and Science on Christian Eschatology

The PACT series is a set of publications of the Public and Contextual Theology (PACT) Strategic Research Centre, Charles Sturt University, Australia. Each volume in the series focuses on an issue or series of related issues in the disciplines of public and contextual theologies. The series explores how public and contextual theologies are worked out in the Australasian region, in collaboration with similar centres in South Africa, Western Europe and North America.

Editorial Committee
William Emilsen
Tom Frame
James Haire
Elizabeth MacKinlay
Clive Pearson

1. *Dodging Angels on Saturday*, Graeme Garrett, 2005
2. *'Into the World You Love'*, edited by Graeme Garrett, 2002

From Resurrection to Return:
Perspectives from Theology and Science on Christian Eschatology

edited by
James Haire
Christine Ledger
and
Stephen Pickard

ATF Press
Adelaide

Text copyright © 2007 remains with the individual authors for all papers in this volume and with ATF Press for the collection and introduction.

All rights reserved. Except for any fair dealing permitted under the Copyright Act, no part of this book may be reproduced by any means without prior permission. Inquiries should be made to the publisher.

First published 2007

National Library of Australia
Cataloguing-in-Publication data

> From resurrection to return : perspectives from theology
> and science on Christian eschatology.

ISBN 9781920691820 (pbk.).

1. Eschatology. 2. Natural Theology. 3. Theology. 4. Religion and science. I. Haire, James, 1946- . II. Ledger, Christine, 1956- . III. Pickard, Stephen K. IV. Title.

236

Published by
ATF Press
An imprint of the Australasian Theological Forum
PO Box 504
Hindmarsh
SA 5007
ABN 68 314 074 034
www.atfpress.com

Cover design by Astrid Sengkey

Contents

Contributors   vii

Introduction   1

Cosmic Future: Progress or Despair?   5
    NT Wright

When He Appears   32
    NT Wright

The Bodily Resurrection of Jesus as a First Instantiation of a
    New Law of the New Creation: Wright's Visionary New
    Paradigm in Dialogue with Physics and Cosmology   54
    Robert John Russell

Between the First and Second Comings   95
    Ted Peters

Resurrection and the Costs of Evolution: A Dialogue with
    Rahner on Noninterventionist Theology   112
    Denis Edwards

A Purposeful Creation: Evolution, Convergence and Eschatology   134
    Graham J O'Brien

Resurrection and Cosmic Eschatology   157
    Neil Ormerod

The Invasion of Memory: A Psychological Perspective on
    Trauma in the Experience of God   172
    Bruce Stevens

Index   185

Contributors

Denis Edwards is a Senior Lecturer in Systematic Theology in the School of Theology of Flinders University. He teaches for the Catholic Theological College within the Adelaide College of Divinity and is a priest of the Roman Catholic Archdiocese of Adelaide. He was actively involved in setting up the Flinders University and Adelaide College of Divinity Centre for Theology Science and Culture and serves on its board, and is a member of the International Society for Science and Religion. Recent publications include *Breath of Life: A Theology of the Creator Spirit* (2004) and *Ecology at the Heart of Faith* (2006), both published by Orbis Books.

James Haire, AM, is Director of the Public and Contextual Theology Strategic Research Centre, Executive Director of the Australian Centre for Christianity and Culture, and Professor of Theology at Charles Sturt University, all based in Canberra, Australia. He is a former President of the Uniting Church in Australia, and a former President of the National Council of Churches in Australia. He served as a theologian in Indonesia for thirteen years, and has been lecturing in Indonesia for the past thirty-five years.

Christine Ledger lectures at St Mark's National Theological Centre and the School of Theology of Charles Sturt University (CSU) in Canberra and is a member of the Public and Contextual Theology Research Centre (PACT) of CSU. Her special areas of interest are the theology of technology, the theology of creation, ecclesiology and ecumenical studies. She has served in the leadership of the World Student Christian Federation, the Christian Conference of Asia and the National Council of Churches in Australia and as Manager of the Australian Centre for Christianity and Culture and Manager of PACT CSU.

Graham O'Brien is an ordained Anglican priest in the Nelson Diocese and has recently been appointed vicar of the Parish of Picton, in the Marlborough Sounds. He has a PhD in cellular and molecular biology (Canterbury University, New Zealand), three years post-doctoral

viii   *From Resurrection to Return*

experience in molecular virology (Auckland University), a bachelor's degree in theology (Auckland University/The College of St John the Evangelist), and is now completing a MTh through the Tyndale-Carey Graduate School. Graham is also member of the InterChurch Bioethics Council, representing the Anglican, Methodist and Presbyterian Churches of Aotearoa New Zealand.

Neil Ormerod is Professor of Theology at the Australian Catholic University. He is widely published in Australia and overseas, with articles in *Theological Studies, Irish Theological Quarterly* and *Heythrop Journal* to name a few. His latest book is *Creation Grace and Redemption* published by Orbis Press. His special areas of interest are the doctrine of the Trinity and ecclesiology. His next major project is a book on globalisation and the mission of the church in collaboration with Australian Pentecostal theologian Shane Clifton.

Ted Peters is Professor of Systematic Theology at Pacific Lutheran Theological Seminary and the Graduate Theological Union in Berkeley, California, USA. He is co-founder and co-editor of *Theology and Science* for the Center for Theology and the Natural Sciences. His writings include *God — The World's Future* (Fortress 2000) and *Anticipating Omega* (Vandenhoeck and Ruprecht 2006). Along with Robert John Russell and Michael Welker, he is co-editor of *Resurrection: Scientific and Theological Perspectives* (Eerdmans 2003).

Stephen Pickard is Assistant Bishop in the Anglican Diocese of Adelaide and Adjunct Associate Professor at Charles Sturt University (CSU). He was previously Associate Professor and Head of the School of Theology of CSU and Director of St Mark's National Theological Centre in Canberra, Australia. He chaired the Science and Theology Focus Group of the CSU Strategic Research Centre for Public and Contextual Theology (PACT), which organised the consultation where the papers in this book were presented. His research interests include science and theology, theology of creation and ecclesiology.

Robert J Russell is founder and Director of the Center for Theology and the Natural Sciences (CTNS) and is the Ian G Barbour Professor of Theology and Science in Residence at the Graduate Theological

Union. He is a leading researcher and spokesperson for the growing international body of theologians and scientists committed to a positive dialogue and creative mutual interaction between these fields. He is the author of *Cosmology, Evolution, and Resurrection Hope: Theology and Science in Creative Mutual Interaction* (Pandora Press, 2006). He has co-edited a five volume CTNS/Vatican Observatory series on science and divine action. He recently co-edited *Resurrection: Theological and Scientific Assessments* (Eerdmans, 2002) and edited *Fifty Years in Science and Religion: Ian G Barbour and His Legacy* (Ashgate, 2004). He is co-editor of the journal *Theology and Science* and principal investigator of 'STARS: Science and Transcendence Advanced Research Series'.

Bruce A Stevens is a clinical and forensic psychologist. He is Director of Counselling at Southern Cross College and an Associate Professor in the Sydney College of Divinity. He has written three books and *Cross Fire! Psychologists Dealing with Cross-examination in Court* will be published by Australian Academic Press in mid-2007. He is an Adjunct Senior Lecturer in Clinical Psychology at University of Canberra. He is married to Jennie with four adult children.

NT (Tom) Wright is Bishop of Durham (Church of England). He taught New Testament studies for twenty years in Cambridge, McGill and Oxford universities before becoming Dean of Lichfield in 1994, Canon of Westminster in 2000 and Bishop of Durham in 2003. He has been a visiting professor at many institutions, including the Hebrew University in Jerusalem, the Harvard Divinity School and the Gregorian University in Rome. He is the author of over forty books at both scholarly and popular levels and has broadcast frequently on radio and television. Tom Wright is married to Maggie and they have four adult children and two grandchildren.

Introduction

The closely related disciplines of public and contextual theologies represent a new and significant way in which theology is being carried out around the world. They presuppose the classical inheritance of the Christian faith and of Christian theology, but recognise the need for a hermeneutic that is responsive to a changing world. We no longer inhabit cultures that take for granted a working knowledge of Christian belief and practice. Our societies are now subject to global movements and are a diverse mixture of cultures, faiths and secularism. On the one hand, there may be a residual Christian frame of reference in some, particularly Western, societies, but the relevance of theology is often no longer self-evident in these societies. On the other hand, in other parts of the world, particularly in Asia, Africa and Latin America, the interactions between Christianity and culture are often quite vibrant.

Public and contextual theologies have arisen partly in protest against the privatisation of Christianity and the dominance of Western culture. They are concerned with how biblical and theological disciplines can both engage particularity and speak to the contemporary world. These forms of theology recognise that theology competes in a public domain in which there are a range of ideologies and philosophies. Public and contextual theologies must be willing to interact with, and respond to, insights from other disciplines. Such theologies are designed to explore the relevance of fundamental Christian beliefs.

We believe that public and contextual theologies are central to the expression of the gospel. The ways in which the good news transforms our social life and enhances civic trust is the burden of our work.

This volume deals with eschatology, a central issue in Christian theology. Indeed, at times in Christian history, eschatology has been the starting point from which all of Christian theology and discipleship have been viewed. It has also been a major impetus to the expression of Christianity in the public sphere. Moreover, eschatology has at times been a driving force in the way in which theology has been expressed contextually.

2   *From Resurrection to Return*

This book is the fruit of a consultation held in Canberra, Australia in March 2006, hosted by the Public and Contextual Theology Strategic Research Centre (PACT) of Charles Sturt University (CSU) in association with the Australasian Theological Forum (ATF), the Centre for Theology, Science and Culture of Flinders University, the Institute for the Study of Christianity in an Age of Science and Technology (ISCAST), St Mark's National Theological Centre and the Australian Centre for Christianity and Culture (ACC&C). The theme was 'From Resurrection to Return: Perspectives from Theology and Science on Christian Eschatology'.

The consultation was fortunate to have three fine internationally renowned speakers to stimulate discussion. They were Bishop NT (Tom) Wright, Bishop of Durham, and a popular New Testament scholar, Professor Ted Peters, professor of systematic theology at Pacific Lutheran Theological Seminary, Berkeley, and Professor Robert Russell, founder and director of the Center for Theology and Natural Sciences, Berkeley. Their knowledge and insight in biblical studies, systematic theology and science and the way in which they engaged each other in conversation set the stage for the whole meeting. Indeed, what was particularly distinctive about this consultation was the fruitful way in which these speakers and their disciplines met each other and engendered a great deal of creative interdisciplinary discussion. This book captures this flavour.

Of the fourteen papers presented by other conference participants, there is room for only four here. Each was chosen on the basis of its closeness to the theme. Together they provide a diversity of perspectives and approaches.

NT Wright challenges two dominant ways in which contemporary Christians understand God's purposes in the world. He calls these 'evolutionary optimism' and 'souls in transit'. The first understands the world as being in a state of progress and the second as heading towards material collapse. While both have profound implications for our eschatological understanding, Wright proposes that they have little in common with the view of early Christians who 'believed that God was going to do for the whole cosmos what he had done for Jesus at Easter'.

He goes on to propose a picture of cosmic redemption and new creation based on the exegesis of key biblical passages.

Introduction 3

NT Wright explores the implications of this picture of cosmic redemption for our understanding of 'the second coming' of Jesus. He suggests that this Jesus' appearing is not like that of a spaceman from another world but rather involves the transformation of the world, of God being all in all. This transformation began with the bodily resurrection of Jesus. Wright likens this resurrection to a 'prototype' of the world's final redemption where heaven and earth meet. He argues that confidence in this transformation should shape the church's worldview and mission in the world.

Robert Russell takes Wright's exposition of the historicity of the bodily resurrection of Jesus and engages it with contemporary discussions of theology and science. He stresses the importance of the empty tomb in illustrating that 'matter matters eschatologically', that is the bodily resurrection of Jesus heralds cosmic transformation. He goes on to propose a new paradigm whereby Jesus' resurrection is understood as a 'first instantiation of a new law of creation'.

Ted Peters develops the theme of transformation introduced by Wright and Russell. In doing so, he explores historical understandings of Jesus' resurrection and theological understandings of our resurrection into the new creation. He concludes that God's promise of a new creation will include the changes in the laws of nature that Russell elaborates. To live in anticipation of such transformation is to engage in what he calls 'beatitudinal living' whereby the church strives to live in the light of God's eschatological promise.

Denis Edwards addresses a theology of divine action that takes into account the costs of evolutionary processes—costs such as the suffering of human beings and other creatures and the loss which accompanies beauty and diversity in these processes. He develops the themes of eschatological power and nonintervention as he elaborates his theology of divine power. He concludes that the resurrection, rather than being a miracle that defies the laws of nature, comes from the creative power of God and gives meaning and direction to the whole universe.

Graham O'Brien proposes a theology of purpose in which evolution is understood as producing 'inevitable humans'. This theology of purpose encompasses an eschatological view of creation moving toward completion and communion with God. O'Brien draws on the thinking of biologist, Simon Conway Morris.

From Resurrection to Return

Neil Ormerod draws the distinction between the end of human history and the end of cosmic history. He maintains that scientific understandings of the size and age of the universe require us to review our theological understandings of the resurrection and eschatology. Ormerod explores physical principles such as the conservation of matter and energy and the implications for our understanding of the origins of the universe and the resurrection. He notes that such questions raise difficult issues for theology that must be grappled with if faith and reason are to be held together.

Bruce Stevens brings a psychological perspective to the conversation on eschatology. In particular, he addresses the themes of trauma and violence in the context of the crucifixion and resurrection of Jesus. In particular, does the resurrected Christ carry the 'memory' of his trauma? Was God changed by these events? This question raises theological questions of the nature of healing, transformation and hope for those who suffer trauma and violence in the world today.

The publication of this book was made possible by the financial contribution of the PACT CSU in cooperation with the ATF Press. It is part of the ATF PACT series.

We are grateful to NT Wright and SPCK for permission to include the two papers by Wright which appears in this volume, which come from a forthcoming publication with SPCK.

James Haire, Christine Ledger, Stephen Pickard

Cosmic Future: Progress or Despair?

NT Wright

I have suggested elsewhere that when we look at the contemporary world and church, we discover great confusion about future hope, but that when we look at the early Christians we find not just faith, but a very precise and specific faith, both about Jesus and his resurrection and about the future life that God had promised to all his people.

This isn't a matter of ancient people being credulous and modern people being sceptical. There is a great deal of credulity in our present world, and there was a great deal of scepticism in the ancient world. It is, rather, something to do with the very specific worldview that was generated by the events concerning Jesus, and supremely the event of Easter itself.

The early Christians looked back with joy to that great event. But precisely because of their very Jewish belief in God as the creator and redeemer, and because they had seen this belief confirmed in the totally unexpected event of Jesus' resurrection, they also looked forward eagerly to an event yet to come in which what began at Easter would be completed. This larger picture of a still-future renewal is the subject of this paper.

It would be possible at this point to jump right in and to speak of the personal hope that the gospel provides for each believer. What God did for Jesus on the first Easter day he has promised to do for each one who is in Christ, each one indwelt by the Spirit of Christ. That is the biblical and historic Christian expectation, in terms of ourselves as human beings. We shall come to this in due course.

But there are good reasons for not starting there. In the last two hundred years Western thought has overemphasised the individual at the expense of the larger picture of God's creation. What is more, in much Western piety, at least since the Middle Ages, the influence of Greek philosophy has been very marked, resulting in a future expectation that bears far more resemblance to Plato's vision of souls entering into disembodied bliss than to the biblical picture of new heavens and new earth. If we start with the future hope of the individual, there is

6 *From Resurrection to Return*

always the risk that we will, at least by implication, understand that as the real centre of everything, and treat the hope of creation as mere embroidery around the edges. That has happened often enough. I am keen to rule it out by the structure of the argument, as well as through the detailed exposition.

The order of the discussion is therefore determined by what seems to me the appropriate arrangement of the material. Instead of looking first at the promise to the individual, and working up from that to the renewal of creation, we begin with the biblical vision of the future world—a vision of the present cosmos renewed from top to bottom by the God who is both creator and redeemer. That is the context within which we will then be able to speak of the 'second coming' of Jesus, and then of the bodily resurrection.[1]

We turn, then, to the large-scale hope of the whole cosmos, the great drama within which our little dramas are, as it were, the play within the play. What is God's purpose for the world as a whole?

To answer this, we must first look at two very popular options before exploring the alternative, which (though you'd never know it from much contemporary Christianity) is the one offered by the New Testament itself.[2]

---

1. Theologians will recognise that I am in implicit dialogue throughout this paper with two of the great German theologians of the last generation: Wolfhart Pannenberg, see, for example, his *Systematic Theology*, volume 3 (Grand Rapids: Eerdmans, and Edinburgh: T&T Clark, 1993), chapter 15 and many other places, and Jürgen Moltmann, for example *Theology of Hope* (London: SCM, 1967), and *The Coming of God: Christian Eschatology* (Minneapolis: Fortress, 1996). There is an entire book to be written as part of this ongoing conversation, but this is not it. On Moltmann see particularly RJ Bauckham, *God Will Be All in All: The Eschatology of Jürgen Moltmann* (Edinburgh: T&T Clark, 2005 [1999]).

2. Sources I have found helpful in this paper include John Polkinghorne and Michael Welker (editors), *The End of the World and the Ends of God: Science and Theology on Eschatology* (Harrisburg: TPI, 2000), John Colwell (editor), *Called to One Hope: Perspectives on Life to Come* (Carlisle: Paternoster, 2000). The latter includes my lecture 'New Heavens, New Earth', originally given in 1993, which anticipates several aspects of this paper. See too my *The Myth of the Millennium* (London: SPCK, 1999), US title *The Millennium Myth* (Louisville: WJKP). Among other recent writers Richard Bauckham is prolific and, in my

Cosmic Future: Progress or Despair? 7

1. Option one: evolutionary optimism

At the risk of gross oversimplification, we may suggest that there have been two quite different ways of looking at the future of the world. Both of these ways have sometimes been confused with the Christian hope, and indeed both have made use of some elements of the Christian hope in telling their grand stories. But neither comes anywhere near the picture we have in the New Testament, and indeed, in flashes, in the Old. The Christian answer lies not so much halfway between as in a biblical answer that combines the strengths, and eliminates the weaknesses, of both.

The first position is the myth of progress. Many people, particularly politicians and secular commentators in the press and elsewhere, still live by this myth, appeal to it and encourage us to believe it. Indeed (if I may digress for a moment) one might suggest that the demise of serious political discourse today consists not least in this, that politicians are still trying to whip up enthusiasm for their versions of this myth—it's the only discourse they know, poor things—while the rest of us have moved on. They are, to that extent, like people trying to row a boat towards the shore while the strong tide pulls them further and further out to sea. Because they face the wrong way they can't see that their efforts are in vain, and they call out to other boats to join them in their splendid shorebound voyage. That is why the relentlessly modernist and progressivist projects that the politicians feel obliged to offer us ('vote for us and things will get better!') have to be dressed up with the relentlessly postmodernist techniques of spin and hype: in the absence of real hope all that is left is feelings. Persuasion will not work, because we're never going to believe it. What we appear to need, and therefore what people give us, is entertainment. As a journalist said recently, our politicians demand to be treated like rock stars, while our rock stars are pretending to be politicians. Sorting out this mess—which the Christian hope, despite current opinion, is well suited to do—should mean, among many other things, a renewal of genuine political discourse, which God knows we badly need.

---

view, largely on the right lines, see, for example, his book with Trevor Hart, *Hope against Hope: Christian Eschatology in Contemporary Context* (Grand Rapids: Eerdmans, 1999).

8   *From Resurrection to Return*

But to return to our main theme. The myth of progress has deep roots in contemporary Western culture, and some of those roots are Christian.[3] The idea that the human project, and indeed the cosmic project, could and would continue to grow and develop, producing unlimited human improvement and marching towards a Utopia, goes back to the Renaissance, and was given its decisive push by the eighteenth-century European Enlightenment. The full flowering of this belief took place in Europe in the nineteenth century, when the combination of scientific and economic advances on the one hand and democratic freedoms and wider education on the other produced a strong sense that history was accelerating towards a wonderful goal. El Dorado was just round the corner, the millennium in which the world would live at peace. Prosperity would spread out from enlightened Europe and America and embrace the world. By no means all thinkers a hundred years ago fitted into this mould, but many, including some of enormous influence such as Hegel, did so enthusiastically. This, again, is precisely where some of our politicians still gain their inspiration.

This Utopian dream is in fact a parody of the Christian vision. The kingdom of God and the kingdoms of the world come together to produce a vision of history moving forwards towards its goal, a goal that will emerge from within rather than being a new gift from elsewhere. Humans can be made perfect, and are indeed evolving inexorably towards that point. The world is ours to discover, exploit and enjoy. Instead of dependence on God's grace, we will become what we have the potential to be by education and hard work. Instead of creation and new creation, science and technology will turn the raw material of this world into the stuff of Utopia. Like the mythical Prometheus, defying the gods and attempting to run the world his own way, liberal modernism has supposed that the world can become everything we could want it to be by working a bit harder and helping forward the great march into the glorious future.

I leave to one side in this brief sketch the role played by Charles Darwin, whose iconic figure continues to haunt several quite different contemporary discussions. One of the strange and perhaps poetically appropriate twists in that story is our increasing recognition that

---

3.   See Richard Bauckham, in Colwell, *Called to One Hope*, 240–51.

Darwin was himself not so much the great new thinker, coming from nowhere to his radical new idea, but rather the exact product of his times, one particular high-water mark in the onward rush of liberal modernist optimism, himself the product of a particular evolution in Western thought. The eagerness with which his ideas were embraced and reapplied, not only in the narrow biological sphere in which they belonged but in far wider areas such as society and politics, indicates well enough the mood of the times. The world in general, and humankind in particular, were marching onwards and upwards, in an immanent process that couldn't be stopped and that would result in the great future that lay just around the corner. Evolution, in this more general sense of progress, was already widely believed—it was a deeply convenient philosophy for those who wanted to justify their own massive industrial and imperial expansion. Darwin gave it some apparent scientific legitimacy, which was quickly seized upon and which, within half a century, had been used to justify everything from eugenics to war. The same could be said, of course, *mutatis mutandis*, of Karl Marx.[4]

Many Christian thinkers went along for the ride on this apparently incoming tide of progress. Many embraced Darwin's ideas as a way of solving (for instance) some of the problems they had felt about the Old Testament. Many eagerly expounded social Darwinism as the way forward for the world, with some even encouraging the pursuit of war as the proper way to test who amongst the human species was the fittest and hence the most deserving of survival. Many Christians embraced what they called the 'social gospel', attempting to put into practice in society the promises of the Christian message. An enormous amount of good work was done by this means, though after a century of it we now all know that it isn't the full answer.

But the best known Christian development of the myth of progress was that of Pierre Teilhard de Chardin. This French Jesuit, born in 1881, was a distinguished scientist of human origins, and a fervent Christian mystic who believed that the presence of God was to be dis-

---

4.   On the reasons for the uncritical acceptance of Darwin see, interestingly, Ludwig Wittgenstein, *Lectures and Conversations on Aesthetics, Psychology and Religious Belief*, edited by C Barrett (Berkeley and Los Angeles: University of California Press, no date), 26ff.

10   *From Resurrection to Return*

covered anywhere and everywhere in the natural world. He believed that the living world disclosed itself as an all-encompassing 'cosmic, christic and divine milieu'. Despite the turmoil and suffering of the world he believed that it was being 'animated and drawn up towards God'. The divine spirit, he believed, is involved in the evolutionary process at every stage, so that 'cosmic and human evolution are moving onwards to an ever fuller disclosure of the Spirit, culminating in "Christ-Omega".'[5] All history had been moving towards the Omega-point of the emergence of the Christ, and was now moving towards the climax and goal in which all creation would find its fulfilment in him. Teilhard de Chardin's most famous book, *The Phenomenon of Man*, written before World War II but only published after his death in 1955, became a best seller and has influenced a whole generation of those who have wanted to combine Christian spirituality with scientific thought. One recent enthusiastic writer suggests that 'his powerful affirmation of the Incarnation and his vision of the universal, cosmic Christ within an evolutionary perspective' can now 'reaffirm the core of the Christian faith for our scientific age'.[6] The influence of Teilhard de Chardin may lie behind the recent popularity of a prayer that speaks of 'all things returning to perfection through him from whom they took their origin'.[7]

Teilhard de Chardin's thinking is many-sided and subtle, and this isn't the place to launch an exposition, let alone a critique. It is a caricature to say, as some have done, that he is simply an advance prophet of New Age spirituality. Likewise, though there appear to be pantheistic elements in his thought, Teilhard de Chardin was not himself a pantheist as such. However, he does share the weaknesses of the evolutionary optimism of his times, not least, as we shall see, an inability to factor into his thinking the fact of radical evil (it was, interestingly, an early work on original sin, or rather its absence, that first brought him critical attention in his own church). Teilhard and his supporters have appealed to the Pauline idea of the 'cosmic Christ', as in Colossians

---

5.   Ursula King, 'Teilhard de Chardin, Pierre', in *The Oxford Companion to Christian Thought*, edited by A Hastings (Oxford: OUP, 2000), 695.

6.   King, 'Teilhard de Chardin, Pierre', 696.

7.   The prayer (which begins 'O God of unchangeable power and eternal light . . . ') appears to originate in the 1912 Scottish Book of Common Prayer.

Cosmic Future: Progress or Despair? 11

1:15–20, but Paul's thinking, there and elsewhere, hardly supports the structure Teilhard wishes to erect. In the long run—and of course it was to the long run that he appealed—he may appear as one of the great flowerings, in Christian form, of that evolutionary optimism of which our post-scientific age is now increasingly sceptical. But more of that anon.

The real problem with the myth of progress is, as I just hinted, that it cannot deal with evil. And when I say 'deal with', I don't just mean intellectually, though that is true as well, I mean in practice. It can't develop a strategy that actually addresses the severe problems of evil in the world. This is why all the evolutionary optimism of the last two hundred years remains helpless before world war, drug crime, Auschwitz, apartheid, child pornography and the other interesting sidelines that evolution has thrown up for our entertainment in the twentieth century. We not only can't explain them, given the myth of progress, we can't eradicate them. Marx's own agenda, not to explain the world but to change it, remains unfulfilled. Of course, the twentieth century provides a quite full answer to the myth of progress, as many people (such as Karl Barth) saw during the World War I, but it's remarkable how many others have continued to believe and propagate it nonetheless. Teilhard himself was a stretcher-bearer during World War I, and the experience was influential, not in leading him away from evolution, but in his attempt to factor human suffering into his equation. Part of the problem in our contemporary debates about asylum seekers, or about the Middle East, is that our politicians still want to present us with the dream of progress, the steady forward advance of the golden dream of 'freedom', and when the tide of human misery washes up on our beaches, or when people in cultures very different from our own seem not to want the kind of 'freedom' we had in mind, it is not just socially but ideologically untidy and inconvenient. It reminds the politicians that there is a gap in their thinking. The world is still a sad and wicked place, not a happy upward progress towards the light.[8]

The myth, then, cannot deal with evil, for three reasons. First, it can't stop it—if evolution gave us Hiroshima and the Gulag it can't

---

8. See my *Evil and the Justice of God* (London: SPCK, and Downers Grove: InterVarsity Press, 2006).

12   *From Resurrection to Return*

be all good. There is no observable reason, in science, philosophy, art or anywhere else to suppose that if we simply plough ahead with the Enlightenment dream these glitches will be ironed out and we'll get to Utopia eventually. What's more, today's cutting-edge science is quite clear that, whatever may and may not be true about specifically biological evolution, the cosmos as a whole is simply not evolving towards a golden future. The world that began with the Big Bang is heading either for the Big Cool Down, as energy gradually runs out and the universe expands into the cold, dark beyond, or for the Big Crunch, as gravity reasserts itself and everything slows down, stops, and then rushes back together again. It is quite possible that, before either of these worrying possibilities takes place, a giant meteorite—such as most likely wiped out the dinosaurs—could strike the earth with similar devastating effects. None of these scenarios makes any sense within the myth of progress.[9]

Second, even if 'progress' brought us to Utopia after all, that wouldn't address the *moral* problem of all the evil that's happened to date in the world. Suppose the golden age arrived tomorrow morning. What would that say to those who are being tortured to death today? How would that be a satisfactory solution to the huge and indescribable evils of the last century, let alone all of world history? If, akin to Teilhard de Chardin, we were to make God part of the process of it all, what sort of a god would it be who builds his kingdom on the bones and ashes of those who have suffered along the way? The picture reminds me of the story of the old Oxford don who, whenever the paper on his desk got quite out of control, would simply spread a copy of *The Times* over the lot and start again. After his death they found several layers, like an archaeologist's tell, of matters that had never been dealt with. And after the construction of an evolutionist's kingdom of God, God would be left with precisely the same problem. It was because of this that the ancient Jews began to speak of the resurrection.

The myth of progress fails because it doesn't in fact work, because it would never solve evil retrospectively and, thirdly, because it un-

---

9.   On all this, see Polkinghorne and Welker, *The End of the World and the Ends of God*, 1–13, WR Stoeger, in my *Evil and the Justice of God*, 19–28, and Polkinghorne, in *Evil and the Justice of God*, 29–41. Polkinghorne begins his chapter by questioning the 'scientific' side of Teilhard de Chardin's theory.

Cosmic Future: Progress or Despair?

derestimates the nature and power of evil itself, and thus fails to see the vital importance of the cross, God's 'No' to evil, which then opens the door to his 'Yes' to creation. Only in the Christian story itself—certainly not in the secular stories of modernity—do we find any sense that the problems of the world are solved, not by a straightforward upward movement into the light, but by the creator God going down into the dark, to rescue humankind and the world from its plight.

The myth of progress, then, has been enormously powerful in our culture. In fact, it still is, not least as an implicit belief that can be appealed to to justify any and every 'development' in a supposed liberalising, humanising, freedom-bringing direction. ('Don't you believe in *progress*?' people ask scornfully when someone objects to a new 'moral' proposal. They used to say that when people objected to cutting down ancient trees to build a new road, but we have begun to realise that 'progress' in that sense wasn't always all it was cracked up to be.) Christians have often gone along with the general idea of 'progress', but, though it sometimes runs on parallel lines to Christian hope, it comes from a different origin and veers off towards a very different destination—just as the trains that run from London to Manchester coincide for a stretch with those that run from Southampton to Newcastle, but start and finish somewhere very different. Politicians and the media plug into the myth constantly, though the appliances they run off it frequently subvert it, like someone using a power drill to cut into the very socket where the tool is getting its electricity.

No wonder we live in a world of flying sparks, of self-defeating energy. But before we look at the truly Christian alternative we must examine, more briefly, the other myth, the negative myth, the story that tells us the world is a wicked place and we'd do better to escape it altogether.

2. Option two: souls in transit

Plato remains the most influential thinker in the history of the Western world. For Plato, as for the Buddha, the present world of space, time and matter is a world of illusion, of flickering shadows in a cave, and the most appropriate human task is to get in touch with the true reality, which is beyond space, time and matter. For Plato, this was the eternal Forms, for the Buddha, the eternal Nothingness.

14   *From Resurrection to Return*

To oversimplify once more, we may say that Plato's picture was based on a rejection of the phenomena of matter and transience. The mess and muddle of the space / time / matter world was an offence to the tidy, clean philosophical mind, which dwelt upon eternal realities. It wasn't just evil that was wrong with the world, it was change and decay, the transitoriness of matter: the fact that spring and summer are followed by autumn and winter, that the sunset tails off into darkness, that human blossoming and flourishing are the prelude to suffering and death.

Here worldviews diverge radically. The optimist, the pantheist, the evolutionist, the myth-of-progress school, will all say that these are just the growing pains of something bigger and better. The Platonist, the Buddhist, the Hindu—and, following the Platonic line, the Gnostic, the Manichaean and countless others within variants of the Christian and Jewish traditions—will all say that these are the signs that we are made for something quite different, a world not made of space, time and matter, a world of pure spiritual existence where we shall happily have got rid of the shackles of mortality once and for all. And the way you get rid of mortality, within this worldview, is to get rid of the thing that can decay and die—namely our material selves.

The Platonic strain entered Christian thinking early on, not least with the phenomenon known as Gnosticism. Since the Gnostics have been making something of a comeback recently, a word about them is appropriate.[10] The Gnostics believed, like Plato, that the material world was an inferior and dark place, evil in its very existence, but that within this world were to be found certain people who were meant for something else. These children of light were like fallen stars, tiny pinpricks of light currently hidden within a gross material body. Once they had realised who they were, though, this 'knowledge' (Greek *gnosis*) would enable them to enter into a spiritual existence in which the material world would no longer count.

Having entered upon that spiritual existence, they would then live by it, through death, and into the infinite world beyond space, time and matter. 'We are stardust,' sang Joni Mitchell, plugging in to this millennia-old mythology, 'we are golden, and we've got to get our-

---

10.   See too my *Judas and the Gospel of Jesus* (London: SPCK, Grand Rapids: Baker, 2006) and other works referred to there.

selves back to the garden'.[11] The Gnostic myth often suggests that the way out of our mess is to return to our primeval state, before the creation of the world. In this view, creation itself is the 'fall', producing matter, which is the real evil. I hope it is clear both how closely this view parodies some aspects of Christianity and how deeply and thoroughly it diverges from it.

Though most people in today's world have probably only a sketchy idea of what Gnosticism might be, assuming they've heard of it at all, it has been argued with some plausibility that some elements of it at least—and Gnosticism is always a very eclectic phenomenon—are to be found in some of the seminal thinkers and writers of the last two hundred years in our culture. The writer and playwright Stuart Holroyd, himself an unashamed apologist for Gnosticism, lists Blake, Goethe, Melville, Yeats and Jung among others as representing this stream in the modern West, and though their insights have often been cross-fertilised with other different types he has a point that should not be ignored. Basically, if you move away from materialistic optimism but without embracing Judaism or Christianity, you are quite likely to land up with some kind of Gnosticism. It should be no surprise that certain elements of the Romantic movement, and some of their more recent heirs, have been prone to this.[12] The discovery of the Nag Hammadi scrolls (a library of Gnostic texts found in Upper Egypt) has in our day fuelled a desire to reinterpret Christianity itself in terms of a supposedly original Gnostic spirituality that contrasts sharply with the very concrete kingdom-of-God-on-earth announced by the Jesus of the canonical gospels. Travel far enough down that road, and you will end up with the blatant and outrageous conspiracy theories of a book like *The Da Vinci Code*. But there are many who, without going that far, have come to assume that some kind of Gnosticism is what genuine Christianity was supposed to be about.

Most Western Christians—and most Western non-Christians, for that matter—have in fact supposed that Christianity was committed to at least a soft version of Plato's position. A good many Christian hymns and poems wander off unthinkingly in the direction of Bud-

---

11.   Joni Mitchell, 'Woodstock' (1970).

12.   See Stuart Holroyd, *The Elements of Gnosticism* (Shaftesbury: Element, 1994), especially chapters 1 and 7.

16   *From Resurrection to Return*

dhism. The 'just passing through' spirituality (as in the spiritual 'This world is not my home / I'm just a'passin' through'), though it has of course some affinities with classical Christianity, encourages precisely a Gnostic attitude: the created world is at best an irrelevance, at worst a dark, evil, gloomy place, and we immortal souls, who existed originally in a different sphere, are looking forward to returning to it as soon as we're allowed to. There has been such a massive assumption made in Western Christianity that the purpose of being a Christian is simply, or at least mainly, to 'go to heaven when you die', that texts that don't say that, but which mention heaven, are read as if they did say it, and that texts which say the opposite, like Romans 8:18–25 and Revelation 21–22, are simply screened out as if they didn't exist.[13]

The results are all around us in the Western church and in the worldviews that Western Christianity has generated. Secularists often criticise Christians for having contributed to ecological disaster, and there's more than a grain of truth in the charge. I have heard it seriously argued in North America that since God intends to destroy the present space / time universe, and moreover since he intends to do so quite soon, it really doesn't matter whether we emit twice as many greenhouse gases as we do now, whether we destroy the rain forests and the Arctic tundra, whether we fill our skies with acid rain. That is a peculiarly modern form of would-be Christian negativity about the world, and of course its skin-deep 'spiritual' viewpoint is entirely in thrall to the heart-deep materialism of the business interests that will be served, in however short a term, by such hazardous practices.

I shall come to that sort of thing in more detail later on. My point for now is to notice that in many parts of the world an appeal to a Christian view of the future is taken to mean an appeal to the eventual demise of the created order and to a destiny that is purely 'spiritual' in the sense of being completely non-material. That remains the popular perception, both from inside and outside the church, of what we Christians are supposed to believe when we speak of 'heaven', and when we talk of the hope that is ours in Christ.

Over against both these popular and mistaken views, the central Christian affirmation is that what the creator God has done in Jesus Christ, and supremely in his resurrection, is what he intends to do for

---

13.   On Philippians 3:20ff, 1 Peter 1 and the like see below.

Cosmic Future: Progress or Despair?

the whole world—meaning, by 'world', the entire cosmos with all its history. It is to this hope that I turn to now.

3. The Christian hope

The early Christians did not believe in 'progress'. They did not think the world was getting better and better under its own steam—or even under the steady influence of God. They knew God had to do something fresh to put it to rights.

But nor did they believe that the world was getting worse and worse and that their task was to escape it altogether. They were not dualists.

Since most people who think about these things today tend towards one or other of those two points of view, it comes as something of a surprise to discover that the early Christians held a quite different view. They believed that God was going to do for the whole cosmos what he had done for Jesus at Easter. This is such a surprising belief, and so little reflected on even in Christian circles, still less outside the church, that we must set it out step by step and show how the different early writers developed different images that together add up to a stunning picture of a future for which, so they insisted, the whole world was waiting on tiptoe.

4. Fundamental structures of hope

The clearest statements of the large-scale Christian hope are to be found in the New Testament, in Paul and in the book of Revelation. I want to explore these now, drawing out as we do so the ways in which they answer the two opposite views I have sketched. We need to notice, in particular, the way in which three themes come out.

First, the *goodness of creation*. Granted the swirling currents of alternative worldviews available in the first century, it is a remarkable feature of the earliest Christianity known to us that it refused to lapse at any point into a cosmological dualism in which the created world is regarded as less than good and God-given. But it is good as *creation*, not as an independent or self-sufficient 'nature'. There is no suggestion of pantheism, or even panentheism. God and the world are not the same thing, nor is everything simply held within something called 'god'. Within biblical theology it remains the case that the one living God created a world that is other than himself, not contained within himself. Creation was from the beginning an act of love, of affirming the goodness of the other. God saw all that he had made, and it was very good, but it was not itself divine. At its height, which according to Genesis 1 is the creation of humans, it was designed to *reflect* God, both to reflect God back to God in worship and to reflect God into the rest of creation in stewardship. But this imagebearing capacity of humankind is not in itself the same thing as divinity. Collapsing this distinction means taking a large step towards a pantheism within which there is no way of understanding, let alone addressing, the problem of evil.

Second, then, the *nature of evil*. Evil is real and powerful, within biblical theology, but it consists neither in the fact of being created, nor in the fact of being other than God (since being loved into life by the one God is quite good enough!), nor yet in the fact that it's made of physical matter and belongs within space and time, instead of being pure spirit in an eternal heaven. Nor—and this is crucial— does evil consist in being transient, made to decay. There is nothing wrong with the tree dropping its leaves in the autumn. There is nothing wrong with the sunset fading away into darkness. Evil consists in none of those things—indeed, it is precisely the transience of the good creation that serves as a pointer to its larger purpose. Creation was good, but it always had a forward look. Transience acts as a God-given signpost, pointing not from the material world to a non-material world, but from the world *as it is* to the world *as it is meant one day to be*—pointing, in other words, from the present to the future that God has in store. The human project, of bringing wise order to the garden, is not yet complete, and without transience we might the more easily be led into idolatry, treating the creature as though it was the creator—which, goodness knows, is all too easy as it is. This harks back to what I have suggested elsewhere. What matters is eschatological duality (the present age and the age to come), not ontological dualism (an evil 'earth' and a good 'heaven').

Evil then consists, not in being created, but in the rebellious idolatry by which humans worship and honour elements of the natural world rather than the God who made them. The result is that the cosmos is out of joint. Instead of humans being God's wise vice-regents over creation, they ignore the creator and try to worship something less demanding, something that will give them a short-term fix of power or pleasure. The result is that death, which was always part of the natural transience of the good creation, gains a second dimension, which the Bible sometimes calls 'spiritual death'. In Genesis, and indeed for much of the Old Testament, the controlling image for death is exile. Adam and Eve were told that they would die on the day they ate the fruit—what actually happened was that they were expelled from the garden. Turning away from the worship of the living God is turning towards that which has no life in itself. Worship that which is transient, and it can only give you death. But when you do commit that idolatry, evil is unleashed into the world, setting off chain reactions with incalculable consequences. Mysteriously, this out-of-jointness seems to become entangled with the transience and decay necessary within the good-but-incomplete creation, so that what we perhaps misleadingly call 'natural evil' can be seen as, among other things, the advance signs of that final 'shaking' of heaven and earth that the prophets understood to be necessary if God's eventual new world was to be born.[14]

Thirdly, the *plan of redemption*. Precisely because creation is the work of God's love, redemption is not something alien to the creator, but something he will undertake with delight and glad self-giving. The point about redemption is that it doesn't mean scrapping what's there and starting again from a clean slate, but rather liberating what has come to be enslaved. And, because of the analysis of evil not as materiality but as rebellion, the slavery of humans and of the world does not consist in embodiment, redemption from which would mean the death of the body and the consequent release of the soul or spirit. The slavery consists, rather, in sin, redemption from which must ultimately involve not just goodness of soul or spirit but a newly embodied life.

This is the plan which, throughout the Bible, is articulated in terms of God's choice of Israel as the means of redemption, and then, after the long and chequered story of God and Israel, God's sending of his son, Jesus. Incarnation—already adumbrated in the Jewish tradition in terms not least of the Temple as the place where God chooses to live

---

14.   See Haggai 2:6ff. See also Romans 8:18–26.

20   *From Resurrection to Return*

on earth—is not a category mistake, as Platonists ancient and modern imagine. It is the centre and fulfilment of the long-term plan of the good and wise creator.

If you tell this story from the point of view of the good creation, the coming of Jesus emerges as the moment all creation had been waiting for. Humans were made to be God's stewards over creation, so the one through whom all things were made, the eternal son, the eternal wisdom, becomes human, so that he might truly become God's steward, ruler over all his world. Equally, if you tell the story from the point of view of human rebellion and the consequent sin and death that has engulfed the whole world, this again emerges as the moment all creation had been waiting for: the eternal expression of the father's love became the incarnate expression of the father's love, so that by his self-giving to death, even the death of the cross, the whole creation can be reconciled to God. If you put these two ways of telling the story together, and cast them into poetry, you will find you have rewritten Colossians 1:15–20. This is the real 'cosmic Christology' of the New Testament—not a kind of pantheism, running under its own steam, and cut off from the real Jesus, but a retelling of the Jewish story of wisdom in terms of Jesus himself, focusing on the cross itself as the act whereby the good creation is brought back into harmony with the wise creator.

The balance of the clauses in the poem in Colossians 1 shows the extent to which Paul has insisted on holding together creation and redemption.[15] Redemption is not simply making creation a bit better, as the optimistic evolutionist would try to suggest. Nor is it rescuing spirits and souls from an evil material world, as the Gnostic would want to say. It is the remaking of creation, having dealt with the evil that is defacing and distorting it. And it is accomplished by the same God, now known in Jesus Christ, through whom it was made in the first place. It is highly significant that in the passage just after the great poem of Colossians 1:15–20, Paul declares that the gospel has already been announced to every creature under heaven (1:23). What has happened in the death and resurrection of Jesus Christ, in other words, is

---

15. On Colossians 1 see also my *The Climax of the Covenant* (Edinburgh: T&T Clark, Minneapolis: Fortress, 1992), chapter 5. The relevant passage is set out in full at the end of this paper.

by no means limited to its effects on those human beings who believe the gospel and thereby find new life here and hereafter. It resonates out, in ways that we can't fully see or understand, into the vast recesses of the universe.

Creation, evil, and the plan of redemption, revealed in action in Jesus Christ: these are the constant themes that the New Testament writers, particularly Paul and the author of Revelation, struggle to express. I now want to explore the key New Testament texts that speak of the cosmic dimension of Christian hope. There are six main themes to be explored. Several of these are themselves powerful images taken from the world of creation. If you're going to speak of God doing something new that nevertheless affirms the old, what better way than to speak of seedtime and harvest, of birth and new life, and of marriage. We begin with the first of these, seedtime and harvest.

5. Seedtime and harvest

In 1 Corinthians 15 Paul uses the image of the 'firstfruits'.[16] This goes back to the Jewish festivals of Passover and Pentecost, which in their developed forms at least were both agricultural and salvation-historical festivals. Passover was the time when the first crop of barley was presented before the Lord. Pentecost, seven weeks later, was the time when the first fruits of the wheat harvest were presented. The offering of the firstfruits signifies the great harvest still to come. At the salvation-historical level, of course, Passover commemorated Israel coming out of Egypt, while Pentecost, seven weeks later, commemorated the arrival at Sinai and the giving of Torah. The two strands were woven together, since part of God's promise in liberating Israel and giving it the law was that Israel would inherit the land and that the land would be fruitful.

Paul applies this Passover-image to Jesus. He is the firstfruits, the first to rise from the dead. But this isn't an isolated instance. The point of the firstfruits is that there will be many, many more. Jesus' Passover, that is Calvary and Easter, which occurred of course at Passover time and was from very early on interpreted in the light of that festival,

---

16. 1 Corinthians 15:20, 23. See also Romans 8:23, 11:16 and 16:5, 1 Corinthians 16:15, 2 Thessalonians 2:13 and James 1:18.

22   *From Resurrection to Return*

indicated that the great slavemaster, the great Egypt, sin and death themselves, had been defeated when Jesus came through the Red Sea of death and out the other side. And Paul goes on, later in the chapter, to expound the nature of the Christian's resurrection body on the basis of the new body of Jesus. Please note, over against any move towards Gnosticism, how this imagery indicates continuity as well as discontinuity. Note too, over against any kind of evolutionary optimism, that moving from seed sown to crop harvested involves discontinuity as well as continuity, and in particular that the Exodus from Egypt, symbolised by this story, could only be seen as an act of pure grace. 'Progress', left to itself, could never have brought it about.[17]

6. The victorious battle

1 Corinthians then continues with a quite different image, one not so organically related to the natural order of creation, but with many biblical antecedents: that of a king establishing his kingdom by subduing all possible enemies.

Paul is careful to stress both that Jesus will rule until every single power in the cosmos has been subjected to him, and that God the Father is not included in that category. Whatever we say about the implied Christology of this passage, Paul is clearly articulating a theology of *new creation*. Every force, every authority in the whole cosmos will be subjected to the Messiah, and finally death itself will give up its power. In other words, that which we are tempted to regard as the permanent state of the cosmos—entropy, threatening chaos and dissolution—will be defeated by the Messiah, acting as the agent of the creator God. If evolutionary optimism is squelched by, among other things, the sober estimates of the scientists that the universe as we know it today is running out of steam and cannot last for ever, the gospel of Jesus Christ announces that what God did for Jesus at Easter

---

17.   There are attempts from time to time to imply that even Jesus' resurrection might be evidence of a new strand in some sort of evolutionary process: Jesus had 'developed' further than the rest of us, so that he was able, by 'natural' means, to pass through death and on into a new life: for example Stephen Holt, in *Resurrection*, edited by SE Porter, MA Hayes and D Tombs (JSNT Supplement Series 186) (Sheffield: Sheffield Academic Press, 1999), 11.

Cosmic Future: Progress or Despair? 23

he will do, not only for all those who are 'in Christ', but for the entire cosmos. It will be an act of new creation, parallel to and derived from the act of new creation when God raised Jesus from the dead.

Here we find, coming into full view, one of the direct results of saying that Jesus was raised bodily from the dead, rather than saying that upon his death he began to exist in a new, non-bodily mode. As I have argued elsewhere, if after his death he had gone into some kind of non-bodily existence, death would not be defeated. It would remain intact, it would merely be redescribed. Jesus, humankind and the world itself could not look forward to any future within a created and embodied mode such as we now know. But this is precisely what Paul is denying. Death is the last enemy, not a good part of the good creation, and therefore death must be defeated if the lifegiving God is to be honoured as the true lord of the world.[18] When this has happened, and only then, Jesus the Messiah, the Lord of the world, will hand over the rule of the kingdom to his father, and God will be all in all. We shall return to this presently.

7. Citizens of heaven—colonising the earth

Before we get to that, we look across to another royal image, found in Philippians 3:20–1. It is very close in theme to 1 Corinthians 15, quoting in fact at the crucial point from the same psalm (Psalm 8), emphasising Jesus' authority over all other powers.

Philippi was a Roman colony. Augustus had settled his veterans there after the battles of Philippi (42 BC) and Actium (31 BC). Not all residents of Philippi were Roman citizens, but all would know what citizenship meant. The point of creating colonies was twofold. First, it was aimed at extending Roman influence around the Mediterranean world, creating cells and networks of people loyal to Caesar in the wider culture. Second, it was one way of avoiding the problems of overcrowding in the capital itself. The emperor certainly did not want retired soldiers, with time (and blood) on their hands, hanging around Rome ready to cause trouble. Much better for them to be establishing farms and businesses elsewhere.

---

18. Contra Kathryn Tanner in Polkinghorne and Welker, *The End of the World and the Ends of God*, 232.

24 *From Resurrection to Return*

So when Paul says we are 'citizens of heaven', he doesn't at all mean that when we're done with this life we'll be going off to live in heaven.[19] What he means is that the Saviour, the Lord, Jesus the King—all of those were of course imperial titles—will come *from* heaven *to* earth, to change the present situation and state of his people. The key word here is 'transform': 'he will transform our present humble bodies to be like his glorious body'. Jesus will not declare that present physicality is redundant and can be scrapped. Nor will he simply improve it, perhaps by speeding up its evolutionary cycle. In a great act of power—the same power that accomplished Jesus' own resurrection, as Paul says in Ephesians 1:19–20—he will *change* the present body into the one that corresponds in kind to his own, as part of his work of bringing all things into subjection to himself. Philippians 3, though it is primarily speaking of human resurrection, indicates that this will take place within the context of God's victorious transformation of the whole cosmos.[20]

8. God will be all in all

Turning back to 1 Corinthians 15, we find Paul declaring that, as the goal of all history, God will be 'everything in everything', or if you like 'all in all' (15:28). This is one of the clearest statements of the very centre of the future-orientated New Testament worldview.

At this level, the problem with a Teilhardian evolutionary optimism, as well as with any form of actual pantheism, is that it collapses the entire future into the present, and indeed into the past. God *will be* all in all. The tense is future. Until the final victory over evil, and particularly over death, this moment has not arrived. To suggest that, it has is to collude with evil, and with death itself.

How then can we think wisely about God's present relation to the created order? If God is indeed the creator of the world, it matters

---

19. This is taken for granted by, for example, Alister McGrath, in *A Brief History of Heaven* (Oxford: Blackwell, 2003), 12ff. McGrath goes so far as to suggest that this (mis)interpretation is 'one of the leading themes of Paul's theology'.

20. On Philippians 3:20ff. see my *The Resurrection of the Son of God*, volume 3 of *Christian Origins and the Question of God* (London: SPCK, Minneapolis: Fortress, 2003), 229–36.

that creation is other than God. This is not a moral problem, as has sometimes been thought (if a good God makes something that is not himself, it must be less than good, and therefore he is not a good God for making it). Nor is it a logical one (if, in the beginning, God is all that there is, how can there be ontological room for anything or anyone else?).

As we said earlier, if creation was a work of love, it must have involved the creation of something other than God. That same love then allows creation to be itself, sustaining it in providence and wisdom but not overpowering it. Logic cannot comprehend love, so much the worse for logic.

That, though, is not the end of the story. God intends, in the end, to fill all creation with his own presence and love. This is part at least of an answer to Jürgen Moltmann's proposal to revive the Rabbinic doctrine of *zimzum*, in which God, as it were, retreats, creates space within himself, so that there is ontological space for there to be something else other than him.[21] If I am right, it works the other way round. God's creative love, precisely by being love, creates *new* space for there to be things that are genuinely other than God.

The New Testament develops the doctrine of the Spirit in just this direction, but the future glimpse is already provided in Isaiah. In chapter 11, anticipating the 'new creation' passage in chapters 65 and 66, the prophet declares that 'the earth will be full of the knowledge of the Lord as the waters cover the sea'.[22] As it stands that is a remarkable statement. How can the waters cover the sea? They *are* the sea. It looks as though God intends to flood the universe with himself, as though the universe, the entire cosmos, was designed as a receptacle for his love. We might even suggest, as part of a Christian aesthetic, that the world is beautiful, not just because it hauntingly reminds us of its creator, but because it is pointing forwards: it is designed to be filled, flooded, drenched in God, as a chalice is beautiful not least because of what we know it is designed to contain, or as a violin is beautiful not least because we know the music of which it is capable. I shall return to this later.

---

21. See, for example, J Moltmann, *God in Creation: An Ecological Doctrine of Creation* (London: SCM Press, 1985), 86–93.

22. Isaiah 11:9 and Habakkuk 2:14.

26   *From Resurrection to Return*

The answer to the pantheism of the evolutionary or progressive optimist on the one hand, and to the dualism of the Gnostic or Manichee on the other, now begins to come into full view in the form of the cosmic eschatology offered in the New Testament. The world is created good *but incomplete*. One day, when all forces of rebellion have been defeated, and the creation responds freely and gladly to the love of its creator, God will fill it with himself, so that it will *both* remain an independent being, other than God, *and also* will be flooded with God's own life. This is part of the paradox of love, in which love freely given creates a context for love to be freely returned, and so on in a cycle where complete freedom and complete union do not cancel each other out, but rather celebrate each other and make one another whole.

9. New birth

This brings us to Romans 8, where we find a further image deeply embedded within the created order itself: that of new birth. This passage has routinely been marginalised for centuries by exegetes and theologians who have tried to turn Romans into a book simply about how individual sinners get individually saved. But it is in fact one of the great climaxes of the letter, and indeed of all Paul's thought.

In this passage, Paul again uses the imagery of the Exodus from Egypt, but this time in relation not to Jesus, nor even to ourselves, but to creation as a whole. Creation, he says (verse 21) is in slavery at the moment, like the children of Israel. God's design was to rule creation in lifegiving wisdom through his imagebearing human creatures. But this was always a promise for the future, a promise that one day the true human being, the Image of God himself, God's incarnate son, would come to lead the human race into their true identity. Meanwhile, the creation was subjected to futility, to transience and decay, until the time when God's children are glorified, when what happened to Jesus at Easter happens to all Jesus' people. This is where Romans 8 dovetails with 1 Corinthians 15. The whole creation, as he says in verse 19, is on tiptoe with expectation, longing for the day when God's children are revealed, when their resurrection will herald its own new life.

Paul then uses the image of birthpangs—a well-known Jewish metaphor for the coming of God's new age—not only of the church

Cosmic Future: Progress or Despair?

in verse 23, and of the Spirit a couple of verses later, but here in verse 22 of creation itself. Once again this highlights both continuity and discontinuity. This is no smooth evolutionary transitition, in which creation simply moves up another gear into a higher mode of life. This is traumatic, involving convulsions and contractions and the radical discontinuity in which mother and child are parted and become not one being but two. But nor is this a dualistic rejection of physicality as though, because the present creation is transient and full of decay and death, God must throw it away and start again from scratch. The very metaphor that Paul chooses for this decisive moment in his argument shows that what he has in mind is not the unmaking of creation, nor simply its steady development, but the drastic and dramatic birth of new creation from the womb of the old.

10. The marriage of heaven and earth

We thus arrive at the last and perhaps the greatest image of new creation, of cosmic renewal, in the whole Bible. This scene, set out in Revelation 21–2, is not well enough known or pondered (perhaps because, in order to earn the right to read it, one should really read the rest of the Revelation to John first, which proves too daunting for many). This time the image is that of marriage. The New Jerusalem comes down out of heaven like a bride adorned for her husband.

We notice right away how drastically different this is from all those would-be Christian scenarios in which the end of the story is the Christian going off to heaven as a soul, naked and unadorned, to meet its maker in fear and trembling. As in Philippians 3, it is not we who go to heaven—it is heaven that comes to earth. Indeed, it is the church itself, the heavenly Jerusalem,[23] that comes down to earth. This is the ultimate rejection of all types of Gnosticism, of every worldview that sees the final goal as the separation of the world from God, of the physical from the spiritual, of earth from heaven. It is the final answer to the Lord's Prayer, that God's kingdom would come and his will be done on earth as in heaven. It is what Paul is talking about in Ephesians 1:10, that God's design and promise was to sum up all things in Christ, things both in heaven and on earth. It is the final fulfilment, in

---

23.   Paul of course also knows this idea: Galatians 4:26. See also Hebrews 12:22–4.

28   *From Resurrection to Return*

richly symbolic imagery, of the promise of Genesis 1, that the creation of male and female would together reflect God's image into the world. And it is the final accomplishment of God's great design, to defeat and abolish death for ever—which can only mean the rescue of creation from its present plight of decay.

Heaven and earth, it seems, are not after all poles apart, needing to be separated for ever when all the children of heaven have been rescued from this wicked earth. Nor are they simply different ways of looking at the same thing, as would be implied by some kinds of pantheism. No: they are different, radically different, but they are made for each other in the same way (Revelation is suggesting) as male and female. And, when they finally come together, that will be cause for rejoicing in the same way that a wedding is: a creational sign that God's project is going forwards, that opposite poles within creation are made for union, not competition, that love and not hate have the last word in the universe, that fruitfulness and not sterility is God's will for creation.

What is promised in this passage, then, is what Isaiah foresaw: a new heaven and a new earth, replacing the old heaven and the old earth, which were bound to decay. This doesn't mean, as I have stressed throughout, that God will wipe the slate clean and start again. If that were so, there would be no celebration, no conquest of death, no long preparation now at last complete. As the chapter develops, the bride, the wife of the Lamb, is described lovingly: she is the new Jerusalem promised by the prophets of the Exile, especially Ezekiel. But, unlike in Ezekiel's vision, where the rebuilt Temple takes eventual centre stage, there is no Temple in this city (21:22). The Temple in Jerusalem was always designed, it seems, as a pointer to, and an advance symbol for, the presence of God himself. When the reality is there, the signpost is no longer necessary. As in Romans and 1 Corinthians, the living God will dwell with and amongst his people, filling the city with his life and love, and pouring out grace and healing in the river of life that flows from the city out to the nations. There is a sign here of the future project that awaits the redeemed, in God's eventual new world. So far from sitting on clouds playing harps, as people often imagine, the redeemed people of God in the new world will be the agents of his love going out in new ways, to accomplish new creative tasks, to celebrate and extend the glory of his love.

11. Conclusion

There are of course other passages in the New Testament that speak of new creation. Ideally one would want to factor in the glorious picture of the city that is to come, at present in heaven but destined for earth, that we find in Hebrews 11 and 12. One would certainly want to discuss the famous passage in 2 Peter that, echoing Isaiah, speaks of waiting for new heavens and a new earth in which justice will dwell. I have discussed these, of course, in my big book on the resurrection. We should certainly place here Ephesians 1:15–23, one of the grandest of all statements of the theme. But I come back, as I have often done over the years, to the great poem in Colossians 1. It has often been squashed into a shallow-level picture of a supposed 'cosmic Christ', legitimating a dehistoricised Jesus and an easygoing transition away from a Jewish creation-theology and towards various soft versions of Teilhardian and similar thought. But it stands there as a rebuke to all such attempts, not least because, if it is Jesus who is the key to the cosmos, it is of course the crucified and risen Jesus we are talking about:

> [15]He is the image of God, the invisible one,
>> the firstborn of all creation.

> [16]For in him all things were created,
>> in the heavens and here on the earth.

> Things we can see and things we cannot—
>> thrones and lordships and rulers and powers—

> All were created both through him and for him.
>> [17]And he is ahead, prior to all else,
>>> and in him all things hold together;
>> [18]And he himself is supreme, the head
>>> over the body, the church.

> He is the start of it all,
>> firstborn from realms of the dead;
>> so in all things he might be the chief.

30   *From Resurrection to Return*

[19]For in him all the Fullness was glad to dwell
    [20]and through him to reconcile all to himself,
    making peace through the blood of his cross,
through him—yes, things on the earth,
    and also the things in the heavens.[24]

It is of course only through imagery, through metaphor and symbol, that we can imagine the new world that God intends to make. That is right and proper. All our language about the future, as I have said, is like a set of signposts pointing into a bright mist. The signpost doesn't provide a photograph of what we will find when we arrive, but a true indication of the direction we should be travelling in. What I am proposing is that the New Testament image of the future hope of the whole cosmos, grounded in the resurrection of Jesus, gives as coherent a picture as we need or could have of the future that is promised to the whole world, a future in which, under the sovereign and wise rule of the creator God, decay and death will be done away, and a new creation born to which the present one will stand as mother to child. This picture, as some recent writers like John Polkinghorne have shown, gives a shape to the Christian hope that can address, and enter into dialogue with, cutting-edge physics in a way that the synthesis offered by Teilhard de Chardin and others simply cannot do. What creation needs is not abandonment on the one hand, nor evolution on the other, but redemption and renewal, and this is both promised and guaranteed by the resurrection of Jesus from the dead. This is what the whole world is waiting for.

This, in turn, clears the way for the other topics concerning the Christian future hope: God's putting all things to rights through the coming of Jesus, and the bodily resurrection itself.

As I reflect on God's future plans for the world, I am reminded of the great teacher and pastor Bishop Lesslie Newbigin. Someone once asked him whether, as he looked to the future, he was optimistic or pessimistic. His reply was simple and characteristic. 'I am,' he said, 'neither an optimist nor a pessimist. Jesus Christ is risen from the dead!' This paper is a way of saying 'Amen' to that. The whole world

---

24.   This translation is taken from my *Paul for Everyone: The Prison Letters* (London: SPCK, Louisville: WJKP, 2002), 148.

Cosmic Future: Progress or Despair?

is waiting, on tiptoe with expectation, for the moment when that resurrection life and power sweeps through it, filling it with the glory of God as the waters cover the sea.

Before we get to the topic of resurrection itself, however, we must turn to the other vital element of the New Testament picture of God's ultimate future. Central to the unveiling of God's new world will be the personal presence of Jesus himself. That is the subject of my next paper.

When He Appears

NT Wright

In the previous paper I sketched the big picture of cosmic redemption that the New Testament invites us to make our own. God will redeem the whole universe, Jesus' resurrection is the beginning of that new life, the fresh grass growing through the concrete of corruption and decay in the old world. That final redemption will be the moment when heaven and earth are joined together at last, in a burst of God's creative energy for which Easter is the prototype and source. When we put together that big picture with what we've said in the previous paper about the ascension of Jesus, what do we get? Why, of course, the personal *presence* of Jesus, as opposed to his current *absence*.

The presence we know at the moment—the presence of Jesus with his people in word and sacrament, by the Spirit, through prayer, in the faces of the poor—is of course related to that future presence, but the distinction between them is important and striking. Jesus' appearing will be, for those of us who have known and loved him here, like meeting face to face someone who we have only ever known by letter, telephone or perhaps email. Communication theorists insist that for full human communication you need not only words on a page but a tone of voice. That's why a telephone call can say more than a letter, not in quantity but in quality. But for full communication between human beings you need not only a tone of voice but also body language, facial language and the thousand small ways in which, without realising it, we relate to one another. At the moment, by the Spirit, the word, the sacraments and prayer, and in those in need whom we are called to serve for his sake, the absent Jesus is present to us, but one day he will be there with us, face to face. Mrs Alexander got it partly right in a classic nineteenth-century compromise:

> And our eyes at last shall see him,
> Through his own redeeming love,
> For that child so dear and gentle
> Is our Lord in heaven above.

When He Appears   33

Unless we feel the pull and yearning of those lines, we may not yet have learnt to know him as we may know him in the present, or to feel the tension between our present knowing and that which is promised in the future. But the hymn is quite wrong to suggest that for this knowledge *we* need to go and find *him*:

> And he leads his children on
> To the place where he is gone.

This is indeed true, as we shall see, of what happens to his people after death, in the interim state. But it isn't the main truth that the New Testament teaches, the main emphasis that the early Christians insisted on over and over again. The main truth is that *he* will come back to *us*.[1] That is the thing of which we must now speak, in two main movements. He will come again, and he will come again as judge.

1. Coming, appearing, revealing, royal presence

We still speak, in our culture, about the sun 'rising' and 'setting', even though we know that in fact it is we (or at least our planet) who are moving in relation to the sun rather than the other way round. In the same way, the early Christians often spoke of Jesus 'coming', or 'returning', indeed, at least in John's gospel, Jesus himself speaks in that way. But the larger picture they use suggests that if we are to understand them properly, that language, common and even credal though it is, may not be the most helpful way today of getting at the truth it affirms.

In fact, the New Testament uses quite a variety of language and imagery to express the truth that Jesus and his people will one day be personally present to each other, as full and renewed human beings. It is perhaps an accident of history that the phrase 'the second coming',

---

1. And another thing, while we're deconstructing that lovely hymn: neither in the Bible nor Christian tradition (Hebrews 2:13, quoting Isaiah 8:18, is the only possible exception) are Jesus' followers described as his *children*. 'His brethren' would be better, perhaps, in this politically sensitive age, 'his siblings'. This is, perhaps, the implicit docetism of the hymn peeping through, not for the only time, collapsing the vital distinction between Jesus and the Father.

34 *From Resurrection to Return*

which is very rare in the New Testament, has come to dominate discussion. When that phrase is identified, as it has often been in America in particular, with a particular view of that 'coming' as a literal downward descent, meeting halfway with the redeemed who are making a simultaneous upward journey, all sorts of problems arise that are avoided if we take the New Testament's multiple witness as a whole.

The first thing to get clear is that, despite widespread opinion to the contrary, during his earthly ministry Jesus said nothing about his return. I have argued this position at length and in detail in my various books about Jesus and don't have space to substantiate it here. Let me just say two things, quite baldly.[2]

First, when Jesus speaks of 'the son of man coming on the clouds', he is not talking about the second coming, but, in line with the Daniel 7 text he is quoting, about his vindication after suffering. The 'coming' is an upward, not a downward, movement. In context, the key texts mean that, though Jesus is going to his death, he will be vindicated by events that will take place afterwards.[3] What those events are remains cryptic from the point of view of the passages in question, which is one good reason for thinking them authentic, but they certainly include Jesus' resurrection on the one hand and the destruction of the Temple, the system that has opposed him and his mission, on the other. And the language, significantly, is precisely the language that the early church used as the least inadequate way of talking about the strange thing that happened after Jesus' resurrection: his 'ascension', his glorification, his 'coming', not to earth, but to heaven, to the Father.

Second, the stories Jesus tells about a king, or master, who goes away for a while and leaves his subjects or servants to trade with his money in his absence were not originally meant to refer to Jesus going away and leaving the church with tasks to get on with until his eventual second coming, even though they were read in that way from fairly early on.[4] They belong in the Jewish world of the first century,

---

2. See my *Jesus and the Victory of God*, volume 2 of *Christian Origins and the Question of God* (London: SPCK, Minneapolis: Fortress, 2003), chapters 8 and 13, and my *The Challenge of Jesus* (London: SPCK, Downers Grove: IVP, 2000), chapters 2 and 5.

3. Mark 13:26 and 14:62 (and parallels).

4. For example Matthew 25:14–30/Luke 19:11–27 and the small scenarios in Luke

When He Appears

where everyone would at once 'hear' the story to be about God himself, having left Israel and the Temple at the time of the exile, coming back again at last, as the post-exilic prophets had said he would,[5] back to Israel, back to Zion, back to the Temple. In their original setting, the point of these stories is that Israel's God, YHWH, is indeed coming at last to Jerusalem, to the Temple—in and as the human person Jesus of Nazareth. The stories are not, in that sense, about the second coming of Jesus, but about the first one. They are explaining, albeit cryptically, Jesus' own belief, that what he was doing in coming to Jerusalem to enact both judgment and salvation was what YHWH had said in scripture that he would do in person.

These two historical moves, about the 'son of man' sayings and about the parables of the returning master or king, have left me open to the attack, particularly from American readers, that I have thereby given up believing or teaching the second coming. This is absurd, as the present paper will make clear. The fact that Jesus didn't teach it doesn't mean it isn't true. (Similarly, the fact that I have written books about Jesus without mentioning it doesn't mean I don't believe in it. When a football commentator goes through a whole game without mentioning cricket, that doesn't mean he doesn't believe it exists, or that he doesn't rate it highly as a sport.) Jesus was having a hard enough time explaining to his disciples that he had to die—they never really grasped that at all—and they certainly didn't take his language about his own resurrection as anything more than the general hope of all Jewish martyrs. How could they possibly have understood him saying something about further events in what would have been, for them, a still more unthinkable future?

Of course, when Jesus came to Zion as Israel's rightful Lord in the first century, that event did indeed point forward to his eventual return as the rightful Lord of the whole world. This means that, if we are careful what we are doing, we can read the parables I've mentioned in this new way if we so desire. The reason we need to be careful, though, is because they don't quite fit. Nowhere in the New Testament does any writer say that at Jesus' final coming there will be some of

---

12:35–48 and elsewhere. On these, see my *Jesus and the Victory of God*.

5.   For example Malachi 3:1. See also Zechariah 14:5. Other texts in my *Jesus and the Victory of God*.

36 *From Resurrection to Return*

his servants, some actual believing Christians, who will be judged in the way that the wicked servant was judged for hiding his master's money in a napkin.

Nor will it do to say, as some have said who have grasped part of the point but not worked it through, that the events of 70 AD were themselves the 'second coming' of Jesus, so that ever since then we have been living in God's new age, and there is no further 'coming' to await. This may seem to many readers, as indeed it seems to me, a bizarre position to hold, but there are some who not only hold it but eagerly propagate it, and use some of my arguments to support it. This results from a confusion: if the texts that speak of 'the son of man coming on the clouds' refer to 70 AD, as I have argued that (in part) they do, this doesn't mean that 70 AD was the 'second coming'—because the 'son of man' texts aren't 'second coming' texts at all, despite their frequent misreading that way. They are about Jesus' vindication. And Jesus' vindication—in his resurrection, ascension and judgment on Jerusalem—requires a still further event for everything to be complete. Let me say it quite emphatically for the sake of those who have been confused on the point (and to the amusement, no doubt, of those who haven't been): the 'second coming' has not yet occurred.

So: if the gospel accounts of Jesus' teaching do not refer to the second coming, where does the idea come from? Quite simply, from the rest of the New Testament. As soon as Jesus had been vindicated, raised and exalted, the church firmly believed and taught that he would return. 'This same Jesus who has gone from you into heaven,' said the angel to the disciples, 'will return in the same way that you saw him go into heaven'.[6] And, though Acts doesn't often refer again to this belief, clearly the whole book takes place under this rubric. This is what the disciples are doing to make Jesus' lordship known in all the world against the day when he will come once more to renew all things.[7]

But of course the primary witness is Paul. Paul's letters are full of the future coming or appearing of Jesus.[8] His worldview, his theology,

---

6. Acts 1:11.

7. See especially, for example, Acts 3:19–21.

8. See especially my *Paul: Fresh Perspectives* (London: SPCK, 2003), US title *Paul in Fresh Perspective* (Minneapolis: Fortress, 2003), chapter 7.

When He Appears 37

his missionary practice, his devotion are all inconceivable without it. Yet what he has to say about this great event has often been misunderstood, not least by the 'rapture' theology I have mentioned. It's almost time to address this directly, but first a word about another major and often misunderstood technical term.

Scholars and simple folk alike can get led astray by the use of a single word to refer to something when that word in its original setting means both more and less than the use to which it is subsequently put. In this case the word in question is the Greek word *parousia*. This is usually translated 'coming', but literally it means 'presence'—that is 'presence' as opposed to 'absence'.

The word *parousia* occurs in two of the key passages in Paul (1 Thessalonians 4:15 and 1 Corinthians 15:23), and it is found frequently elsewhere in Paul and the New Testament. It seems clear that the early Christians knew the word well, and knew what was meant by it. People often assume that the early church used *parousia* simply to mean 'the second coming of Jesus', and that by this event they all envisaged, in a quite literal fashion, the scenario of 1 Thessalonians 4:16–7 (Jesus coming down on a cloud and people flying upwards to meet him). Neither of these assumptions is in fact correct.

On the one hand, the word *parousia* had two lively meanings in non-Christian discourse at the time. Both of these seem to have influenced it in its Christian meaning.

The first meaning was the mysterious presence of a god or divinity, particularly when the power of this god was revealed in healing. People would suddenly be aware of a supernatural and powerful 'presence', and the obvious word for this was *parousia*. Josephus sometimes uses this word when he is talking about YHWH coming to the rescue of Israel.[9] God's powerful, saving presence is revealed in action, for instance when Israel under King Hezekiah was miraculously defended against the Assyrians.

The second meaning emerges when a person of high rank makes a visit to a subject state, particularly when a king or emperor visits a colony or province. The word for such a visit is 'royal presence': in Greek, *parousia*. In neither setting, we note, obviously but importantly, is there the slightest suggestion of anybody flying around on a cloud.

---

9.   See, for example, Josephus, *Antiquities*, 3.80, 203.

38 *From Resurrection to Return*

Nor is there any hint of the imminent collapse or destruction of the space-time universe.

Now supposing Paul, and for that matter the rest of the early church, wanted to say two things. On the one hand, supposing they wanted to say that the Jesus they worshipped was near in spirit but absent in body, but that one day he would be present in body, and that then the whole world, themselves included, would know the sudden transforming power of that presence. A natural word to use for this would be *parousia*.

On the other hand, supposing they wanted to say that the Jesus who had been raised from the dead and exalted to God's right hand was the rightful Lord of the world, the true emperor before whom all other emperors would shake in their shoes and bow their knees in fear and wonder. And supposing they wanted to say that, just as Caesar might one day visit a colony like Philippi or Thessalonica or Corinth (the normally absent but ruling emperor appearing and ruling in person) so the absent but ruling Lord of the world would one day appear and rule in person within this world, with all the consequences that would result. Again, the natural word to use for this would be *parousia*. (This was particularly significant in that Paul and the others were keen to say that Jesus was the true Lord and that Caesar was a sham.)

Now these things are not just suppositions. This is exactly how it was. Paul and the others used the word *parousia* because they wanted to evoke these worlds. But they evoke them within a different context. For neither the first nor the last time, the Jewish storyline and the Greco-Roman allusions and confrontations meet like two tectonic plates, throwing up the craggy mountain range we call New Testament theology.

The Jewish storyline in question was, of course, the story of the Day of the Lord, the Day of YHWH, the Day when YHWH would defeat all Israel's enemies and rescue his people once and for all. Paul and the other writers regularly refer to 'the Day of the Lord', and now of course they mean it in a Christian sense: 'the Lord' here is Jesus himself.[10] In this sense, and in this sense only, there is a solid Jewish background for the Christian doctrine of the 'second coming' of

---

10. 1 Thessalonians 5:2, 1 Corinthians 1:8 and 5:5, 2 Corinthians 1:14, Philippians 1:6, 10 and 2:16 and 2 Peter 3:10.

Jesus.[11] Of course, there could be nothing stronger, because pre-Christian Judaism, including the disciples during Jesus' lifetime, never envisaged the death of the Messiah. That is why they never thought of his resurrection, let alone an interim period between such events and the final consummation, during which he would be installed as the world's true Lord while still awaiting that sovereign rule to take full effect.

What happened, it seems, was this. The early Christians had lived within, and breathed and prayed, that old Jewish story line. In the resurrection and ascension of Jesus, shocking and unexpected though they were, they grasped the fact that in this way Israel's God had indeed done what he'd always intended, though it hadn't looked like they thought it would. Through this they came to see that Jesus, as Israel's Messiah, was already the world's true Lord, and that his secret presence by his Spirit in the present time was only a hint of what was still to come, when he would finally be revealed as the one whose power would trump all other powers both earthly and heavenly. The Jesus-story thus created a radical intensification and transformation from within the Jewish story, and the language that results in describing the Jesus-event that is yet to come is the language that says, in relation to the future: Jesus is Lord and Caesar isn't.

Parousia is itself, in fact, one of those terms in which Paul is able to say that Jesus is the reality of which Caesar is the parody. His theology of the second coming is part of his political theology of Jesus as Lord.[12] In other words, we have the language of *parousia*, of royal presence, sitting in a typically Pauline juxtaposition with the language of Jewish apocalyptic. This would not, I think, have presented many problems for Paul's first hearers. It has certainly created problems for subsequent readers, not least in the last century or so.

This is so especially when we read 1 Thessalonians 4:16–7:

> The Lord himself will come down from heaven with
> a shouted order, with the voice of an archangel and

---

11. See CJ Setzer, in JT Carroll, *The Return of Jesus in Early Christianity* (Peabody: Hendrickson, 2000), 169–83.

12. See further my *Paul: Fresh Perspectives*, chapter 4, and other material referred to there.

40 *From Resurrection to Return*

> the sound of God's trumpet. The Messiah's dead will rise first; then we who are alive, who are left, will be snatched up with them among the clouds, to meet the Lord in the air. And in this way we shall always be with the Lord.

The point to notice above all about these tricky verses is that they are *not* to be taken as a literal description of what Paul thinks will happen. They are simply a different way of saying what he is saying in 1 Corinthians 15:23–7 and 51–4, and in Philippians 3:20–1.

We had better get those other passages straight in our minds to start with. In 1 Corinthians 15:23–7 Paul speaks of the *parousia* of the Messiah as the time of the resurrection of the dead, the time when his present though secret rule will become manifest in the conquest of the last enemies, especially death. Then in verses 51–4 he speaks of what will happen to those who, at Jesus' coming, are not yet dead. They will be *changed*, transformed. This is clearly the same event as he is speaking of in 1 Thessalonians 4, we have the trumpet in both, and the resurrection of the dead in both, but whereas in 1 Thessalonians he speaks of those presently alive being 'snatched up in the air', in 1 Corinthians he speaks of them being 'transformed'. So too in Philippians 3:21, where the context is quite explicitly ranging Jesus over against Caesar, Paul speaks of the *transformation* of the present lowly body to be like Jesus' glorious body, as a result of his all-conquering power.

So why does Paul speak in this peculiar way in 1 Thessalonians, about the Lord descending and the living saints being snatched up in the air?

I suggest that he is finding richly metaphorical ways of alluding to three other stories that he is deliberately bringing together. (Paul was good at richly mixed metaphors: in the next chapter, 1 Thessalonians 5, he says that the thief will come in the night, so the woman will go into labour, so you mustn't get drunk but must stay awake and put on your armour. As the television programs say, don't try that one at home.)

We must remind ourselves yet once more that all Christian language about the future is a set of signposts pointing into a mist. Signposts don't normally provide you with advance photographs of what you'll find at the end of the road, but that doesn't mean they aren't

When He Appears

pointing in the right direction. They are telling you the truth, the particular sort of truth that can be told about the future.

The three stories that Paul is here bringing together start with the story of Moses coming down the mountain. The trumpet sounds, a loud voice is heard, and after a long wait Moses appears and descends from the mountain to see what's been going on in his absence.

Then there is the story of Daniel 7, in which the persecuted people of God are vindicated over their pagan enemy by being raised up on the clouds to sit with God in glory. This 'raising up on the clouds', which Jesus applies to himself in the gospels, is now applied by Paul to the Christians who are presently suffering persecution.[13]

Putting these two stories together, in a typically outrageous mix of metaphors, enables Paul to bring in the third story, to which we have already alluded. When the emperor visited a colony or province, the citizens of the country would go to meet him at some distance from the city. It would be disrespectful to have him actually arrive at the gates as though they his subjects couldn't be bothered to greet him properly. When they met him, they wouldn't then stay out in the open country—they would escort him royally into the city itself. When Paul speaks of 'meeting' the Lord 'in the air', the point is precisely not—as in the popular rapture-theology—that the saved believers would then stay up in the air somewhere, away from earth. The point is that, having gone out to meet their returning Lord, they will escort him royally into his domain, that is, back to the place they have come from. Even when we realise that this is highly charged metaphor, not literal description, the meaning is the same as in the parallel in Philippians 3:20. Being citizens of heaven, as the Philippians would know, doesn't mean that one is expecting to go back to the mother city, but rather that one is expecting the emperor to come *from* the mother city to give the colony its full dignity, to rescue it if need be, to subdue local enemies and put everything to rights.

These two verses in 1 Thessalonians 4, then, have been grievously abused by those who have constructed out of them a big picture of a supposed 'rapture'. This has had its effect not only on popular fundamentalism, but on a fair amount of New Testament scholarship, which

---

13. For the persecution of the Thessalonians see, for example, 1 Thessalonians 1:6, 2:14 and 3:3ff.

42 *From Resurrection to Return*

has assumed that Paul really meant what the fundamentalists think he meant. Only when we put together the several different things that he says on the same topic does the truth emerge. This is a typical piece of highly charged and multiply allusive rhetoric. The reality to which it refers is this: Jesus will be personally present, the dead will be raised, and the living Christians will be transformed. That, as we shall now see, is pretty much what the rest of the New Testament says as well.

Note, though, something else of great significance about the whole Christian theology of resurrection, ascension, second coming and hope. This theology was born out of confrontation with the political authorities, out of the conviction that Jesus was already the true Lord of the world who would one day be manifested as such. The 'rapture' theology avoids this confrontation, because it suggests that Christians will miraculously be removed from this wicked world. Perhaps that is why such theology is often gnostic in its tendency towards a private dualistic spirituality, and towards a political *laissez-faire* quietism. And perhaps that is partly why such theology, with its dreams of Armageddon, has quietly supported the political *status quo* in a way that Paul would never have done.

Before turning away from Paul, notice a significant pair of passages. First, at the end of 1 Corinthians, Paul suddenly writes a phrase in Aramaic: *Marana tha*.[14] It means, 'Our Lord, come!', and goes back (like the word *Abba*, 'father') to the very early Aramaic-speaking church. There is no reason why the Greek-speaking church would have invented a prayer in Aramaic—we must be in touch at this point with extremely early and pre-Pauline tradition. The early church was from the beginning praying to Jesus that he would return.

Second, a very different passage in Colossians 3. Here we have in a nutshell Paul's theology of resurrection and ascension, as applied to present Christian living and future Christian hope:

> If you've been raised with the Messiah, seek the things that are above, because that's where the Messiah is, sitting at God's right hand. Think about the things above, not about the things below; for you died, and your life is hidden with the Messiah in

---

14.   1 Corinthians 16:22.

When He Appears

> God. When the Messiah appears [*hotan ho Christos phanerōthē*], the one who is your life, then you too will appear with him in glory.[15]

This is clearly in the same ballpark as the other texts we've been looking at. But notice the key thing: that instead of 'coming', or the blessed word *parousia*, Paul can here use the word 'appear'. It's the same thing from a different angle, and this helps us to demystify the idea that the 'coming' of Jesus means that he will descend like a space-man from the sky. Jesus is at present in heaven. But, as we saw earlier, heaven, being God's space, is not somewhere within the space of our world, but is rather a different though closely related space. The promise is not that Jesus will simply reappear within the present world order, but that, when heaven and earth are joined together in the new way God has promised, then he will appear to us—and we will appear to him, and to one another, in our own true identity.

This is, in fact, remarkably close to a key passage in the first letter of John:

> 2[28]Now, children, abide in him; so that, when he appears [*ean phanerōthē*], we may have confidence and not shrink from him in shame at his presence [*parousia*] . . . 3[2]Beloved, we are now God's children; and it has not yet appeared [*oupō ephanerōthē*] what we shall be; but we know that when he appears [*ean phanerōthē*], we shall be like him, because we shall see him just as he is.

Here we have more or less exactly the same picture as in Colossians, though this time with 'appearing' and *parousia* happily side by side. Of course, when he 'appears' he will be 'present'. But the point of stressing 'appearing' here is that, though in one sense it will seem to us that he is 'coming', he will in fact be 'appearing' right where he presently is—not a long way away within our own space-time world, but in his own world, God's world, the world we call 'heaven'. This world is different from ours ('earth'), but intersects with it in countless

---

15. Colossians 3:1–4 (the author's own traslation has been used in this chapter).

44   *From Resurrection to Return*

ways, not least in the inner lives of Christians themselves. One day the two worlds will be integrated completely, and be fully visible to one another, producing that transformation of which both Paul and John speak.

Of course, Paul and John are not the only writers to mention all this. The Revelation of St John the Divine also speaks of the coming of Jesus, and here we find the word 'come' itself. The Spirit and the Bride say, 'Come,' and the closing prayer of the book, as with 1 Corinthians, is that the Lord Jesus will come, and come soon. The same theme is scattered elsewhere in the book.[16] There is no space here to look at these in detail, or indeed at the relevant passages in the other, smaller, New Testament books.[17] 2 Peter 3, famously, is the one place in the New Testament where the issue of delay is addressed head on, and it's worth noting that those who reckon this a problem are precisely, in context, those who are arguing for a rather different, non-historical, form of Christianity.[18]

What we have here, with minor variations, is a remarkably unanimous view spread throughout the early Christianity known to us. There will come a time, which might indeed come at any time, when, in the great renewal of the world that Easter itself foreshadowed, Jesus himself will be personally present, and will be the agent and model of the transformation that will happen both to the whole world and also to believers. This expectation and hope, expressed so clearly in the New Testament, continues undiminished in the second and subsequent centuries. Mainstream Christians throughout the early period were not worried by the fact that the event had not happened within a generation. The idea that the problem of 'delay' set out in 2 Peter 3

---

16.   Revelation 1:7, 2:25, 3:11, 16:15 and 22:7, 12 and 20.

17.   James 5:7–8 is important, as is Hebrews 9:28. 1 Peter 1:20ff and 5:4 use the word 'appear' both for the first and the second coming of Jesus.

18.   See CH Talbert in *Vigilae Christianae*, 20, 1966, 142 (quoted by J Siker, in JT Carroll (editor), *The Return of Jesus*, 148). And for all these passages, see the relevant places in my *The New Testament and the People of God*, volume 1 of *Christian Origins and the Question of God* (London: SPCK, Minneapolis: Fortress 1992), in particular for 2 Peter 3:5–13 see my *The Resurrection of the Son of God*, volume 3 of *Christian Origins and the Question of God* (London: SPCK, Minneapolis: Fortress, 2003), 462ff.

When He Appears

was widespread in second-generation Christianity is a modern scholars' myth rather than a historical reality.[19] Nor was the idea of Jesus' 'appearing' or 'coming' simply part of a tradition that was passed on uncritically without later generations really tuning in to what it was saying. As with the Ascension, so with Jesus' appearing: it was seen as a vital part of a full presentation of the Jesus who was, and is, and is to come. Without it the church's proclamation makes no sense. Take it away, and all sorts of things start to unravel. The early Christians saw this as clearly as anyone since, and we would do well to learn from them.

But it is now high time to look at the second aspect of the appearing or coming of Jesus. When he comes, according to the same biblically-grounded tradition, he will have a specific role to play: that of judge.

2. Jesus the coming judge

From the very beginning of Christianity—it's already there in some of the earliest traditions—we discover the belief that the Jesus who will appear at the end will take the role of judge. This is not an isolated belief. Indeed, within its Jewish context, it is more readily explicable than the *parousia* itself. However, it's important that we explore its meaning within early Christianity, and its significance for today and tomorrow.

The picture of Jesus as the coming judge is the central feature of another absolutely vital and non-negotiable Christian belief: that there will indeed *be* a judgment in which the creator God will set the world right once and for all. The word 'judgment' has carried negative overtones for a good many people in our liberal and postliberal world. We need to remind ourselves that throughout the Bible, not least in the Psalms, God's coming judgment is a good thing, something to be celebrated, longed for, yearned over. It causes people to shout for joy, and indeed the trees of the field to clap their hands.[20] In a world of systematic injustice, bullying, violence, arrogance and oppression, the

---

19. See Siker in Carroll, *The Return of Jesus*, and especially my *The New Testament and the People of God*, 459–64.

20. Psalm 98:8. The whole psalm is relevant, as are several others in that section of the Psalter.

46   *From Resurrection to Return*

thought that there might be a coming day when the wicked are firmly put in their place and the poor and weak are given their due is the best news there can be. Faced with a world in rebellion, a world full of exploitation and wickedness, a good God *must* be a God of judgment. The liberal optimism of the nineteenth century had a long run for its money, outlasting some of the more obvious counter-arguments provided by the huge systemic evil of the twentieth century. But more recent theology has returned to the theme of judgment, recognising that the biblical analysis of evil corresponds more closely to reality.[21]

The Old Testament hope for the creator God to bring judgment and justice to the world, to set the world right, became focused in the later biblical period on Israel's longing to see God overturn the oppressive regimes of the pagan world. It would be like a great, cosmic law court scene. Israel (or at least the righteous within Israel) would play the part of the helpless defendant. The Gentiles (or at least the particularly wicked ones) would play the part of the arrogant bullies who would at last meet their match, and get the justice (the 'judgment') they deserved.

The most famous scenario that expresses all this is Daniel 7. There, the gentile nations are depicted as huge, powerful monsters, while Israel, or the righteous within Israel, are depicted as an apparently defenceless human being, 'one like a son of man'. The scene is a great law court setting, whose climax comes when the judge, the Ancient of Days, takes his seat and finds in favour of the Son of Man against the monsters, of Israel against the pagan empires. The Son of Man is then given authority and dominion over all the nations, in a deliberate echo of Adam being given authority over the animals in Genesis 1 and 2.

What happens when this is transposed to the New Testament? Answer: we find Jesus himself taking on the role of the 'Son of Man', suffering then vindicated. Then, as in Daniel, he receives from the Supreme Judge the task of bringing this judgment to bear on the world. This accords with numerous biblical and postbiblical passages in which Israel's Messiah, the one who represents Israel in person, is given the task of judgment. In Isaiah 11, the Messiah's judgment creates a

---

21. See, particularly, Miroslav Volf, *Exclusion and Embrace: A Theological Exploration of Identity, Otherness and Reconciliation* (Nashville: Abingdon Press, 1994).

When He Appears 47

world where the wolf and the lamb lie down side by side. In Psalm 2, the Gentiles tremble when the Messiah is enthroned. Again and again the Messiah is stated to be God's agent to bring the whole world, not just Israel, back into the state of justice and truth for which God longs as much as we do. So the early Christians, who had concluded from Easter that Jesus was indeed the Messiah, naturally identified him as the one through whom God would put the world to rights. They didn't simply deduce this from their belief in his future coming or appearing. Actually, it may have been the other way round: their belief in Jesus' Messiahship may have been a decisive factor in the emergence of the belief in his final coming as judge.

Certainly by the time of Paul this belief is well established. The summary of what Paul said on the Areopagus in Athens concludes with the statement that God has fixed a day on which he will judge the world by a man whom he has appointed, giving assurance of the fact by raising him from the dead.[22] Paul can refer almost casually (in Romans 2:16) to the fact that, according to the gospel he preaches, God will judge the secrets of all hearts through Jesus the Messiah. Although people often suppose that, because Paul taught justification by faith, not works, there can be no room for a future judgment 'according to works', this only goes to show how much some have radically misunderstood him. The future judgment according to deeds, a judgment exercised by Jesus at his 'judgment seat', is clearly taught in, for instance, Romans 14:9–10, 2 Corinthians 5:10 and elsewhere. Equally important, these are not isolated places where Paul is quoting a tradition that doesn't fully fit with his developed theology. They are fully and tightly integrated into his thinking and preaching. For him, as much as for anyone else in the early church, the final judgment, exercised by Jesus the Messiah, was a vital element, without which all sorts of other things simply wouldn't stand up.

In particular (though there isn't space to develop this here) this picture of future judgment according to works is actually the *basis* of Paul's theology of justification by faith.[23] The point of justification by

---

22. Acts 17:31. See also 10:42.

23. On all this, see my *What St Paul Really Said* (Grand Rapids: Eerdmans, 1997), chapter 7, and my *Paul: Fresh Perspectives*, chapter 6. See also 'Redemption from the New Perspective', in *Redemption*, edited by ST Davis, D Kendall and

48   *From Resurrection to Return*

faith isn't that God suddenly ceases to care about good behaviour or morality. Justification by faith cannot be collapsed, as so many in the last two centuries have effectively tried to do, either into a generalised liberal view of a laissez-faire morality or into the romantic view that what we do outwardly doesn't matter at all since the only thing that matters is what we're like inwardly. (Those who overanxiously defend a doctrine from which all mention of 'works' has been rigorously excluded should consider with whom they are colluding at this point!) No: justification by faith is what happens in the *present time,* anticipating the verdict of the *future day* when God judges the world. It is God's advance declaration that, when someone believes the gospel, that person is already a member of his family no matter who their parents were, that their sins are forgiven because of Jesus' death, and that on the future day, as Paul says, 'there is now no condemnation' (Romans 8:1). Clearly there are further questions to be asked about how the verdict issued in the present can so confidently be supposed to anticipate correctly the verdict issued in the future on the basis of the entire life led. Paul addresses those questions in several ways at several points, particularly in his expositions of the work of the Holy Spirit. But for Paul (and this is the only point I am making in the present context) there was no clash between present justification by faith and future judgment according to works. The two actually need, and depend upon, one another. To go any further would demand a fairly thorough exposition of Romans and Galatians, for which there is obviously no space here.[24]

G O'Collins (Oxford: Oxford University Press, 2003), 69–100, '4QMMT and Paul: Justification, "Works," and Eschatology', in *History and Exegesis: New Testament Essays in Honor of Dr E Earle Ellis for His 80th Birthday*, edited by Aang-Won (Aaron) Son (New York and London: T&T Clark, 2006), 104–32, and 'New Perspectives on Paul', in *Justification in Perspective: Historical Developments and Contemporary Challenges*, edited by Bruce L McCormack (Grand Rapids: Baker Academic, 2006), 243–64.

24. See my 'Romans' in the *New Interpreter's Bible*, volume X (Nashville: Abingdon, 2002), 393–770, the various volumes of my *Paul for Everyone* (London: SPCK, Louisville: WJKP) (*Galatians and Thessalonians*, 2002, *The Prison Letters*, 2002, *1 Corinthians* and *2 Corinthians*, both 2003, *Romans* (2 volumes), 2004), and *The Climax of the Covenant* (Edinburgh: T&T Clark, Minneapolis: Fortress,

When He Appears   49

Once again, the Pauline picture is filled out by other references in the New Testament. This is no flash in the pan or Pauline idiosyncrasy—it is common early Christian belief.[25] It is the central point in that long paragraph in John 5 that caused so many headaches to those earlier scholars who tried to make John's gospel teach simply a present eternal life, rather than also the future one:

> The father doesn't judge anyone, he has handed over all judgment to the son, so that everyone should honour the son just as they honour the father. Anyone who doesn't honour the son doesn't honour the father who sent him. I'm telling you the solemn truth: anyone who hears my word, and believes in the one who sent me, has eternal life. Such a person won't come into judgment; they will have passed out of death into life. I'm telling you the solemn truth: the time is coming—in fact, it's here already!—when the dead will hear the voice of God's son, and those who hear it will live. You see, just as the father has life in himself, in the same way he has given the son the privilege of having life in himself. He has even given him authority to pass judgment, because he is the son of man. Don't be surprised at this. The time is coming, you see, when everyone in the tombs will hear his voice. They will come out—those who have done good, to the resurrection of life, and those who have done evil, to the resurrection of judgment. I can't do anything on my own authority. I judge on the basis of what I hear. And my judgment is just, because I'm not trying to carry out my own wishes, but the wishes of the one who sent me.[26]

The main point to notice, once more, is that all the future judgment is highlighted basically as good news, not bad. Why so? It is good

---

1992), especially chapters 7, 8, 10 and 13.

25.   See also, for example, 2 Timothy 4:1 and 1 Peter 4:5.

26.   John 5:22–30.

50　　　　　*From Resurrection to Return*

news, first, because the one through whom God's justice will finally sweep the world is not a hard-hearted, arrogant or vengeful tyrant, but the Man of Sorrows, who was acquainted with grief, the Jesus who loved sinners and died for them, the Messiah who himself took the world's judgment upon himself on the cross. Of course, this also means that he is quite uniquely placed to judge the systems and rulers that have carved up the world between them, and the New Testament points this out here and there.[27] In particular, as we have already seen and as some mediaeval theologians and artists highlighted, Jesus comes as judge much as Moses descended the mountain into the camp where idolatry and revelry was in full swing. The Sistine Chapel itself reminds us of the day when careless and casual living, as well as downright wickedness, will be brought to book.[28]

Within the New Testament, and within subsequent Christian theology, this judgment is *anticipated* under certain circumstances. I have already spoken of justification by faith. The same is true, in 1 Corinthians, for the Eucharist: eating and drinking the body and blood of Jesus means confronting here and now the one who is the judge as well as the saviour of all.[29] And the same is true, of course, of the work of the Spirit, as we see once more in John 16. When the Spirit comes, declares Jesus, he will convict the world of sin, of righteousness and judgment.[30] The final judgment, in other words, will be anticipated in the present world through the Spirit-led work and witness of Jesus' followers.

3. Second coming and judgment

The so-called second coming of Jesus, then, when properly understood in the New Testament and subsequent Christian teaching, is no

---

27. For example John 16:8–11, about which there is no space to say more at this point.

28. See Douglas Farrow, *Ascension and Ecclesia: On the Significance of the Doctrine of the Ascension for Ecclesiology and Christian Cosmology* (Grand Rapids: Eerdmans, 1999), 271.

29. 1 Corinthians 11:27–34.

30. See especially TF Torrance, *Space, Time and Resurrection* (Edinburgh: Handsel Press, 1976), 158.

When He Appears 51

afterthought to the basic Christian message. It hasn't been as it were bolted on to the outside of a gospel message that could stand complete without it. We cannot relegate it to the margins of our thinking, our living and our praying—if we do, we shall pull everything else out of shape.

I now want, briefly, to draw out a few final points of relevance for us today.

First, the appearing or coming of Jesus offers the complete answer to the literalist fundamentalists on the one hand and to the proponents of the 'cosmic Christ' idea I outlined in the previous paper. Jesus remains other than the church, other than the world, even while being present to both by the Spirit. He confronts the world in the present, and will do so personally and visibly in the future. He is the one to whom every knee shall bow (Philippians 2:10–1), as well as the one who took the form of a servant and was obedient to the death of the cross (Philippians 2:6–8). Indeed, as Paul stresses, he is the first *because* he did the second. In his appearing we find neither a dualist rejection of the present world, nor simply his arrival like a spaceman into the present world, but the *transformation* of the present world, and ourselves within it, so that it will at last be put to rights, and we with it. Death and decay will themselves be overcome, and God will be all in all.

This means, second, that a proper shape and balance are given to the Christian worldview. Like the Jewish worldview, but radically opposed to the Stoic, the Platonic, the Hindu and the Buddhist worldviews, Christians tell a story with a beginning, a middle and an end. Not to have closure at the end of the story—to be left with a potentially endless cycle, round and round with either the same things happening again and again, or simply perhaps the long outworking of karma—would be the very antithesis of the story told by the apostles, and by the long line of their Jewish predecessors. And, precisely because Jesus is not collapsed into the church, or indeed the world, we can renounce on the one hand the triumphalism that conveniently makes his sovereign lordship an excuse for its own, and on the other hand the despair that comes when we see such hopes dashed, as they always will be, in the follies and failings of even the best and greatest Christian organisations, structures, leaders and followers. Because we live between Ascension and appearing, joined to Jesus Christ by the

52   *From Resurrection to Return*

Spirit but still awaiting his final coming and presence, we can be *both* properly humble *and* properly confident. 'We proclaim not ourselves, but Jesus Christ as Lord, and ourselves as your servants through Jesus.'[31]

Thirdly, following directly from this, the task of the church between Ascension and Parousia is therefore set free both from the self-driven energy that imagines it has to build God's kingdom all by itself, and the despair that supposes it can't do anything until Jesus comes again. We do not 'build the kingdom' all by ourselves, but we do build *for* the kingdom. All that we do in faith, hope and love in the present, in obedience to our ascended Lord and in the power of his Spirit, will be enhanced and transformed at his appearing.[32] This too brings a note of judgment, of course, as Paul makes clear in 1 Corinthians 3:10–7. The 'day' will disclose what sort of work each builder has done.

In particular, the present rule of the ascended Jesus Christ and the assurance of his final appearing in judgment should give us—which goodness knows we need today—some clarity and realism in our political discourse. Far too often Christians slide into a vaguely spiritualised version of one or other major political system or party. What would happen if we were to take seriously our stated belief that Jesus Christ is already the Lord of the world, and that at his name, one day, every knee would bow?

You might suppose that this would inject merely a note of pietism, and make us then avoid the real issues—or, indeed, to attempt a theocratic takeover bid. But to think in either of those ways would only show how deeply we have been conditioned by the Enlightenment split between religion and politics. What happens if we reintegrate them? As with specifically Christian work, so with political work done in Jesus' name: confessing Jesus as the ascended and coming Lord frees up the political task from the necessity to pretend that this or that program or leader has the key to Utopia (if only we would elect them). Equally, it frees up our corporate life from the despair that comes when we realise that, once again, our political systems let us down. The Ascension and appearing of Jesus constitute a radical

---

31.   2 Corinthians 4:5.

32.   This is the logic behind, for example, 1 Corinthians 15:58. See my *The Way of the Lord* (Grand Rapids: Eeerdmans, 1999) chapter 9 and below, chapter 13.

When He Appears 53

challenge to the entire thought-structure of the Enlightenment (and of course several other movements). And, since our present Western politics is very much the creation of the Enlightenment, we should think seriously about the ways in which, as thinking Christians, we can and should bring that challenge to bear. I know this is giving a huge hostage to fortune, raising questions to which I certainly don't know the answer, but I do know that unless I point all this out one might easily get the impression that these ancient doctrines are of theoretical or abstract interest only. They aren't. People who believe that Jesus is already Lord, and that he will appear again as judge of the world are called and equipped (to put it mildly) to think and act quite differently in the world from those who don't.

In particular, of course, the hope of Jesus' coming as judge, to put right all that is wrong in the world and to give new life to the dead, is the context for one of the central themes of all Christian faith—the hope of the resurrection of the body. But that is another subject for another time.

The Bodily Resurrection of Jesus as a First Instantiation of a New Law of the New Creation: Wright's Visionary New Paradigm in Dialogue with Physics and Cosmology

Robert John Russell

'If it is impossible, it cannot be true. But if it is true, it cannot be impossible.' NT Wright's new paradigm for the historicity of the bodily resurrection of Jesus offers us a bold and inspiring new vision of the truth of Christian faith and a robust agenda for understanding and championing that faith in today's secular world, particularly in the context of historical research.

The goal of this working paper is to connect Wright's paradigm with the international discussions of 'theology and science'. My hope is that such a connection will enhance Wright's work through the resources and discoveries of the theology and science community, and that Wright's paradigm will inspire and ground the creative interaction between theology and science through his arguments for the historicity of the resurrection.

In Part 1 I offer some constructive comments on Wright's critique of the principle of analogy in historical research. Then in Part 2 I turn to the version of the principle of analogy based on science and its philosophical interpretations and suggest ways in which this version is even further undermined—surprisingly, perhaps—by science itself. In Part 3 I move to the central issue of this paper: the apparent challenge from cosmology to eschatology and the possibilities for moving beyond this to genuine creative interaction between science and theology.

I have included excerpts from previous publications that provide background for the work in Part 3 as an appendix. I hope this paper serves as a basis for an engaging conversation and critical feedback on 'research in progress'.

The Bodily Resurrection of Jesus

55

1. Wright's new paradigm: breaking the principle of analogy in historical science

In the third book in his landmark trilogy on Christians origins, *The Resurrection of the Son of God*, NT Wright lays out his new paradigm for the historicity of the bodily resurrection of Jesus with this bold claim:

> [T]he *only* possible reason why early Christianity began and took the shape it did is that the tomb really was empty and that people really did meet Jesus, alive again, and . . . though admitting it involves accepting a challenge at the level of worldview itself, the best historical explanation for all these phenomena is that Jesus was indeed bodily raised from the dead.[1]

This claim actually includes two proposals: (a) the resurrection of Jesus functions as an historical explanation, and (b) the resurrection of Jesus calls for a change in our overall worldview. In this first part of my paper I want to focus on Wright's first proposal and offer my own reasons for supporting the argument for why the resurrection of Jesus *can* function as an historical explanation. I will then turn to proposal (b) that deals with the change in worldview and the problem of science in the second part of the paper.

1.1 The resurrection of Jesus serves as a historical explanation and the challenge to the principle of analogy

With roots in nineteenth-century liberal Protestant theology and biblical criticism, particularly in the work of Ernst Troeltsch, and continuing in such twentieth-century figures as Rudolf Bultmann and John Dominic Crosson, we find an insistence that ancient history must be

---

1.   NT Wright, *The Resurrection of the Son of God*, volume 3 of *Christian Origins and the Question of God* (London: SPCK, Minneapolis: Fortress Press, 2003), 8. Note: Peters cites and supports this in his paper for the conference as well. See also Ted Peters, 'The Future of the Resurrection', in *The Resurrection of Jesus: John Dominic Crossan and NT Wright in Dialogue*, edited by Robert B Stewart (Minneapolis: Fortress Press, 2006), 149–69.

56   *From Resurrection to Return*

understood by analogy to present historical experience. Claude Welch summarises the importance of Troeltsch's contribution to this argument in the following way:

> ... Troeltsch may rightly be looked upon as the outcome of Protestant thought in the nineteenth century, the one who most effectively posed the problems facing twentieth century theology ... in their acutest form and laid out certain directions of thought that cannot be evaded by subsequent generations ... [O]ne cannot go around him in the attempt to recover a prior state of theological reflection; one must rather go through the critical perspective that he embodied ... [H]e put the questions in an inescapable way.[2]

In a brief article on historical and dogmatic method in theology (1900), Troeltsch listed the principle of analogy as the second of three elements in critical method:[3]

> Analogy with what happens before our eyes and what is given within ourselves is the key to criticism ... Agreement with normal, ordinary, repeatedly attested modes of occurrence and conditions as we know them is the mark of probability for the occurrences that the critic can either acknowledge really to have happened or leave on one side. The observation of analogies between past occurrences of the same sort makes it possible to ascribe probability to them and to interpret the one that is unknown from what is known of the other.[4]

---

2.   Claude Welch, *Protestant Thought in the Nineteenth Century*, volume 2 (New Haven: Yale University Press, 1985), 266–7.

3.   The other two are often referred to as the principles of criticism and of correlation.

4.   Ernst Troeltsch, 'Der Historismus und Seine Probleme', in *Gesammelte Schriften* (Tubingen, 1922), 221–693, especially 656ff as found in translation in Wolfhart

The Bodily Resurrection of Jesus

In his ground-breaking work, *Theology of Hope*, Jürgen Moltmann underscored the 'grave difficulties' posed by Troeltsch's principle of analogy if it were to be accepted in theological reflections on the resurrection of Jesus. Instead Moltmann urged that:

> . . . theology has the possibility of constructing its own concept of history and its own view of the tale of history on the basis of a theological and eschatological understanding of the reality of the resurrection. Then the theology of the resurrection would no longer be fitted in with an existing concept of history, but an attempt would have to be made . . . to arrive at a new understanding of history with the ultimate possibilities and hopes that attach to it on the presupposition of the raising of Christ from the dead. In conflict with other concepts of history, an *intellectus fidei resurrectionis* must then be developed which makes it possible to speak 'Christianly' of God, history and nature . . . The resurrection of Christ does not offer itself as an analogy to that which can be experienced any time and anywhere, but as an analogy to what is to come to all . . . It is called historic because . . . it *makes* history . . . [and] discloses an eschatological future.[5]

I am appreciative of Moltmann's response to the challenge posed by Troeltsch, but I would prefer to view the resurrection of Jesus not only as disclosing a future eschaton in sharp contrast to the present world but also as an eschatological event realised in part within the flowing context of history, beginning at Easter, an event whose empirical elements such as the empty tomb are open to historical inquiry. For this and other reasons, I turn to an early work by Wolfhart Pannen-

---

Pannenberg, *Basic Questions in Theology*, translated by George H Kehm (Minneapolis: Fortress Press, 1970), 43–4.

5. Jürgen Moltmann, *Theology of Hope: On the Ground and the Implications of a Christian Eschatology*, translated by James W Leitch (New York: Harper & Row, 1975), 177–81.

58   *From Resurrection to Return*

berg, 'Redemptive Event and History'. Here Pannenberg offered his own distinctive response to the threat posed by the move to treat the method of analogy as a general principle of historical explanation:

> A constriction of historical-critical inquiry, in the sense of domination by a biased world view, first occurs when, instead of pointing out analogies from case to case, one postulates a fundamental homogeneity of all reality with the current range of experience and research . . .

The end result is that:

> [Troeltsch] spoke of an 'omnipotence of analogy' . . . which includes a 'fundamental homogeneity of all historical events' . . . [t]he leveling of historical particularity, brought about by one-sided emphasis on the typical and analogous, threatens to elevate the postulate of the homogeneity of all events to the status of a principle.[6]

Pannenberg returned to this problem two decades later in volume 2 of his *Systematic Theology* (1994), where he wrote simply and unambiguously:

> Historicity does not necessarily mean that what is said to have taken place historically must be like other known events. The claim to historicity that is inseparable from the assertion of the facticity of an event simply involves the fact that it happened at a specific time. The question whether it is like other events may play a role in critical evaluation of the truth of the claim but is not itself a condition of the actual truth claim the assertion makes.[7]

---

6.   Pannenberg, *Basic Questions*, 47.
7.   Wolfhart Pannenberg, *Systematic Theology*, volume 2, translated by GW Bromiley (Grand Rapids: Eerdmans, 1994), 360–1.

The Bodily Resurrection of Jesus   59

If Pannenberg is correct, all one needs to do is offer convincing reasons for claiming that a purported event actually happened in history whether or not it is analogous to other historical events. If we can discover such reasons in regard to the resurrection of Jesus, we will be in a position to claim that the resurrection is a historical event. That in turn will lead to a fundamental change in our general worldview of both history and nature.

Here the voluminous work of NT Wright takes centre stage and becomes of crucial importance for the Christian church. Wright has constructed a new paradigm that offers robust reasons for treating the resurrection as having happened objectively in history, and not just as a narrative code for the strictly subjective religious experience of the early disciples.

If Wright's arguments can be sustained, we will genuinely be in a new era of Christian scholarship and apologetics, particularly if we can make his case not only to historical research but perhaps even more importantly to science, where the principle of analogy might be taken for granted as unassailable—and thus pitting science against a theology of bodily resurrection.

Wright first offers a more nuanced and generous reading of Troeltsch than did Pannenberg: 'Jesus' resurrection might have occurred . . . we simply cannot say anything about it.' But then he challenges even this claim: Even if we can only speak of things that are analogous to our experience, is there no way in which the resurrection of Jesus could be analogous? Wright's response is that the resurrection of Jesus did fit within the prevailing Jewish worldview. In addition, it could be thought of as partly analogous to other liberating works of God in the history of Israel, even though it was more than this. Finally, it had at least partial precedents in the healings and resuscitations recounted in the Old Testament.[8] So if partial analogy counts, then it would seem that we can address the resurrection of Jesus as an historical event.

Suppose, however, partial analogies don't count. In a brilliant move, Wright then wields Troeltsch against Troeltsch: the rise of the early church is so strikingly *sui generis* that if Troeltsch were correct and partial analogies didn't count, we could say nothing about it either! Thus:

---

8.   Wright, *Resurrection*, 17.

60 *From Resurrection to Return*

> The rise of the early church thus constitutes in itself a counter-example to Troeltsch's general point. If we are to speak truly about the early church, we must describe something for which there was no precedent and of which there remains no subsequent example. In addition, as we shall see, the early church by its very existence forces upon us the question which we, as historians, must ask: what precisely happened after Jesus' crucifixion that caused early Christianity to come into being? Ironically, then, it is precisely the uniqueness of the rise of the early church that forces us to say: never mind analogies, what happened?[9]

Wright then answers this for us in his crucial move that encapsulates his new paradigm:

> [T]he *only* possible reason why early Christianity began and took the shape it did is that the tomb really was empty and that people really did meet Jesus, alive again, and . . . that, though admitting it involves accepting a challenge at the level of worldview itself, the best historical explanation for all these phenomena is that Jesus was indeed bodily raised from the dead.[10]

1.2 *A brief comment on Wright's argument*

I would like to offer a brief comment on Wright's use the phrase 'historical explanation' for the resurrection of Jesus before turning to the challenges from science and its version of the principle of analogy. As already stated, I agree with him that we should dismiss the **principle of analogy** as a normative criterion for historical explanation even while maintaining the **heuristic of analogy** by which our hermeneutics of suspicion are roused without an *a priori* decision about events that fall outside its purview. I am reminded here of that oft-quoted visionary

---

9.   Wright, *Resurrection*, 18.
10. Wright, *Resurrection*, 8.

The Bodily Resurrection of Jesus 61

statement by Pope John Paul II on the right relations between science and religion: 'Science can purify religion from error and superstition; religion can purify science from idolatry and false absolutes.'[11] If as a heuristic the disanalogies between biblical claims and modern inquiry lead to a cleansing of merely mythic elements (in Barth's, not Bultmann's sense), so much the better. A sweeping program of 'demythologisation', based on the principle of analogy, however, would treat science itself idolatrously and should be rejected, not embraced, by theology.

Where I want to raise a question and offer a suggestion to Wright is about the term 'historical explanation'. As he clearly shows, the rise of the early church as an historical event leads, immediately, to the question about its explanation: whatever explanation we proffer, should it be considered historical since it is purportedly an explanation of an historical event?

Wright says yes: he claims that the best explanation is the bodily resurrection of Jesus, including the empty tomb, and he claims this is therefore a 'historical explanation'.

My concern is about a possible play on words here. I agree with Wright that the bodily resurrection of Jesus is the best explanation of the rise of the early church. My question is whether the bodily resurrection should be considered a historical explanation or whether it is better considered a theological explanation of the historical fact of the rise of the early church. By 'theological explanation' I do not mean an 'unhistorical' explanation, that is one insulated from the data of history or the events that secular (non-confessional) historical inquiry view as having actually happened in time and place. As Moltmann rightly says, we must not allow *fides quaerens intellectum* to 'give up all claim to an *intellectus fidei* in the realm of history' because this, in turn, 'leaves the knowledge of history to all possible kinds of pantheistic or atheistic principles . . . '[12]

---

11. John Paul II, 'Message to the Pontifical Academy of Sciences', in *Evolutionary and Molecular Biology: Scientific Perspectives on Divine Action*, edited by Robert John Russell, William R Stoeger and Francisco J Ayala (Vatican City State: Vatican Observatory Publications, Berkeley: Center for Theology and the Natural Sciences, 1998), M13.

12. Moltmann, *Theology of Hope*, 177–8.

62   *From Resurrection to Return*

Instead I view a theological explanation as one that is irreducibly theological yet one that embraces the 'data' of secular historical inquiry (as well as 'data' from other sources). On the one hand it is irreducible in the epistemic sense that I will discuss in more detail later: it cannot be restated exhaustively through the concepts of the subdisciplines that it includes yet transcends. Arthur Peacocke, a leading figure in theology and science, draws specifically on his extensive discussion of critical realism in support of holistic epistemology to claim that the theological term 'resurrection' may in fact be one of these irreducible terms in theology, one that cannot be reduced entirely to the field of psychology and thus to the psychological experience of the disciples, even though the term 'resurrection' includes reference to the psychological experience of the disciples to the resurrection of Jesus.[13] Yet on the other hand it embraces, and is not in a separate linguistic sphere from, such historical reports as the visit of the women to the tomb of Jesus, the tomb being empty, the journey to Emmaus and the breaking of the bread, and so on (this is not a neo-Orthodox or Wittgensteinian 'two language' move). These reports are open to secular historical investigation and could, in principle, be disproven (for example, Crossan's claim that the body of Jesus was eaten by dogs could in principle be proven). To the extent that they are not disproven, they can be presumed to be data for which theology offers, as the best explanation, the resurrection of Jesus. Hence when I ask whether the resurrection is a theological, rather than an historical, explanation, I would prefer to say that the term 'resurrection' is irreducibly theological because it is qualified and constrained by the results of historical, psychological and natural scientific analysis.

In passing, I would point out that it can also be seen as historical in the temporal-sequence sense that the resurrection of Jesus follows upon his death and burial, both of which are historical events in every

---

13.   This is a particularly poignant claim since Peacocke goes on allow for a non-bodily interpretation of the resurrection of Jesus (that is the empty tomb is irrelevant to the resurrection of Jesus), which, in my view, can be seen as evacuating the resurrection of its central and shocking claim, namely that 'matter matters'. See Arthur Peacocke, *Theology for a Scientific Age: Being and Becoming—Natural, Divine and Human*, Enlarged Edition (Minneapolis: Fortress Press, 1993), 279–88.

The Bodily Resurrection of Jesus 63

ordinary sense. However, the resurrection as the series of reported events—visions and appearances of the risen Lord—would be of a mixed historical/non-historical account: historical in that they happened at a time and place of ordinary depiction, like the Upper Room or the Road to Emmaus and the breaking of the bread, but non-historical in that they assume theological categories, like the revelation of Jesus' identity as the Son of God in the breaking of the bread.[14]

In sum, then, I think the best way to respond to this question is 'both/and': In one sense the resurrection of Jesus is historical since it is the best explanation of the historical fact of the rise of the early church. I take it that this is the sense in which Wright calls it a 'historical explanation'.

Yet in another sense the resurrection of Jesus transcends secular historical categories of explanation and opens up to a theological explanation as that which embraces but transcends, and cannot be reduced to, an historical explanation.[15]

2. Factoring the methods and discoveries of science into the problematic of the resurrection of Jesus

2.1 A critique of the principle of analogy as represented in the methodology of science

It might seem, at first blush, that science, particularly the philosophical assumptions all too often brought to it, raises even stronger arguments in favour of its version of the principle of analogy than historical research.

---

14. For a lucid analysis of the historicity of the resurrection and a comparison of Protestant and Roman Catholic views, see Gerald O'Collins, SJ, *Jesus Risen: An Historical, Fundamental and Systematic Examination of Christ's Resurrection* (New York: Paulist Press, 1987).

15. A parallel in science might be the absolute beginning of the universe at time t = 0 according to standard Big Bang cosmology. It is a physical event open to scientific investigation in the sense of it being the cause of the following effects (that is those for t > 0), but in principle it is not a physical event in the sense of being the effect of a previous cause (that is the effect of a cause at t < 0, since in standard Big Bang cosmology we cannot refer meaningfully to events preceding t = 0). Thus it is both physical and non-physical.

64   *From Resurrection to Return*

Epistemic reductionism. Physics is now, or at least one day will be, the only route to true knowledge. Every other form of intellectual inquiry is, essentially, empty and only of temporary and pragmatic value. In particular, the concepts in theology can be restated without remainder in the concepts of an underlying discipline, either psychology (that is the resurrection as merely the experience of hope for the disciples), existentialist philosophy (that is the resurrection is merely the encounter of faith in the present moment of personal existence), secular history (that is the resurrection is simply the incentive for political/social liberation), and ultimately natural science (that is the resurrection as a function of the pattern of neuronal firings under certain physiological conditions).

Nomological universality. The laws of nature are timeless and universal: they are the same everywhere in the universe and at all times in the past and future. Actually this concept should be factored into two distinct concepts: spatial nomological universality, that the laws are the same everywhere in the universe at the same moment in time, and temporal nomological universality, that the laws are the same in the past, present and future of the universe at a given place in the universe.[16] Roughly equivalent to this is the claim that the predictions of science, based on these universal laws, are apodeictic: unless they are technically incorrect (that is the result of a mathematical error or erroneous data used to make them), they necessarily apply in the future even as they correctly describe and explain the past.

The combined effect of epistemic reductionism and nomological universality is to open the doors to metaphysical naturalism: nature is all there is and God, if the term is still meaningful, is at most to be understood in terms of deism. Clearly if the laws are the same everywhere and at all times, if their predictions based solely on natural

---

16. What I am calling spatial nomological universality is related to what scientists call the cosmological principle: that the universe is homogeneous (the same at all places) and isotropic (the same in all directions) at each given moment. What I am calling temporal nomological universality is related to what scientists call the perfect cosmological principle, that the universe is the same, not only at each moment, but in the past, present and future. Big Bang cosmology represents the cosmological principle, while Einstein's static cosmology and Hoyle's steady state cosmology represent the perfect cosmological principle.

The Bodily Resurrection of Jesus

causes are to hold apodeictically, and if the concepts of theology are essentially empty, then science will provide the adequate explanatory paradigm not only for nature but even for all human experience, and there can be no appeal to divine action in unique historical events— whether or not God even exists (metaphysical naturalism).

I would like to discuss several reasons drawn from the 'theology and science' scholarship which challenge these claims and in this way add further support to Wright's rejection of the principle of analogy in historical research.

Epistemic reductionism. It is self-evident that analogy can serve as a heuristic device for the discovery of new knowledge within and across disciplines. As a heuristic, one tries to see how much can be learned by seeking to explain the unknown in terms of the known. As a working assumption or 'rule of thumb', reasoning by analogy is ubiquitous to all academic disciplines.[17] Indeed as scholars from Paul Ricoeur to Lakoff have convincingly argued, the tension between analogy and disanalogy (or simile and dissimile) constitutes the structure of language as metaphor and conveys its epistemic truth claims.[18] Exploration of the unknown by way of analogy with the known is clearly a form of 'methodological reductionism': the program to analyse the whole in terms of its parts and to use a known theory to explain as much of the new and unknown as possible. Of the various forms of reductionism—epistemological, ontological/metaphysical, eliminative, causal, amongst others—methodological reductionism is the only one that is universally accepted and employed by scholars in theology and science.[19]

---

17. For the general role of analogy in science, where it serves in the construction of models and finally theories, see the writings of Ian G Barbour, notably his early work, Ian G Barbour, *Myths, Models, and Paradigms: A Comparative Study in Science and Religion* (New York: Harper & Row, 1974). For the role of analogy in the writings of one of the twentieth century's most influential theologians, see David Tracy, *The Analogical Imagination: Christian Theology and the Culture of Pluralism* (New York: Crossroad, 1981).

18. See for example George Lakoff and Mark Johnson, *Metaphors We Live By* (Chicago: University of Chicago Press, 1980).

19. Interestingly, methodological reductionism is based on a combination of two intellectual traditions: nature as rational and intelligible, as found in Hellenistic thought, and nature

From Resurrection to Return

Clearly, however, what must be opposed is the elevation of analogy from its constructive role as a heuristic to a universal principle limiting what can be considered historical or natural to what can be known through direct experience today of human history and the natural world. The claim that the unknown **must** be reducible to the known is actually a form of epistemological reductionism as mentioned above. Actually epistemic reduction takes on two distinct meanings: (1) interdisciplinary reductionism—it is reductionistic in the inter-disciplinary sense that the higher disciplines, such as psychology or sociology, can be reduced without remainder, or translated down into, lower disciplines, such as neuroscience or biology, and (2) temporal reductionism—it is reductionistic in the temporal sense by assuming that although more complex phenomena seem to appear in the history of the world, they cannot be genuinely novel. There can be no truly unknown or truly new to be discovered, just the as-yet unrecognised known. All knowledge is given in the present.

Epistemic reductionism has received universal criticism from scholars in theology and science. They counter it with various arguments for epistemic holism / epistemic emergence by emphasising the fact that new properties and processes occur at higher levels of organisation in nature and history.[20] As I will argue below, contemporary science, with its dynamic worldview of the evolution of life on earth and the unique sequence of unrepeatable epochs in the history of the universe, radically undercut the principle of analogy in its guise as epistemic reductionism. Instead, I will propose that the history of emergent, new phenomena in nature, and the fact that their appearance which cannot be predicted by what has come before them, suggests that they represent the first instance of a new 'law of nature'.

---

as created *ex nihilo*, as found in the three Abrahamic monotheistic traditions. If the universe is God's free creation and not something coeternal with God (as in the Platonic creation narratives), then we must experiment to gain knowledge of it. If the universe is created by the divine Logos, then it will be rational and, if we are created in the *imago dei*, we will have the ability to understand its rationality. The empirical method, methodological naturalism, and the use of mathematics in theoretical science, embody then this confluence between Athens and Jerusalem. So there are good theological reasons for seeing science as the inheritor of the Biblical and Greek traditions.

20. For a helpful discussion of holistic epistemology see Peacocke, *Theology for a Scientific Age*.

The Bodily Resurrection of Jesus

Nomological universality. As a heuristic, nomological universalism is essential to science. One cannot falsify a theory against evidence if its predictions need not hold, if the theory is insulated from such anomalies by makeshift qualifications that the theory really shouldn't hold in these cases. Scientific theories are held, as Polanyi argued, with 'universal intent'.

Nevertheless there is a distinction between a prediction holding for the purpose of falsifying a scientific theory and a prediction holding apodeictically against any 'all else being equal' arguments. We shall return to this near the end of this paper when we deal the predictions for the 'freeze or fry' of the cosmological future in light of eschatology and the claim that if God acts in a new way, this new way of acting (which underlies natural regularities and their expression as laws of nature) does not violate the predictions of science but changes the framework in which science operates. The task will be to combine nomological universality as a necessary assumption for scientists in their research and a necessary assumption for theologians when integrating science into theology in its explanations of the past history of the universe, and nomological universality as a tentative and provisional assumption which can be set aside by theologians when they are focusing on the eschatological reality of the future new creation based proleptically on the resurrection of Jesus.

2.2 Resurrection as 'a proleptic first instance of the coming new creation'

> Blessed be the God and Father of our Lord Jesus Christ! By his great mercy he has given us a new birth into a living hope through the resurrection of Jesus Christ from the dead. (1 Peter 1:3)

> Our generation must be obedient . . . to what *God* has chosen to do in Jesus; and we cannot impose on that picture what we think God should have done. (Raymond E Brown[21])

---

21. Raymond E Brown, *The Virginal Conception and Bodily Resurrection of Jesus* (New York: Paulist Press, 1973), 72.

68   *From Resurrection to Return*

What about the discoveries of science: are they 'friend or foe' to the historical understanding of the resurrection that Wright proposes? We first need to discuss, briefly, the bodily character of the resurrection and the empty tomb narratives before turning to them.

The empty tomb as a key to explaining the rise of the early Christian faith. A number of New Testament scholars and systematic theologians argue in support of the bodily resurrection of Jesus of Nazareth. Along with Raymond Brown, Gerald O'Collins, William Craig, Jürgen Moltmann, Wolfhart Pannenberg, Ted Peters, Sandra Schneiders and many others, Wright views the resurrection of Jesus as neither a resuscitation (for example the daughter of Jairus—Mark 5:22, Lazarus—John 11:1) nor a spiritual, disembodied gnostic escape from this world. Instead it irreducibly involves a transformation of the human person, Jesus, into eternal life with God.

As Wright emphasises, Paul uses of the term *soma* to refer to 'the entire human being, much as our modern word "person" might do'[22] Because of this, the resurrection involves a 'transformation', 'transfiguration' or 'identity-in-transformation',[23] which holds together in tension elements of continuity and elements of discontinuity between Jesus of Nazareth and the risen Christ. According to Wright, 'the Easter stories in the gospels provide a model for [both continuity and transformation], in their strange portrait of a Jesus who is definitely embodied but whose body as unprecedented, indeed hitherto unimagined, properties.'

What can account for the fact that early Christians believed in this kind of resurrection? Here we come to Wright's central argument, which I will restate again here:

> We are left with the conclusion that the combination of empty tomb and appearances of the living Jesus forms a set of circumstances which is itself *both necessary and sufficient* for the rise of early Christian belief. Without these phenomena, we cannot explain why this belief came into existence, and took the

---

22. Wright, *Resurrection*, 264.
23. Gerald O'Collins, SJ, *The Resurrection of Jesus Christ* (Valley Forge: The Judson Press, 1973), 95.

The Bodily Resurrection of Jesus

shape it did. With them, we can explain it exactly and precisely.[24]

With Wright I want to draw attention to the empty tomb account not as a basis for faith (no one 'believes' in the empty tomb per se) but as one of the two factors (the other being the appearances traditions) that together serve as an explanation of the faith found historically in the very early Christian community. What, then, does the empty tomb as such imply about the eschatological significance of the resurrection of Jesus?

The empty tomb and the connection between the resurrection of Christ and the general resurrection: matter matters. The empty tomb, as a part of the explanation of the rise of Christianity, has a direct implication for what I take to be the hermeneutical context for understanding the resurrection of Jesus, namely the general resurrection of the dead at the end of the age. The logic of Paul makes it transparently clear that the affirmation of the truth of Jesus' resurrection depends entirely on the affirmation of the truth of the general resurrection. Look at the italicised portions of the following text taken from Paul's epistle to the Corinthians (1 Corinthians 15:12–20, 22):

> Now if Christ is preached that He has been raised from the dead, how do some among you say that there is no resurrection of the dead? But *if there is no resurrection of the dead, then Christ is not risen.* And if Christ is not risen, then our preaching is empty and your faith is also empty. Yes, and we are found false witnesses of God, because we have testified of God that He raised up Christ, whom He did not raise up—if in fact the dead do not rise. For *if the dead do not rise, then Christ is not risen.* And if Christ is not risen, your faith is futile; you are still in your sins! Then also those who have fallen asleep in Christ have perished. If in this life only we have hope in Christ, we are of all men the most pitiable. But now Christ is risen from the dead, and has become the

---

24. Wright, *Resurrection*, 696. The italics are in Wright's text.

70   *From Resurrection to Return*

> first fruits of those who have fallen asleep . . . For as
> in Adam all die, even so in Christ all shall be made
> alive.

Paul is unambiguous here: Jesus cannot be risen if the general resurrection of the dead at the end of the age proves to be false. As Ted Peters writes in his paper in this book:

> The Easter resurrection of Jesus is a past event,
> an event available for historical study. Yet, Easter
> could not be what it was without the accompanying
> promise of the eschatological kingdom of God. The
> past cannot be what it is without its future.[25]

If the resurrection of Jesus is the best explanation for the rise of Christian faith, and if the empty tomb and the appearances are irreducibly connected with it in defining what 'bodily' means regarding the resurrection of Jesus, then the truth of the empty tomb is an irreducible clue to the meaning of the general resurrection as the background out of which the resurrection of Jesus makes sense. Far from being a basis of faith, the empty tomb thus plays a defining, even if indirect, role in the meaning of the **general** resurrection. The tomb being empty means that everything about Jesus as *soma* counts—nothing is irrelevant. This in turn means that the 'materiality' of the *soma* of Jesus of Nazareth is in an irreducible, even if highly partial, element of continuity with the *soma* of the risen Christ. Matter matters eschatologically. Just how it does is the subject of major future research.

The empty tomb as a proleptic event, the first instantiation of a new law of the eschatological new creation. Following Pannenberg we can view the resurrection of Jesus, including the empty tomb tradition and the appearances narratives, as a presence, manifestation and revelation within the flow of ordinary history and nature during the first Eastertide, of what will one day be the eternal new creation, including the general resurrection and the Lordship of the Father bequeathed back to him by the Son through the power of the Spirit. Pannenberg refers to the revelation in history at Easter of the eschatological future of

---

25. Page 98.

The Bodily Resurrection of Jesus   71

the world by the term 'prolepsis'[26]: Precisely because of its proleptic nature, the truth of the resurrection is best understood as 'hypothetical' in relation to our present reality, even while it will be known to be true in relation to the eschatological future, and therefore it will always have been true. Following Pannenberg's approach to eschatology, Peters defines prolepsis as 'the future consummation of all things has appeared ahead of time in the Christ-event'.[27]

My way of stating this is that the resurrection of Jesus, particularly as it is characterised by the empty tomb, is the first instantiation of what will one day be a universal new regularity of the world as it is transformed into the eschatological new creation, or in short, the first instantiation of a new law of the eschatological new creation. The empty tomb points to a radically new phenomenon in this world, yet one which will one day be entirely normal in the new creation.

Conclusions: The empty tomb—'matter matters eschatologically'. Thus the empty tomb, which serves as part of the explanation of early Christian faith for Wright, and the conceptual connection between the reference of that faith—the resurrection of Jesus—and its hermeneutical context of meaning—the general resurrection—together entail that for Christian faith in the bodily resurrection to be intelligible, the future of the world must be an eschatological transformation of the universe into the new creation. In particularly, the empty tomb, perhaps more even than the appearances, tells us that if the resurrection as transformation includes elements of continuity (even if overshadowed by elements of discontinuity), there must be, included in those elements of continuity, elements of material continuity. Just what material continuity means is, in my view, an open question requiring extensive further research, but one thing it tells us in a still highly gnostic twentieth and now twenty-first century is this: 'Matter matters eschatologically.' Indeed, the goodness of creation, a universal affirmation of the Christian theology of creation *ex nihilo* that, against the early Manichaens, includes the goodness of materiality, must hold not only for the present creation but for the future creation, the 'new

---

26. See for example Wolfhart Pannenberg, *Systematic Theology*, volume 1, translated by GW Bromiley (Grand Rapids: Eerdmans, 1991), 250.

27. Ted Peters, *God—the World's Future: Systematic Theology for a Postmodern Era* (Minneapolis: Fortress Press, 1992), 194–5.

creation': the goodness of the matter of our world—better said, our universe—matters eternally. The first evidence of this eternal goodness of matter is the empty tomb. Had it not been empty, the resurrection of Jesus would have (at a minimum) been robbed not only of its materiality and left to the ghostly emptiness of a merely existentialist/demythologised or a Platonised account, the proclamation of the goodness of the physical universe (and with it the Christian basis for environmental ethics) would have been severely challenged, for it is really only sin, and not anything created (including matter), which will cease to be in the new creation (where we 'cannot sin', according to Augustine).

How then do we bring science into the conversation?

2.3 What about twentieth century. physics? From Newtonian determinism to an open world in which God can act without intervening

> I need to see the worldly events as linked by cause and effect . . . there remains no room for God's working. (Rudolf Bultmann[28])

Is the standard scientific worldview, based on a philosophical interpretation of fundamental scientific theory, open to constructive dialogue with a theology of the bodily resurrection? To answer in the affirmative we have to recall that the Newtonian, mechanistic worldview contributed to the rise of the principle of analogy in history and thus the rejection of the bodily resurrection by liberal Protestant theologians in the nineteenth and twentieth centuries. How then do we introduce science into this discussion without succumbing to this same fate?

My starting point is to recognise that even while science rightly restricts its explanatory framework to natural causes, we certainly no longer live in a mechanistic universe characterised by Laplacian determinism. On the one hand, science *is* based on methodological naturalism, the commitment to explain events in nature as the result of natural causes and to rule out of bounds an interventionist account of God's supernatural action as part of a *scientific* explanation of events

---

28. Rudolf Bultmann, *Jesus Christ and Mythology* (New York: Charles Scribner's Sons, 1958).

The Bodily Resurrection of Jesus 73

in the world. For example, this rules out intelligent design as a scientific theory,[29] but it does not require that we elevate methodological naturalism to metaphysical naturalism and its atheistic implications. On the other hand, unlike Bultmann (and the Jesus Seminar), I also claim that science cannot rule out a *theological* account of God as acting objectively in nature if such divine action occurs without divine intervention—where intervention is understood as breaking the laws of nature or equivalently as interfering with the regular processes of nature, and thus, in either sense of the term, challenging the theories of natural science. Such an account of divine action that is compatible with science and its foundations in methodological naturalism goes by the acronym 'NIODA' for 'non-interventionist objective divine action'.

Is it possible to construct a non-interventionist account of objective divine action? This is an open question being subjected to extensive and ongoing research in the field of theology and science.[30] What is required for NIODA is that we can argue for ontological indeterminism, and not just epistemic unpredictability, at some level in nature based on a philosophical interpretation of a solid scientific theory appropriate to that level. Such indeterminism would mean that there are domains in nature where nature lacks an efficient natural cause to bring about specific events.[31] If we can argue this way, then, along

---

29. For example, the presence of $t = 0$ in standard Big Bang cosmology led some scientists to construct modified cosmologies which did away with $t = 0$, such as inflationary Big Bang cosmology and now quantum cosmology.

30. The Center for Theology and the Natural Sciences and the Vatican Observatory have jointly sponsored a decade-long series of research conferences and scholarly publication, one of whose key purposes was to explore this possibility in depth. For summaries of the approximately 100 chapters in this series, see http://www.ctns.org/books.html.

31. A case in point would be quantum mechanics, where according to the Heisenberg interpretation, nature does not offer a sufficient efficient natural cause of certain subatomic events, like radioactive decay. See Robert John Russell, 'Divine Action and Quantum Mechanics: A Fresh Assessment', in *Quantum Mechanics: Scientific Perspectives on Divine Action*, edited by Robert John Russell et al. (Vatican City State: Vatican Observatory Publications, Berkeley: Center for Theology and the Natural Sciences, 2001), 293–328.

74   *From Resurrection to Return*

with God's general action in creating and sustaining the world ('general providence') here at least God can act in specific events in unique ways to bring them about without intervening in nature and without contradicting science ('special providence').

Areas in science that might admit ontological indeterminism include chaos theory (holistic chaos), as explored by John Polkinghorne, the mind/brain problem, as discussed by Philip Clayton and Nancey Murphy, cosmology (the 'world-as-a-whole') as described by Arthur Peacocke and quantum mechanics (QM), analysed by George Ellis, Nancey Murphy, Tom Tracy and myself. I am quite certain that a QM-NIODA is a viable candidate, and its great outcome is that it offers a robust version of theistic evolution (making intelligent design unnecessary and undermining the atheistic claim that evolution is intrinsically atheistic).[32]

Is NIODA, then, a way to understand the resurrection of Jesus in light of science? Actually there are good theological reasons for answering 'no'. The resurrection of Jesus is clearly 'much more than' what is meant by noninterventionist objective divine action: an unusual natural event that nevertheless is consistent with science and only attributable by faith to God's action hidden within the flux of nature. Indeed, the resurrection of Jesus is even more than a 'miracle,' where by miracle I mean the resurrection of Lazarus or the daughter of Jairus as resuscitations, with death eventually and inevitably to follow one day.

Instead New Testament scholars who take the bodily resurrection of Jesus seriously are almost unanimous in describing it as involving a change in the entire natural environment leading to a change, as Wright puts it, in our **world view**. The resurrection of Jesus is what I refer to as a 'megamiracle'. And so NIODA cannot be of much, if any, help with the agenda of bringing science into conversation with the resurrection of Jesus in **this** way. If the resurrection of Jesus is 'more than a miracle' then NIODA is 'less than a miracle'. In this sense, incidently, O'Collins is both right and wrong in his critique of NIODA for not dealing with miracles, let along the resurrection.[33] In my mind it

---

32.   See the five-volume CTNS-VO publications summarised at: http://www.ctns.org/books.html.

33.   O'Collins, 'The Resurrection', 21, footnote 52.

The Bodily Resurrection of Jesus 75

was never intended to, from the outset it was clearly not going to be adequate to that task.

2.4 What about twentieth-century physics and cosmology? From a timeless Newtonian universe to the Big Bang universe as natural history

> The cosmos is a unique and irreversible sequence of events. Our account of it must take a historical form rather than consist of general laws alone. (Ian G Barbour[34])

What about physics and cosmology: don't they even more fully embody the principle of analogy in nature and thus undermine a theology of resurrection eschatology? Here I will suggest that while physics and cosmology are based on methodological naturalism, and thus do not appeal to divine causality as part of its scientific explanatory framework, they each in their own way undercut the principle of analogy even while being based on methodological naturalism. In essence, the universe is more like a historical process than a timeless reality, one which might be amenable to a theological interpretation that includes the bodily resurrection of Jesus.

The universe as historical even though physics is non-historical. In my view, inflationary (hot) Big Bang cosmology thoroughly undermines the principle of analogy, at least at the level of phenomenology, since it points to a universe of epochs and stages of development that are radically different from the universe we see today. Hence the universe is more like a historical reality described by a time-irreversible narrative cosmology than a repeatable reality subsumed as in classical mechanics by the underlying, time-reversible laws of physics.

This is a brief listing of some key epochs and stages of development of the universe:

- Big Bang marked by infinite temperature, infinite density, radical expansion, often referred to as the beginning of time, t = 0: 13.7 billion years ago.

---

34. Ian G Barbour, *Religion and Science: Historical and Contemporary Issues* (San Francisco: HarperSanFrancisco, 1997), 212.

76　　　　　*From Resurrection to Return*

- Inflation, first 10–36 seconds after t = 0, produces many 'domains' (for example our visible universe) within the overall mega-universe.
- First 3 minutes: formation of hydrogen and helium.
- After 400,000 years: universe cool enough for photons to decouple from matter, forming what today is the 2.7°K microwave background radiation.
- After 150–500 million years, quasars, galaxies and first generation stars begin to form.
- After 8–10 billion years, first generation stars supernova, producing all the heavy elements, and second generation stars with planets begin to form, including our solar system.
- About 3.85 billion years ago, evolution of life began on earth.

Of course a given area in physics, such as electromagnetism or gravity, displays the conventional non-historical aspects we associate with physics: uniformity, reversibility, predictability—although even here the strictly statistical predictability of quantum mechanics (and its implications of an underlying ontological indeterminism) which characterises all of fundamental physics introduces an element of historicity to physics proper. Moreover the fundamental laws of physics are also historical in a phenomenological sense.

- t = 0: all four fundamental forces (gravity, strong nuclear force, weak nuclear force, electromagnetism) are unified in a single force ('supersymmetry').
- t = 10^{-43} sec: gravity separates out from the remaining three unified forces.
- t = 10^{-35} sec: strong nuclear forces separate out from the electroweak unified force.
- t = 10^{-10} sec: weak and electromagnetic forces separate out, leaving all four forces as separate kinds of fundamental interactions.

The universe as characterised by a series of 'first instantiations of a new law of nature' and the future of nature as the hermeneutical context for nature's present. The developmental character of the history of the universe and the irreversibility of quantum mechanics as it underlies all of contemporary physics both lend themselves to viewing the emergence for the first time of new, *sui generis* phenomena as 'first instantiations of a new law of nature'. The first time atoms form, or quasars,

The Bodily Resurrection of Jesus

or planetary systems, let alone the first signs of life on a planet like ours, all represent transitions to new, emergent phenomena in nature that cannot be predicted in advance, although they can be explained retroactively once the new phenomena are known and embraced by new laws of nature.

Chemistry, for example, shows such emergent novelty. A simple example is the wetness of water: wetness of the water as a liquid does not arise from a minuscule property of wetness adhering to each H_2O molecule and it cannot be predicted or described by the underlying laws of quantum mechanics alone, although the quantum mechanical properties of the H_2O molecule make possible the viscosity of water as an emergent, holistic property of the aggregate of 10^{26} molecules. Biology, even more clearly, includes phenomena that originate some 10 billion years after the Big Bang. For all this time the universe was lifeless, but it always had within its laws and constants the eventual possibility of life. As Peters writes:

> New laws of nature have already appeared in physical history. From the era of the Big Bang to the onset of life, no laws governing life were in effect. The onset of biological processes began only well into the history of the cosmos. Many aeons since the Big Bang 13.7 billion years ago had to pass lifelessly before the first sign of life on planet earth, only 3.8 billion years ago. With the arrival of life forms, so also came the arrival of life processes and the first instantiation of biological laws of nature. Nature has a history, and new chapters are genuinely new. A precedent has been set.[35]

This idea of a 'new law of nature' not only undermines the claim that science is based on one of the ways that science is interpreted by analogy with the principle of analogy: what I've previously referred to as nomological universality. It leads to a much more surprising view of the historicity of nature: namely that the future of nature is the best hermeneutic for understanding the meaning of nature's past. Why

---

35. Pages 109–10.

78   *From Resurrection to Return*

is this so? First of all, as just pointed out, we cannot predict biology from physics even though biology is consistent with and incorporates the constraints placed on it by the laws of physics even while transcending them. Secondly and more subtly, the requirements for biology place strict constraints on the characteristics of physics. Put more precisely, we start with the so-called 'fine-tuning' of the universe: the specific form of the laws of physics (for example quantum mechanics, special relativity) and the precise values of the constants of nature (for example Planck's constant, h, found in quantum mechanics, the speed of light, c, based in special relativity, among others) that characterise our universe must be just as they are (typically to less than one part per million) if the evolution of life is to be possible in the universe. What I am suggesting is that the unpredictability of biology based on physics alone combined with the 'fine-tuning' of the physics of the universe by the requirements of biology together yield the claim that the true meaning of physics—its particular laws and values of the constants of nature—is only to be found in the future of the early universe, namely the evolution of life once planetary systems formed. We can know something about the meaning of nature from the physics of its early epoch, but not all. The future of nature provides the interpretive key to nature's past and the hermeneutic principle for understanding nature's past, present and future.[36]

Biology thus discloses the inner meaning of physics. It shows us *that* the universe is 'fine-tuned' for life, but we could only know that if we first had encountered the phenomenon of life. Physics—the particular physics of this universe—provides the possibility for life, but not the explanatory framework for describing it, let alone for telling us

---

36.   In almost all of the literature in theology and science, fine-tuning is used as an argument for the existence of God, framed in what is usually called the 'strong Anthropic Principle'. I am not using it in this way here. For references, see Robert John Russell, Nancey C Murphy, and Chris J Isham, editors, *Quantum Cosmology and the Laws of Nature: Scientific Perspectives on Divine Action*, Scientific Perspectives on Divine Action Series, Part V (Vatican City State: Vatican Observatory Publications, Berkeley: Center for Theology and the Natural Sciences, 1993), 468, and Nancey Murphy and George F Ellis, *On the Moral Nature of the Universe: Theology, Cosmology, and Ethics*, Theology and the Sciences Series (Minneapolis: Fortress Press, 1996).

The Bodily Resurrection of Jesus

that it provides this possibility. Life is both a new law of nature, with the origins of life a first instantiation of that new law that presupposes, is constrained by, even while transcending, the laws of physics. Life is also the interpretive and disclosive context for the inner meaning of physics, a meaning that can never be exhumed from physics alone. Analogously, that the empty tomb is empty is cortically significant, but we can never tell what is missing from the empty tomb simply by its being empty.

Another way of saying this is that emergence in time assumes an underlying continuity in nature of a very special sort: it is a continuity in the laws of physics and the constants of nature that is 'fine-tuned' to provide the context precisely required for the occurrence of the radically discontinuous, the radically new, a radically new that cannot be predicted—not even imagined—from the framework of the underlying continuity from the past.

We can go further along this path. As Francisco Ayala has argued, evolutionary biology provides the basis for the appearance in complex creatures like hominids of both reason and moral capacity, but not the content of moral norms (for example by analogy, evolution provides the capability for language but not the specifics of Spanish vs Japanese).[37] For this we need revelation and/or philosophical ethics. Indeed if Ted Peters is correct, we can only really know how to shape our ethics if that revelation is grounded in the eschatological vision of the future, or what Ted calls 'proleptic ethics'.[38]

In conclusion, we have good scientific reasons to throw out the principle of analogy in cosmology and to limit it for physics in light of the historicity of physics, without abandoning science and its explanations of the world. The key is to stay with methodological naturalism and to resist metaphysical/ontological naturalism. Yet resurrection remains beyond emergence ('more than a miracle' while emergence is 'less than a miracle'), involving a fundamental change in the background/physical laws and world view. Cosmology as such cannot

---

37. Francisco J Ayala, 'Human Nature: One Evolutionist's View', in *Whatever Happened to the Soul? Scientific and Theological Portraits of Human Nature*, edited by Warren S Brown, Nancey Murphy and and H Newton Malony (Minneapolis: Fortress Press, 1998), 31–48.

38. Peters, *God—the World's Future*, chapter 12.

80 *From Resurrection to Return*

provide a sufficient framework for a theology of bodily resurrection, but it can plan a role in helping us understand what some of the elements of continuity might be in that cosmic transformation. Together, physics and cosmology can offer a view of explanation as future-based that anticipates the proleptic role of eschatology as the hermeneutics of the present based on the future in theology.

3. Bodily resurrection, an eschatology of transformation and the challenge and opportunities for engaging science

Cosmology also raises a fundamental challenge to the intelligibility of eschatology, with its general resurrection of the dead and the coming of the new creation: it predicts a future which seems to make Christian eschatology impossible. How do we respond to this challenge and at the same time appropriate science as an invaluable dialogue partner with theology concerning eschatology?

3.1 Challenge/conflict with science: cosmological future, freeze or fry
The visible universe from the Planck time to the present is described by Big Bang cosmology (whether or not inflation and/or quantum cosmology wins the day scientifically), and there are two scenarios for the universe's far future: freeze or fry. *Freeze:* If the universe is open or flat, it will expand forever and continue to cool from its present temperature (about 2.7°K), asymptotically approaching absolute zero. *Fry:* If it is closed, it will expand to a maximum size in another one to five hundred billion years, then re-collapse to an arbitrarily small size and unendingly higher temperatures. (Although the presence of a cosmological constant (Λ)—understood as 'dark matter'—could either accelerate its expansion rate as current astronomical evidence strongly suggests, or, possibly, close the universe, the far future scenarios are still freeze or fry.) In either case, the overall picture for life in the far future is bleak, regardless of whether it is open or closed (that is freeze or fry). According to Frank Tipler and John Barrow:[39]

---

39.   John D Barrow and Frank J Tipler, *The Anthropic Cosmological Principle* (Oxford: Clarendon Press, 1986), chapter 10. See also William R Stoeger, SJ, 'Scientific Accounts of Ultimate Catastrophes in Our Life-Bearing Universe', in *The End of the World and the Ends of God: Science and Theology on Eschatology*, edited by

The Bodily Resurrection of Jesus

- In 5 billion years, the sun will become a red giant, engulfing the orbit of the earth and Mars, eventually becoming a white dwarf.
- In 40–50 billion years, star formation will have ended in our galaxy.
- In 10^{12} years, all massive stars will have become neutron stars or black holes.[40]
- In 10^{19} years, dead stars near the galactic edge will drift off into intergalactic space, and stars near the centre will collapse together forming a massive black hole.
- In 10^{31} years, protons and neutrons will decay into positrons, electrons, neutrinos and photons.
- In 10^{34} years, dead planets, black dwarfs and neutron stars will disappear, their mass completely converted into energy, leaving only black holes, electron-positron plasma and radiation, and all carbon-based life-forms will be extinct. Beyond this, solar mass, galactic mass, and finally supercluster mass black holes will evaporate by Hawking radiation.

The upshot is clear: 'Proton decay spells ultimate doom for ... *Homo sapiens* and all forms of life constructed of atoms ... '[41]

As I have already stated, the resurrection of Jesus, as underscored by Pannenberg, Peters and Wright, is both a singular event requiring a historical explanation and an event irreducibly connected to the eschatological worldview for the transformation of the universe, including the general resurrection of the dead, a transformation of this present creation into the new creation modeled roughly on the bodily resurrection of Jesus (the inner logic of 1 Corinthians 15). It is this eschatological worldview as a radically changed worldview, as Wright emphasises, that we must take on board, and it is this changed worldview that runs up against these stark scientific predictions for the cosmological far future. Here science cannot be ignored—while a once-

---

John Polkinghorne and Michael Welker (Harrisburg: Trinity Press International, 2000).

40. If the universe is closed, then in 1,012 years the universe will have reached its maximum size and recollapse back to a singularity like the original hot Big Bang.

41. Barrow and Tipler, *The Anthropic Cosmological Principle*, 648.

82   *From Resurrection to Return*

off historical event like the resurrection of Jesus might be set aside as a contingent event that doesn't fit the general structure of physical laws, when it comes to the general resurrection we are dealing conceptually with a universe-wide future phenomenon.

3.2   Responding to the challenge

How do we meet this challenge? Actually, it is a 'dual challenge' for the theological claim, if viewed (as I do) as a truth-claim (that is one capable of being true or false but not meaningless), pushes back against cosmology too.

The challenge from cosmology to eschatology: If the predictions of contemporary scientific cosmology come to pass there will never be a general resurrection. Therefore Christ has not been raised from the dead, and our hope is in vain.

The challenge from eschatology to cosmology: If it is true that Jesus rose bodily from the dead, then the general resurrection will occur. Therefore the future of the universe will not be what scientific cosmology predicts.

In previous writings I have laid out a series of 'guidelines' that hopefully will help us distinguish between the kind of responses we could construct to this challenge that would not work from those that potentially could work.[42] They are placed here in an appendix for further discussion and as background for Part 3. They are based on what I am calling 'the method of creative mutual interaction' in which

---

42.   Robert John Russell, 'Eschatology and Physical Cosmology: A Preliminary Reflection', in *The Far Future: Eschatology from a Cosmic Perspective*, edited by George FR Ellis (Philadelphia: Templeton Foundation Press, 2002), 266–315, Robert John Russell, 'Bodily Resurrection, Eschatology and Scientific Cosmology: The Mutual Interaction of Christian Theology and Science', in *Resurrection: Theological and Scientific Assessments*, edited by Ted Peters, Robert John Russell and Michael Welker (Grand Rapids: Eerdmans Publishing Company, 2002), 3–30, Robert John Russell, 'Sin, Salvation, and Scientific Cosmology: Is Christian Eschatology Credible Today?' in *Sin and Salvation*, edited by Duncan Reid and Mark Worthing (Australia: ATF Press, 2002), Robert John Russell, 'Eschatology and Scientific Cosmology: From Conflict to Interaction', in *What God Knows: Time, Eternity and Divine Knowledge*, edited by Harry Lee Poe and J Stanley Mattson (Waco: Baylor University Press, 2006).

The Bodily Resurrection of Jesus

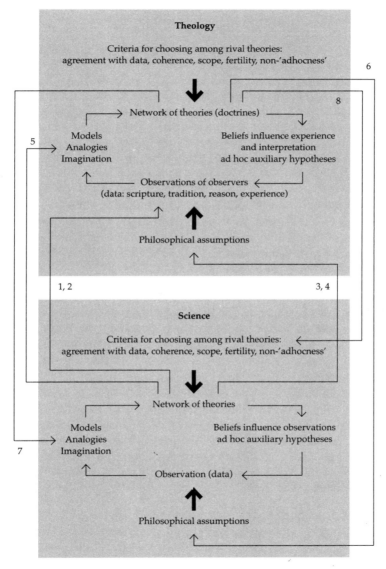

Figure 1: Method of creative mutual interaction

84   *From Resurrection to Return*

theology has something to offer to science as well as something to be learned from science. Figure 1 sketches this method, including numbered paths from one area to the other. These are the paths referred to in the guidelines that follow.

Here I would like to draw on them briefly to develop them further in terms of the themes of this present chapter.

Rejection of the principle of analogy and its generalisation as nomological universality. In order to get beyond the double challenge (above) we need to recognise that the challenge is not from science but from the philosophical assumptions that we routinely bring to science, namely that scientific predictions hold without qualification. As discussed in the previous part of this paper, this assumption involves two arguments: (1) at its most fundamental level, the future will be just like the past (that is a version of Troeltsch's 'principle of analogy' applied to nature rather than history), and (2) the same laws of nature which govern the past and present will govern the future as well, or what I have been calling 'temporal nomological universality'.

It is quite possible, however, to accept a very different assumption about the future predictions of science while accepting all that science describes and explains about the past history of the universe (as long as we resist any move from methodological to metaphysical naturalism).

The first step is deciding whether the laws of nature are descriptive or prescriptive, and, as William Stoeger argues, science alone cannot settle the matter.[43] A strong case can then be made on philosophical grounds that the laws of nature are descriptive. One can, in turn, claim on theological grounds that the processes of nature that science describes are the result of God's ongoing action as Creator. Their regularity is the result of God's faithfulness. But God is free to act in radically new ways, not only in human history, but also in the ongoing history of the universe, God's creation.

---

43. William R Stoeger, SJ, 'Contemporary Physics and the Ontological Status of the Laws of Nature', in *Quantum Cosmology and the Laws of Nature: Scientific Perspectives on Divine Action*, edited by Robert J Russell, Nancey C Murphy and Chris J. Isham, Scientific Perspectives on Divine Action Series (Vatican City State: Vatican Observatory Publications, Berkeley: Center for Theology and the Natural Sciences, 1993), 209–34.

The Bodily Resurrection of Jesus

Another way of making this case is to recognise that all scientific laws carry *a ceteris paribus* clause, that is their predictions hold 'all else being equal'. But if God's regular action accounts for what we describe through the laws of nature, and if God will act in radically new ways to transform then world, then of course all else is not equal.[44] We could say that the 'freeze or fry' predictions for the cosmological future might have been applicable had God not acted in Easter and if God were not to continue to act to bring forth the ongoing eschatological transformation of the universe.

Guideline 1 also places a crucial limitation on nomological universality. The limitation is that, though they are clearly applicable to the universe as a whole in its past and present, the laws of nature as we now know them cannot be arbitrarily extended to the future. In short, we could say that the 'freeze or fry' predictions for the cosmological future might have applied had God not acted in Easter and were God not to continue to act to bring forth the ongoing eschatological transformation of the universe.

The resurrection of Jesus, particularly in light of the empty tomb, as a proleptic event, the first instantiation of a new law of the eschatological new creation. The position I want to explore here is the relation between the emergence of new phenomena within the present created order, the transformation of this present order into the new creation, and the resurrection of Jesus as a proleptic event of that transformed new creation within the history of the present created order.

In discussing the resurrection as 'transformation' I referred to both elements of continuity and elements of discontinuity entailed in that transformation. I also suggested that the resurrection as transformation could provide a way of thinking of the eschatological transformation of the creation into the new creation. Hence, in order to compare emergence with transformation, I would like to stress that the relative importance of these elements of continuity and discontinuity can provide a useful way to conceptualise the difference between emergence and transformation and, in turn, the difference between first instantiations within the present universe and the resurrection as a first instantiation of the new creation within the present creation.

---

44. I am grateful to Nancey Murphy for pointing this argument out to me. (Private communications.)

86 *From Resurrection to Return*

What I propose is the following: with emergence, the discontinuous and the novel, like biological life, is set within the wider continuing context of the repeatable and universal, like the laws of physics (pace that even they display elements of irreversibility). Moreover, what emerges is not the miraculous, in the Humean sense of violating the underlying laws of physics. Rather it is something whose possibility is already given in the underlying laws, the elements of continuity, even though its actuality only emerges in time (again, unlike a Humean view of static nature). It is these underlying laws that allow us to distinguish the radically new such as results from NIODA, which is entirely consistent with them even if not predictable, or even understandable, in terms of them (think the first instance of life compared to a lifeless universe of mere physics) and the radically new in terms of a miracle, which violates the background, underlying laws of nature.

The transformation of the creation into the new creation by God's radically new action, on the other hand, is something like the converse of emergence: the elements of continuity are embraced within the more inclusive elements of discontinuity. The background conditions, the underlying laws of physics and biology, are changed in the process of this transformation. Put more carefully, the radical newness of God's Easter-based action will lead to new regularities in the new creation (for example life without death) that will, in turn, allow for radically new descriptions of them (for example new laws of a new nature). It is 'more than a miracle', it is more like a 'miraculous transformation of the miraculous.' In essence, the **environment** is eschatologised, and not just the individual event in that environment.

Now imagine this process of transformation, and the new creation that results, as happening both in 'the future' and as reaching back like a 'wormhole' to occur in the context of the present creation—the proleptic event of the first Easter. In this very striking sense the resurrection of Jesus as a historical event, particularly as it is characterised by the empty tomb (and therefore the promise to include all of creation in the new creation), is a proleptic event, the first instantiation of a new law not of this present creation but the first instantiation of a fundamentally new law of the eschatologically new creation.

The eschatological future of nature provides the 'double hermeneutical principle' for nature's present and past. We have seen that emergence in time assumes an underlying and continuing continuity in nature of a

The Bodily Resurrection of Jesus 87

very special sort: it is a continuity that is 'fine-tuned' to provide the context precisely required for the occurrence of the radically discontinuous, the radically new, a radically new that cannot be predicted—perhaps not even imagined—from the framework of the underlying continuity from the past. What I have stressed about this is that the future of nature provides the interpretive key, the hermeneutic principle, for nature's past.

When we consider the eschatological future, we find an even more profound sense in which the future interprets the present and the past. Here we find a concept of the future of all creation, termed new creation, as brought about by God's radical transformation of the present creation. This is not just the future that emerges from the present given the underlying, present laws of nature, even allowing for the relatively new that so emerges, such as biology from physics. This is the radically new future that comes about from the future acting in each present moment through God's transforming, resurrection power. Peters refers here to the eschatological future as *adventus* or *venturum*, and contrasts this with the ordinary sense of the future emerging from the past, *futurum*.[45] As he frames it, prolepsis brings together these two distinct views of the future in the Christ-event: 'Time itself becomes christologised and eschatologised.' Because of this, Peters argues that the linear notion of time as embraced by science is incapable of representing this 'interweaving' of *futurum* and *venturum*. I strongly agree with Peters, and believe that one of the tasks for future research is to find ways in mathematics to represent the more complex view of time that Peters and Pannenberg describe and see, in turn, whether it would be helpful for research in theoretical physics.

If this future, this eschatological future, is to be the true interpreter of the real meaning of the present creation of already 13.7 billion years, and the real hope for all life in the universe, how are we to know what its interpretation holds? Our only hope is that God will give us a clue, an early sign, a prophecy, not just from the ordinary future but from this eschatological future, and this is just what is claimed in the argument that the resurrection of Jesus is the proleptic presence in our creation's history of our creation's transformed future. In this sense, not only does the future of creation serve as the hermeneutic of the

---

45. Peters, *God—the World's Future*, 308–9.

present of creation (for example biology to physics), but the eschatological future of creation as new creation serves as the hermeneutic of the hermeneutic of the present creation, or the 'double hermeneutic' of the world we now know.

The new creation as creation ex vetera *and the implications for today's science.* The new creation as a transformation of the present creation carries with it a crucial theological assumption: it is not a separate creation, a second *ex nihilo*. Instead God's act of creation *ex nihilo* includes the present and the new creation intertwined in the complex temporality of *futurum/venturum*. As John Polkinghorne so nicely says, the new creation is really a creation *ex vetera*, a creation 'out of the old.'[46] This in turn means that the elements of continuity between 'now and then' work 'both ways': any conception we can gain about the eschatologically new creation might tell us something new and different about just what is of lasting value in this present creation. Here, once again but in a new way, science enters into the discussion, and in two ways: (1) science might help us recognise something about the universe which will be an element of continuity into the new creation, and (2) our thinking about the new creation might lead to new questions to pose to science about the universe as it is now, questions that we might not ask without such an eschatological perspective. Peters suggests one about time being more complex than the linear view of time embodied in today's science. Pannenberg implies that the pre-Augustinian view of time as duration and embedded in a Trinitarian doctrine of God might offer rich insights about nature that contemporary science has overlooked.[47] These are exciting research agendas for the creative mutual interaction between theology and science, agendas which I hope to continue to pursue in future work.[48]

---

46.   John C Polkinghorne, *The Faith of a Physicist: Reflections of a Bottom-up Thinker* (New Jersey: Princeton University Press, 1994), chapter 9, John Polkinghorne, *The God of Hope and the End of the World* (New Haven: Yale University Press, 2002).

47.   Wolfhart Pannenberg, *Metaphysics and the Idea of God*, translated by Philip Clayton (Grand Rapids: Eerdmans, 1990). For further references and analysis see Robert John Russell, 'Time in Eternity', *Dialog* 39.1 (March 2000), 46–55.

48.   Russell, 'Eschatology and Physical Cosmology', Russell, 'Bodily Resurrection, Eschatology and Scientific Cosmology'.

The Bodily Resurrection of Jesus

Appendix: Guidelines for pursuing the discussion of resurrection, eschatology and cosmology through the method of creative mutual interaction.

Guideline 1: Rejection of two philosophical assumptions about science: the principle of analogy and its representation as nomological universality
My response is to recognise that the challenge is not from science but from the philosophical assumptions that we routinely bring to science, namely that scientific predictions hold without qualification. This assumption involves two arguments: (1) at its most fundamental level, the future will be just like the past (or what I have attributed to Troeltsch as the principle of analogy), and (2) the same laws of nature which govern the past and present will govern the future as well (or what one can call 'nomological universality').

It is quite possible, however, to accept a very different assumption about the future predictions of science while accepting all that science describes and explains about the past history of the universe. The first step is deciding whether the laws of nature are descriptive or prescriptive, and, as William Stoeger argues, science alone cannot settle the matter.[49]

A strong case can then be made on philosophical grounds that the laws of nature are descriptive. One can, in turn, claim on theological grounds that the processes of nature that science describes are the result of God's ongoing action as Creator. Their regularity is the result of God's faithfulness. But God is free to act in radically new ways, not only in human history, but also in the ongoing history of the universe, God's creation.

Another way of making this case is to recognise that all scientific laws carry a *ceteris paribus* clause, that is their predictions hold 'all else being equal'. But if God's regular action accounts for what we describe through the laws of nature, and if God will act in radically new ways to transform then world, then of course all else is not equal. We could say that the 'freeze or fry' predictions for the cosmological future might have been applicable had God not acted in Easter and if God were not to continue to act to bring forth the ongoing eschatological transformation of the universe.

---

49. Stoeger, 'Contemporary Physics'.

90 *From Resurrection to Return*

Guideline 1 also places a crucial limitation on nomological universality. The limitation is that, though they are clearly applicable to the universe as a whole in its past and present, the laws of nature as we now know them cannot be arbitrarily extended to the future. In short, we could say that the 'freeze or fry' predictions for the cosmological future might have applied had God not acted in Easter and were God not to continue to act to bring forth the ongoing eschatological transformation of the universe.

Guideline 2: Eschatology should embrace methodological naturalism regarding the cosmic past and present: the formal argument
Any eschatology that we might construct must be scientific in its description of the past history of the universe. More precisely, it must be constrained by methodological naturalism in its description of the past: it should not invoke God in its explanation of the (secondary) causes, processes and properties of nature.

This guideline is a formal argument. It separates this proposal as sharply as possible from such approaches as 'intelligent design' in so far as they are critical of the physical and/or biological sciences for not including divine agency in its mode of explanation.

Guideline 3: Big Bang and inflationary cosmology as a 'limit condition' on any revise eschatology (Path 1): the material argument
Guideline 3 is a material argument. It follows Path 1 by stating that standard and inflationary Big Bang cosmologies, or other scientific cosmologies (such as quantum cosmology), place a limiting condition on any possible eschatology. All we know of the history and development of the universe and life in it will be data for theology.

Guideline 4: Metaphysical options: limited but not forced
In revising contemporary eschatology there are a variety of metaphysical options from which we may choose. They are not forced on us, or determined by science. On the one hand, since eschatology starts with the presupposition of God, it rules out reductive materialism and metaphysical naturalism. By taking on board natural science, other metaphysical options become unlikely candidates, including Platonic or Cartesian ontological dualism. On the other hand, there are several metaphysical options that are compatible with science and Christian

The Bodily Resurrection of Jesus

theology, including physicalism, emergent monism, dual-aspect monism, ontological emergence and panexperientialism (Whiteheadian metaphysics).

Guidelines for specific theological construction in light of science (G5–G7)

We must now begin the enormous job of revisiting our understanding of eschatology in a way that takes up and incorporates all the findings of science, and particularly scientific cosmology, without falling back into the philosophical problem Guideline 1 is meant to address.

Guideline 5: 'Transformability' and the formal conditions for its possibility (the 'such that' or 'transcendental' argument)

Our starting point is that the new creation is not a replacement of the old creation, or a second and separate creation *ex nihilo*. Instead, God will transform God's creation, the universe, into the new creation *ex vetere*, to use John Polkinghorne's phrase. It follows that God must have created the universe such that it is transformable, that is that it can be transformed by God's action.

Specifically, God must have created it with precisely those conditions and characteristics that it needs as preconditions in order to be transformable by God's new act. Moreover, if it is to be transformed and not replaced, God must have created it with precisely those conditions and characteristics that will be part of the new creation. Since science offers a profound understanding of the past and present history of the universe (Guidelines 2, 3), then science can be of immense help to the theological task of understanding something about that transformation, if we can find a way to identify, with at least some probability, these needed conditions, characteristics and preconditions. Using our previous discussion of the bodily resurrection and the new creation, I will refer to these conditions and characteristics as 'elements of continuity.'

Guideline 5 can be thought of as a transcendental or 'such that' argument. A simple analogy would be that an open ontology could be thought of as providing a precondition for the enactment of voluntarist free will, but certainly not the sufficient grounds for it. Science might also shed light on which conditions and characteristics of the present creation we do not expect to be continued into the new creation. These

92   *From Resurrection to Return*

can be called 'elements of discontinuity' between creation and new creation. Thus physics and cosmology might play a profound role in our attempt to sort out what is truly essential to creation and what is to be left behind in the healing transformation to come.

Guideline 5 gives to the terms 'continuity' and 'discontinuity,' found in the theological literature on the resurrection of Jesus, a more precise meaning and a potential connection with science. With it in place we can move eventually to a material argument and ask just what those elements of continuity and discontinuity might be.

Guideline 6: Continuity within discontinuity: inverting the relationship
Closely related to the previous guideline is a second formal argument about the relative importance of the elements of continuity and discontinuity. So far in theology and science, discontinuity has played a secondary role within the underlying theme of continuity in nature as suggested by the term 'emergence.' Accordingly, irreducibly new processes and properties (that is discontinuity) arise within the overall, pervasive and sustained background of nature (that is continuity).

Thus, biological phenomena evolve out of the nexus of the physical world, the organism is built from its underlying structure of cells and organs, mind arises in the context of neurophysiology, and so on. Now, however, when we come to the resurrection and eschatology, I propose we invert the relation: the elements of continuity will be present, but within a more radical and underlying discontinuity as is denoted by the transformation of the universe by a new act of God *ex vetera*. With this inversion, discontinuity as fundamental signals the break with naturalistic and reductionistic views such as 'physical eschatology,' while continuity, even if secondary, eliminates a 'two-worlds' eschatology.

This has important implications for our search for candidate theories. It eliminates 'non-interventionist objective special divine action' as a candidate since it does not involve a transformation of the whole of nature. Indeed, these approaches presuppose that it is the continual operation of the usual laws of nature that makes objective special divine action possible without the need for the violation or suspension of those laws.

But the bodily resurrection of Jesus directs us towards a much more fundamental view: the radical transformation of the background conditions of space, time, matter and causality, and with this, a permanent change in at least most of the present laws of nature.

Guideline 7: 'Relativistically correct eschatology:' constructing eschatology in light of contemporary physics (Paths 1, 2)
Although we will set aside the predictions Big Bang offers for the cosmic future, we must be prepared to reconstruct current work in eschatology in light of contemporary physics—specifically relativity and quantum physics—as well as what cosmology tells us about the history of the universe, following Paths 1 and 2. I will refer to this project as the attempt to construct a 'relativistically correct Christian eschatology.'

Guidelines for Constructive Work in Science (G8–G10)
Our project also involves the question of whether such revisions in theology might be of any interest to contemporary science—at least for individual scientists who share eschatological concerns such as developed here, and are interested in whether they might stimulate a creative insight into research science. Very different guidelines hold for scientific research. Scientists should set aside the preceding guidelines, which only apply to theological research, and consider instead Guidelines 8–10.

Guideline 8: Theological reconceptualisation of nature leading to philosophical and scientific revisions (Path 6)
Here we move along Path 6 in discovering whether a richer theological conception of nature both as creation and as new creation can generate important revisions in the philosophy of nature that currently underlies the natural sciences, the philosophy of space, time, matter and causality in contemporary physics and cosmology.

Guideline 9: Theology as suggesting criteria of theory choice between existing theories (Path 7)
We can also move along Path 7 to explore philosophical differences in current options in theoretical physics and cosmology. The theological views of research scientists might play a role in selecting which theoretical programs to pursue among those already on the table (for example, the variety of approaches to quantum gravity).

94 From Resurrection to Return

Guideline 10: Theology as suggesting new scientific research programs (Path 8)

Finally we can move along Path 10 and suggest the construction of new scientific research programs whose motivation stems, at least in part, from theological interests.

In closing this section I want to stress that all such programs in science would have to be tested by the scientific communities (what is often called 'the context of justification') without regard for the way theology or philosophy might have played a role in their initiation ('the context of discovery').

Between the First and Second Comings

Ted Peters

The Christian church is an arc between two terminals, a connection between the Easter resurrection of Jesus Christ yesterday and the advent of the kingdom of God tomorrow. The challenge is to keep the spark alive. The spark of the arc brightens our life when we live daily out of God's promise for the future. I call this the 'Life of Beatitude' or 'beatitudinal living'.[1]

Beatitudinal living is not the topic of this paper. Beatitudinal thinking is. Here is the central question: How should we think historically about the Easter resurrection of Jesus, and how should we think theologically about the eschatological promise of our resurrection into the new creation? My answer has to do with prolepsis, with seeing Jesus' Easter resurrection as an anticipation or prefiguration of what God promises for us. 'The resurrection functions as a promise that creation has a future in God,' writes Denis Edwards.[2]

As we explicate this promise theologically, we cannot help but ask: Just what might resurrected existence look like? Might it look like life as we know it now, perhaps tweaked here and there with immortality? Or, might it require such a radical transformation that it defies our imagination? Or, might it lie somewhere in the middle?

To address such questions in the contemporary context within which we find ourselves, the resources of modern science are ready to hand. How might we imagine a resurrected reality in light of what we know about the present reality from the field of physics? How radical a change would we have to expect?

As we proceed to develop an answer, I will draw on the scholarship of biblical historian, NT Wright, systematic theologian Wolfhart Pannenberg and two scholars who reflect theologically on the impli-

---

1.　This essay is adapted from a book I am currently writing, *Anticipating Omega*, forthcoming with Vandenhoeck & Ruprecht.

2.　Denis Edwards, *Breath of Life: A Theology of the Creator Spirit* (Maryknoll: Orbis Books, 2004), 110.

96 *From Resurrection to Return*

cations of physics, John Polkinghorne and Robert John Russell. The physicists agree that the Christian concept of resurrection is not simply one more form of belief in immortality. Rather, it implies a transformation of the entire natural universe. It implies a transformation of the very principles by which the physical universe is governed. It implies a new creation, anticipated by the Easter resurrection. Might we think of the Easter resurrection of Jesus the way Robert John Russell does, as the first instantiation of a new law of nature?

1. The historicity of Easter in NT Wright

The question posed to the New Testament by the renowned British biblical scholar, NT Wright, is this: Why did the early Christian church come into existence? Wright answers: 'The *only* possible reason why early Christianity began and took the shape it did is that the tomb really was empty and that people really did meet Jesus, alive again . . . the best historical explanation for all these phenomena is that Jesus was indeed bodily raised from the dead.'[3] The Easter resurrection of Jesus gave birth to the church. 'The combination of empty tomb and appearances of the living Jesus forms a set of circumstances which is itself *both necessary and sufficient* for the rise of early Christian belief. Without these phenomena, we cannot explain why this belief came into existence, and took the shape it did. With them, we can explain it exactly and precisely.'[4]

Wright's task here is that of the historian, not that of the theologian, at least not directly. Wright's argument proceeds as follows: (1) from the very earliest days Christians shared stories of both the empty tomb and of appearances of the resurrected Jesus, and those early oral stories were very similar to the ones we now have in written form in our Gospels, and (2) Paul, far from offering a different, more spiritual view of Jesus' resurrection, is actually summarising those early stories in the opening verses of 1 Corinthians 15 and elsewhere, and his great contribution was to provide, not a different story, but a theological

---

3. NT Wright, *The Resurrection of the Son of God,* volume 3 of *Christian Origins and the Question of God* (London: SPCK, Minneapolis: Fortress Press, 2003), 8 (Wright's italics).

4. Wright, *Resurrection,* 696 (Wright's italics).

way of thinking about those traditional stories, already well known in his day. 'The gospel stories are not dependent on Paul . . . Irrespective of when the gospels reached their final form, the strong probability is that the Easter stories they contain go back to genuinely early oral tradition.'[5] In summary, Wright contends that the empty tomb combined with the appearances created the church.

An important issue all biblical scholars need to address is this: Is the Easter resurrection a historical event? Many say, 'No,' either sceptically because dead people simply don't rise or faithfully because faith is said to be subjective and not objective. The sceptics argue against historicity on the grounds of analogy: because dead people normally remain dead, Jesus must have remained dead as well. Ernst Troeltsch bequeathed to modern scholarship a formalised principle of analogy—that is, because he has himself not observed a dead person rising he argues, by analogy, neither Jesus nor anybody else could possibly have risen in the past.

Wright does not belong in the sceptic's camp, nor does he allow the principle of analogy to get in the way of pursuing historical study. He concedes that Jesus' Easter resurrection was unique, that it does not have an analogy in common experience. *'The fact that dead people do not ordinarily rise is itself part of early Christian belief*, not an objection to it. The early Christians insisted that what had happened to Jesus was precisely something new, was, indeed, the start of a whole new mode of existence, a new creation.'[6] The uniqueness of what happened to Jesus is part of its significance. 'It is precisely the uniqueness of the rise of the early church that forces us to say: never mind analogies, what happened?'[7]

Wright does not belong in the fideist camp with Rudolf Bultmann and existentialist interpreters. The resurrection of Jesus cannot be reduced to the rise of faith in the disciples of Jesus, or in the renewal of hope among the members of what would become the Christian

---

5. Wright, *Resurrection*, 612.

6. Wright, *Resurrection*, 712 (Wright's italics).

7. Wright, *Resurrection*, 18. For a thorough critique of the Troeltschian overuse of the principle of analogy in historical research, see Wolfhart Pannenberg, *Basic Questions in Theology* (2 volumes), (Minneapolis: Fortress Press, 1970–1971), I:38–53.

98 *From Resurrection to Return*

church. A subjectivist explanation for the appearance of the church is insufficient. The followers of Jesus who began the church experienced a new reality, an objective reality, to which the rise of faith became a response.

2. From history to prolepsis

The Easter resurrection of Jesus is a past event, an event available for historical study. Yet, Easter could not be what it was without the accompanying promise of the eschatological kingdom of God. The past cannot be what it is without its future.

Wright sees accurately that what happened to Jesus can be understood only within the framework of God's promise of our future resurrection into the new creation:

> Early Christianity was a 'resurrection' movement through and through, and that, indeed, it stated much more precisely what exactly 'resurrection' involved (it meant going through death and out into a new kind of bodily existence beyond, and it was happening in two stages, with Jesus first and everyone else later); second, that though the literal 'resurrection' of which the early Christians spoke remained firmly in the future, it coloured and gave shape to present Christian living as well.[8]

The colour this adds to our present life I refer to as beatitudinal living. Our task here in this paper is beatitudinal reflecting.

To aid us in this reflecting, I would like to introduce the concept of prolepsis. This is not a term Wright exploits extensively, yet as a theological concept it moves us from the basic historical experience with Jesus to the eschatological significance or meaning of Jesus:

> The heart and centre of it all, then, is the defeat of death in the future, based on the proleptic defeat inflicted in the resurrection of Jesus himself; or, to put

---

8.   Wright, *Resurrection*, 210.

Between the First and Second Comings 99

> it another way, it is the final completion of the 'age
> to come', which was inaugurated, in the midst of
> the 'present evil age', through the Messiah's death
> and resurrection.[9]

With prolepsis, we are understanding the Easter resurrection of Jesus as an anticipation or even a prefiguration of the advent of the eschatological new creation. This is a theological judgment, already present in the New Testament. It is built right into the meaning of the history of Jesus. We need to take a step from historical judgment toward theological meaning, from reference toward significance. Wright acknowledges the hermeneutical distinction between referent and meaning. By 'referent' he refers to the historical judgment that Jesus rose bodily from the dead. By 'meaning' he draws out its significance, namely, Jesus is the Son of God. 'The resurrection, in other words, declares that Jesus really is God's Son: not only in the sense that he is the Messiah, though Paul certainly intends that here, not only in the sense that he is the world's true lord, though Paul intends that too, but also in the sense that he is the one in whom the living God, Israel's God, has become personally present in the world, has become one of the human creatures that were made from the beginning in the image of this same God.'[10] As we move from exegesis to systematic theology, this proleptic connection between the historical Easter and the eschatological promise is our focus. Yet, we need to ask whether the systematician finds the connection already built into the history, or must resurrection and that systematic theology consists of a constructive interpretation of what scripture says.

The systematic theologian needs to rely on a two-directional hermeneutic. The first direction is backward, back from the biblical text towards speculation about the history that must have given rise to the text as we read it. The second direction is forward towards our contemporary context, towards an explication of the Christian faith within the modern post-Enlightenment horizon of meaning. Both di-

---

9.   Wright, *Resurrection*, 336.

10.   Wright, *Resurrection*, 733. See my chapter, 'The Future of Resurrection', in *The Resurrection: John Dominic Crossan and NT Wright in Dialogue*, edited by Robert Stewart (Minneapolis: Fortress, 2006), 149–70.

100   *From Resurrection to Return*

rections start from the same location, from what scripture says. Both history and explication are interpretations of scripture. The horizon of the future plays a significant role in both.

3. Prolepsis in Wolfhart Pannenberg

To take the next step in developing the proleptic significance of Jesus' resurrection and the accompanying promise of our resurrection, we can draw on the scholarship of Munich systematic theologian Wolfhart Pannenberg.

Pannenberg emphasises that Jesus' Easter resurrection was a pre-realisation of God's eschatological promise. 'The ministry of Jesus shared with prophecy the character of an anticipation, but not only as in prophecy and apocalyptic in the sense of mere pre-*cognition*, but, so to say, as a pre-*realisation* of the future, as its proleptic dawning.'[11]

Actually, according to Pannenberg, we do not first find bare history and then add significance on top of it. Rather, history and significance come together in a single package. Wrapped right within the original meaning of Jesus' Easter resurrection is the dawning of the general or universal resurrection previously anticipated in apocalyptic prophecies. Whether Jewish listeners to Jesus believed or disbelieved in the apocalyptic vision of resurrection, they understood it, and they could understand why what happened to Jesus on Easter would be interpreted within this horizon. Jesus' resurrection is the 'first fruits' of those having 'fallen asleep' (1 Corinthians 15:20). What was expected for all of us has already happened individually to the person of Jesus. 'Jesus' expectation of the speedy realisation of the eschatological reality did not simply fail. It was fulfilled, and thus confirmed, though only in his own person . . . The general human destiny has occurred in Jesus—if he *really* was resurrected from the dead.'[12]

It is important to note how Pannenberg makes his theological assertion contingent upon a historical one: 'If he *really* was resurrected from

---

11.   Wolfhart Pannenberg, 'Focal Essay: The Revelation of God in Jesus of Nazareth', in *Theology As History*, volume III of *New Frontiers in Theology*, edited by James M Robinson and John B Cobb, Jr (New York: Harper, 1967), 112–13 (Pannenberg's italics).

12.   Pannenberg, 'Focal Essay', 114 (Pannenberg's italics).

Between the First and Second Comings   101

the dead.' Theological commitment is dependent upon historicity of the founding event, Jesus' personal resurrection. Faith is dependent on history. Faith, even though it is a subjective appropriation of Christian belief, is not reducible to its subjective character, it requires grounding in the objective realm of fact. This means, among other things, that a historical judgment against the authenticity of the biblical claim regarding Jesus' resurrection would undermine Christian belief.

The implication of Pannenberg's method is that we need a more thorough integration of fact and meaning, what Wright calls 'referent' and 'meaning':

> Such splitting up of historical consciousness into a detection of facts and an evaluation of them . . . is intolerable to Christian faith, not only because the message of the resurrection of Jesus and of God's revelation in him necessarily becomes merely subjective interpretation, but also because it is the reflection of an outmoded and questionable historical method. It is based on the futile aim of the positivist historians to ascertain bare facts without meaning in history . . . Against this we must reinstate today the original unity of facts and their meaning.[13]

Just how close are Wright and Pannenberg on this matter? Is Wright more willing to separate historical fact from its meaning? Is Wright insistent that we first get the historical facts straight, then we proceed to make theological judgments? Or, would it be better to see fact and meaning inextricably united in the historical reports of Jesus' resurrection and then consider our division of fact from meaning to be an abstraction? Pannenberg tips toward the latter.

Theologians such as Pannenberg proceed with the assumption that historical reconstrual of the facts will confirm the historicity of the Easter resurrection. He proceeds accordingly:

> Now let us assume that the historical question concerning the resurrection of Jesus has been decided

---

13.   Pannenberg, 'Focal Essay', 126–27.

102 *From Resurrection to Return*

positively, then the meaning of this event as God's
final revelation is not something that must be added
to it; rather, this is the original meaning inherent in
that event within its own context of history and tradition.[14]

As we explicate the meaning of Jesus' Easter resurrection, we draw
out its significance for Jesus' person and for the eschatological vision.
According to Pannenberg: If Jesus has been raised, then (a) the end of
the world has begun, (b) God himself has confirmed the pre-Easter
activity of Jesus, (c) Jesus is the expected Son of Man, (d) God is ultimately revealed in Jesus, (e) the universality of Israel's God motivates
the gentile mission, and (f) Jesus' words and appearances should be
interpreted as having the same content.[15]

The methodological point is that for both the early oral and written tradition as well as people of Christian faith today, the historical
report of Jesus' Easter resurrection comes prepackaged, so to speak,
with the eschatological promise of new creation and the advent of
God's everlasting kingdom. Both this referent and the meaning of this
historical event are contingent upon their eschatological confirmation
or disconfirmation.

The inextricable connection between past and future, between
what happened to Jesus and what will happen to us and the whole of
reality, is built into the historical question. Adolf Harnack recognised
this in the development of dogma. 'The firm confidence of the disciples in Jesus was rooted in the belief that he did not abide in death, but
was raised by God . . . Consequently, the resurrection of Jesus became
the sure pledge of the resurrection of all believers, that is of their real
personal resurrection.'[16]

Pannenberg explicates it systematically by arguing that the proleptic events surrounding the historical Jesus and the eschatological event

---

14. Pannenberg, 'Focal Essay', 128.

15. Wolfhart Pannenberg, *Jesus—God and Man*, translated by Lewis L Wilkins and
    Duane A Priebe, second edition (Louisville: Westminster/John Knox Press, 1977),
    66–73.

16. Adolf Harnack, *History of Dogma*, translated by Neil Buchanan, 7 volumes (New
    York: Dover, 1961) I:84–5.

Between the First and Second Comings 103

of new creation are a single reality, a single act by an eternal God with a temporal world:

> The coming again of Christ will be the completion of the work of the Spirit that began in the incarnation and with the resurrection of Jesus. From the standpoint of eternity we have here one and the same event because the incarnation is already the inbreaking of the future of God, the entry of eternity into time. For us, however, confession of the incarnation has its basis in Jesus' resurrection, and only at his return will debate concerning the reality of the Easter event be at an end and will that reality definitively and publicly come into force, for the resurrection of Jesus is a proleptic manifestation of the reality of the new, eschatological life of salvation in Jesus himself.[17]

Only in the future will we know the past for certain.

4. Eschatology in John Polkinghorne

As previously mentioned, the systematic theologian needs a two-directional hermeneutic. Beginning with scripture, the theologian goes backward to speculative history and forward to explications of the biblical faith. As we move forward from the biblical horizon to the horizon of understanding of the modern world, we encounter modern science. Science influences if not determines the conceptual apparatus of the contemporary mind. Beatitudinal thinking needs science. Within this context we might ask: Just how can we conceive of the resurrection of the body? Any answer we offer will, like history, be speculative and, thereby, hypothetical and provisional. But explication requires

---

17. Wolfhart Pannenberg, *Systematic Theology*, translated by Geoffrey W Bromily, 3 volumes (Grand Rapids: Eerdmans, 1991–1998), III:627. See Ted Peters, 'Clarity of the Part Versus Meaning of the Whole', in *Beginning with the End: God, Science, and Wolfhart Pannenberg*, edited by Carol Rausch Albright and Joel Haugen (Chicago: Open Court, 1997), 289–302.

104   *From Resurrection to Return*

such theological preconstruction. Perhaps at this juncture we should turn our attention to the creative contributions of Cambridge physicist and theologian John Polkinghorne. Based on his interpretation of the Bible and his knowledge of physical cosmology and evolutionary biology, Polkinghorne is convinced that the eschatological resurrection of the dead cannot arise out of the natural world. Dead people stay dead. Unless, of course, God acts to raise them. Our hope rests solely in God. 'An ultimate hope will have to rest in an ultimate reality, that is to say, in the eternal God himself, and not in his creation.[18]

The scope of the projected transformation is tantamount to the creation of the world in the first place. However, there is a difference. Whereas the present creation arrived *ex nihilo*, out of nothing, the new creation will be *ex vetere*, a transformation of the existing creation. As we saw with Pannenberg earlier, key here is that resurrection of the individual is inextricably tied to the renewal of all things. 'The new creation represents the transformation of that universe when it enters freely into a new and closer relationship with its Creator, so that it becomes a totally sacramental world, suffused with the divine presence.' This suffusion of divine presence translates into healing:

> Its process can be free from suffering, for it is conceivable that the divinely ordained laws of nature appropriate to a world making itself through its own evolving history should give way to a differently constituted form of 'matter', appropriate to a universe 'freely returned' from independence to an existence of integration with its Creator.[19]

When we think of the healing miracles during Jesus' lifetime, we could think of his person 'suffused with the divine presence.' The healing power in Jesus' person prefigures or prerealises the healing power of the entire new creation. Even though Polkinghorne's hermeneutic explicates the faith within the horizon of modern science, he does not

---

18.   John Polkinghorne, '1993–1994 Gifford Lectures', in *The Faith of a Physicist* (Princeton: Princeton University Press, 1994), or *Science and Christian Belief* (London: SPCK, 1994), 162–3.

19.   Polkinghorne, '1993–1994 Gifford Lectures', 167.

Between the First and Second Comings   105

allow the scientific worldview to dictate exhaustively his explication. On theological grounds he argues that the present universe will have its material with its natural laws transformed. We will have new laws conducive to the avoidance of suffering and death. These new natural processes will be healing and life-giving because they will be suffused with the divine presence, the source of healing and life.

This leads to a distinction between evolution and eschatology. The new creation will not evolve on the basis of existing resources within the present creation, says Polkinghorne. Only an eschatological action on the part of God can make this transformation happen. The corollary to this is that our immortality is not inherent in the human soul. Death is total annihilation of the psychosomatic person, at least from our point of view. No quality within us as mortal beings has any purchase on immortality. If we are to rise from the dead, it will be due solely to the exertion of divine power. 'The Christian hope is, therefore, for me not the hope of *survival* of death, the persistence *post mortem* of a spiritual component which possesses, or has been granted, an intrinsic immortality. Rather, the Christian hope is of death and *resurrection*.'[20]

But, we might ask: what about continuity? Will eschatological transformation create such newness that all connection with the past and present will be severed? Here is the way Polkinghorne handles it. He defines the soul as an information-bearing pattern. He places himself in the tradition of Aristotle and Thomas, for whom the soul is the form of the body. What keeps Polkinghorne from garden-variety Platonism is that it is God, not the soul on its own, that remembers our pattern. 'I believe it is a perfectly coherent hope that the pattern that is me will be remembered by God and its instantiation will be recreated by him when he reconstitutes me in a new environment of his choosing. That will be his eschatological act of resurrection.'[21]

On the one hand, death is complete, total. On the other hand, disembodied information perdures. The dissipation of our biological atoms into the surrounding physical environment is complete, total. Who we were physically in the past is not retrieved in its original substance. Resurrection consists of transformation into a spiritual body, the form of which is recalled by God into a new individual existence.

---

20.   Polkinghorne, '1993–1994 Gifford Lectures', 163.

21.   Polkinghorne, '1993–1994 Gifford Lectures'.

God remembers us as information patterns. I still would want to ask Polkinghorne why he limits continuity to the divinely remembered soul or pattern. I recall in Paul's vocabulary it is the body or *soma* that is repeated, no soul or *psyche* survives in the spiritual body, *soma pneumatikon* (1 Corinthians 15:42–4). This text suggests that what will be changed is the material of the new creation making up the future resurrected body. On the one hand, Polkinghorne seems to offer an appropriate explication regarding materiality. The new material will obey new laws of nature, laws of life rather than laws of death.

Yet, on the other hand, our identity is carried forward only by a divinely remembered information pattern, not physically. Be that as it may, such an idea of resurrection 'is both immensely thrilling and deeply mysterious'.[22]

As we have seen, Polkinghorne stresses the totality of death. This is because such totality is natural. Resurrection is not natural, at least as we understand nature today.

Resurrection will require an act of God:

> Thus the Christian hope centres on a real death followed by a real resurrection, brought about through the power and merciful faithfulness of God . . . It is not necessary, however, that the 'matter' of these bodies should be the same matter as makes up the flesh of this present world. In fact, it is essential that it should not be. That is because the material bodies of this world are intrinsically subject to mortality and decay. If the resurrected life is to be a true fulfilment, and not just a repeat of an ultimately futile history, the bodies of that world-to-come must be different, for they will be everlastingly redeemed from mortality. Science knows only the matter of this world but it cannot forbid theology to believe

---

22. Polkinghorne, '1993–1994 Gifford Lectures', 164. See John Polkinghorne, 'Eschatological Credibility: Emergent and Teleological Processes', in *Resurrection: Theological and Scientific Assessments*, edited by Ted Peters, Robert John Russell and Michael Welker (Grand Rapids: Eerdmans, 2002), 43–55.

Between the First and Second Comings 107

that God is capable of bringing about something totally new.[23]

In summary, Polkinghorne thinks of the resurrected spiritual body as material, but not the same material we enjoy presently in our present biological make-up. We have a soul, defined as the form of the body—that is, the complex information-processing pattern of the body.

This soul or pattern, however, is not in itself immortal. Rather, it supplies the form by which the divine mind remembers us and on the basis of which God in the new creation recreates us. Who we are in the new creation is who we are, but this continuity of identity is a gift from God.

This leads me to offer a slight modification of the Polkinghorne view. Polkinghorne places weight on the information pattern that constitutes the human soul and is remembered by God. I would prefer to place the weight on the relationship we temporal beings enjoy with our eternal God. Roland Chia follows this relationalist path with reference to the *imago dei* or image of God. 'The image of God in humanity cannot be destroyed by sin or death.

So long as God maintains his relationship with humanity, so long as he holds fast to humanity, the human person's designation as the

---

23. John Polkinghorne, *Science and Theology: An Introduction* (London and Minneapolis: SPCK and Fortress, 1998), 115–6. One of the related issues not addressed in this paper is the relationship of time to eternity. The Christian eschatological vision assumes a connection, because salvation and fulfilment consists of a transformation of the temporal world. Yet, as Paul Davies points out, it is difficult to conceive of a world going and going through more time after it has made its point, after its fulfilment. 'I believe there is no plausible cosmological model on offer at this time that simultaneously satisfies two widespread but seemingly conflicting desires: that the universe has an ultimate destiny or purpose, and that the universe will exist interestingly for eternity. This fundamental tension between progress and eternity pervades the history of religion, and is solved in classical Christian theology . . . by placing God . . . outside of time altogether.' Paul Davies, 'Eternity: Who Needs It?', in *The Far Future Universe: Eschatology from a Cosmic Perspective*, edited by George FR Ellis (Philadelphia and London: Templeton Foundation Press, 2002), 50.

108 *From Resurrection to Return*

image of God is indissoluble, inalienable, and immortal.'[24] Mark Worthing reiterates this point well. 'We are in the image of God because God relates to us. Not vice versa. The image of God must not only be understood in a primarily relational way, but also radically as gift.'[25] The key, in my judgment, is God's relationship to us, within which the dynamism of transformation takes place.

5. Robert John Russell: the first instantiation of a new law of nature

As we have seen, a historical retrieval of the event of Jesus' Easter resurrection leads immediately to spelling out its significance for the eschatological future of the created universe. If what happened in Jesus' resurrection is a prolepsis of what will happen to us upon resurrection into God's promised new creation, then we must speculate about a future world where dead people don't stay dead. What will resurrected life look like? Polkinghorne has made it clear that, according to present laws of physics, resurrected life is impossible. The laws of nature will need to be transformed.

This is the 'problem of eschatology and cosmology', as Robert John Russell formulates it. This problem is 'intensified to the breaking point if we take the resurrection of Jesus to entail "bodily resurrection", since this view of the resurrection is coupled with an eschatology which entails the transformation of the present creation into a new "heaven and earth".'[26] Russell assumes an inextricable connection between what happened to Jesus at Easter and what will happen to the laws of nature at the advent of the eschaton.

---

24. Roland Chia, 'Biological Essentialism and the Person', in *Beyond Determinism and Reductionism: Genetic Science and the Person*, edited by Mark LY Chan and Roland Chia (Adelaide: Australian Theological Forum, 2003), 186–7.

25. Mark William Worthing, 'Human and Animal Intelligence: A Difference of Degree or Kind?', in *God, Life, Intelligence, and the Universe*, edited by Terrence J Kelly, SJ, and Hilary D Regan (Adelaide: Australian Theological Forum, 2002), 109.

26. Robert John Russell, 'Sin, Salvation, and Scientific Cosmology: Is Christian Eschatology Credible Today?' in *Sin and Salvation*, edited by Duncan Reid and Mark Worthing (Adelaide: Australian Theological Forum, 2003), 131.

Between the First and Second Comings 109

Now we need to ask Russell: Did Jesus' resurrection abide by the current laws of nature, or the expected new ones? Russell answers with this: Jesus' Easter resurrection constitutes 'the first instantiation of a new law of nature' (FINLON). The future new reality has arrived ahead of time, so to speak, in the singular event of Easter. What was true for Jesus on the first Easter will become true for all of physical reality at the advent of the eschaton.

Now is this just plain crazy? Are we talking about a transformation of physical reality so radical that it has no continuity with the present physical world? No. The physical world we currently live in has windows open toward such transformation, anticipations of newness. Specifically, the contingency inherent in natural events just might be a pointer toward eschatological newness.

The context within which Russell developed FINLON was an analysis of the concept of contingency, with special reference to the theory of the resurrection developed by Pannenberg.[27] Russell proposes a threefold typology of (1) global contingency, (2) local contingency,and (3) nomological contingency. Each of these has subtypes. The first, global contingency, yields (1a) global ontological contingency, which asks: Why does the universe exist *per se*? Why is there something and not nothing? Or (1b) global existential contingency, which asks: Why does the universe have such global characteristics as the fundamental laws of physics and the constants of nature? Or, why this particular universe and not another one? The second, local contingency, yields (2a) local ontological contingency, which asks: Why does this particular thing exist and continue to exist? Or, local existential contingency, which asks: Why does this particular thing have the characteristics it has? When Russell turns to the third, nomological contingency, he locates the contingency of nature's laws. He asks: Could the first instance of a new natural process inaugurate a new law of nature?

New laws of nature have already appeared in physical history. From the era of the Big Bang to the onset of life, no laws governing

---

27. Robert John Russell, 'Contingency in Physics and Cosmology: A Critique of the Theology of Wolfhart Pannenberg', *Zygon*, 23:1 (March 1988), 23–44. See chapter one of the forthcoming festschrift for Robert John Russell, *God's Action in Nature's World,* edited by Ted Peters and Nathan Hallanger (Aldershot: Ashgate, 2006).

110   *From Resurrection to Return*

life were in effect. The onset of biological processes began only well into the history of the cosmos. Many aeons since the Big Bang 13.7 billion years ago had to pass lifelessly before the first sign of life on planet earth, only 3.8 billion years ago. With the arrival of life forms, so also came the arrival of life processes and the first instantiation of biological laws of nature. Nature has a history, and new chapters are genuinely new. A precedent has been set.

Now, does the resurrection of Jesus fit this paradigm? Might we think of what happened to Jesus on Easter as the first instantiation of a new natural process that we can expect to become universal at some point in the future? Within the category of nomological contingency Russell places the resurrection as a *first instantiation contingency*.

The first instantiation contingency is linked to our concept of prolepsis. This leads to an epistemological question: Should one aspect of the eschatological future arrive ahead of time within our present eon still governed by what we acknowledge as nature's laws, could we discern it? If the eschatological new creation would include the resurrection of the dead, and if a person would rise from the dead now, could we discern it? Could we understand the Easter resurrection of Jesus as the first instantiation of a new law of nature that will apply universally at the advent of the renewed creation?

In order to discern it, says Russell, we need to suspend two philosophical assumptions made by natural science, namely, analogy and nomological universality. According to the principle of analogy, the future will be just like the past. This means that, based upon analogy from observations about the natural world we make now we can project what the universe will be like sixty-five billion years from now. This needs critique. If in the near or distant future God acts to transform and redeem this world, it would be unpredictable according to the principle of analogy.

According to the principle of nomological universality, the same laws that govern the past and present will govern the future as well. This needs critique. Again, should God the creator re-create the world so that different laws obtain—such as wolves living with lambs and the elimination of death—then existing laws would no longer apply. The law that dead people stay dead would no longer apply. What we need to say about the Easter resurrection of Jesus, according to Russell, is that the future law that dead people will rise into the new creation has occurred ahead of time. Jesus is the 'first fruits of those having fallen asleep' (1 Corinthians 15:20). On Easter, God inaugurated a new law of nature, one that we will see become universal at some point in the future.

Russell finds distinctively theological warrant for holding this view. He claims 'on *theological* grounds that the processes of nature that science describes are the result of God's ongoing action as Creator, their regularity is the result of God's faithfulness. But God is free to act in radically new ways, not only in human history but also in the ongoing history of the universe, God's creation.'[28]

At the moment when God raised Jesus from the grave on the first Easter Sunday, the law that dead people remain dead was still in effect. It remains in effect today. In this context, this divine act leaves us with an anomaly. It could appear to be a miracle, a violation of existing laws of nature. However, Russell wants us to view that original resurrection as the first instance of a general resurrection. The advent of the new creation complete with general resurrection will establish that resurrection is a universal law. Jesus' Easter resurrection was the first instance, the prolepsis. Yet, it looks like a miracle.

6. Conclusion

We live in the era of the church. We live like an arc between two terminals, yesterday's Easter resurrection and tomorrow's resurrection into the eschatological new creation. What happened to Jesus on the first Easter was a prolepsis of what will happen to the entirety of the created universe. God's promise of a new creation will necessarily include changes in the laws of nature to accommodate resurrected existence and harmony among all life forms. What we see in the Easter resurrection is Jesus' incarnation of the first instantiation of that eschatological law of nature where the dead will rise and come to full flower in the kingdom of God. To live now in anticipation of our future resurrection is to live the life of Beatitude.

---

28. Robert John Russell, 'Bodily Resurrection, Eschatology, and Scientific Cosmology', in *Resurrection: Theological and Scientific Assessments*, edited by Ted Peters, Robert John Russell and Michael Welker (Grand Rapids: Eerdmans, 2002), 19.

Resurrection and the Costs of Evolution: A Dialogue with Rahner on Noninterventionist Theology

Denis Edwards

Suffering that springs from natural causes, such as the South Asian tsunami of 26 December 2004, has always raised hard questions for Christian theology. In the current dialogue between science and theology the issue of the suffering of human and nonhuman creatures takes on a new intensity, with science making it clear how predation, competition for survival, death and extinction are built into the 3.8-billion-year history of life on earth. Without creatures drawing energy from their environment, there could be no emergence of life. Without death and the succession of generations, there could be no evolution: there would be no eyes, wings or human brains. The evolution of life in its abundance and beauty is accompanied by terrible costs to human beings and to other species. The costs are built into the process. They are built into the biology, geology and underlying physics of a dynamic, life-bearing planet. The costs of evolution are built into an emergent universe. The awareness of these costs pushes theology to a deeper reflection on the nature of God's action. Theology needs to respond, however inadequately, to the idea that so much that is beautiful and good arises by way of increasing complexity through emergent processes that involve tragic loss. We know, as no generation has known before us, that these costs are intrinsic to the processes that give rise to life on earth in its beauty, fecundity and diversity.

In response to the costs built into evolution, a theology of creation has to be able to offer a view of God working creatively in and through the natural world to bring it to healing and wholeness.[1] I see at least three requirements for such a response. First, with Robert John Russell and others in the science-theology dialogue, I am convinced that a theological response to the costs of evolution must involve eschatology,

---

1.   A version of this paper has appeared in *Theological Studies*, 67 (2006).

even though the claims of Christian eschatology exist in some tension with the predictions of scientific cosmology.[2] What is needed is an objective and powerful theology of both resurrection and the final fulfilment of creation. God's action in creating an emergent universe needs to be understood in the light of the resurrection and its promise that all things will be transformed and redeemed in Christ (Romans 8:19–23, Colossians 1:20, Ephesians 1:10 and Revelation 21:5). A merely psychological or subjective theology of the resurrection cannot offer hope to creation. Only a theology of resurrection that is eschatologically transformative can begin to respond to the suffering that is built into an evolutionary universe.

A second requirement is that this divine action be understood in a noninterventionist way. Of course, it has long been recognised that science becomes impossible if God is thought of as intervening in such a way as to compete with or to overturn the regularities of nature. In addition, the theological problem of suffering is made far worse if God is thought of as arbitrarily intervening to send suffering to some creatures and not to others. Christian theology today must face up to how a particular theology of divine action that runs deep in the Christian tradition can exacerbate the pain of those who suffer because of its implicit model of an interventionist God, who chooses freely to send sufferings to some and lovingly to protect others. Such a theology can contribute to a sense of alienation from God. The culture of an interventionist God is reinforced, sometimes explicitly and sometimes implicitly, by many aspects of church life. The scientific insight that the costs of evolution built into an emergent universe challenges theology to find an alternative to the model of a God who can be thought of as freely modifying the dynamics of tectonic plates to save some from a tsunami, while causing others to suffer it.

The third requirement for a theology of divine action that might offer some response to the costs of evolution would involve an understanding of God's power as constrained by God's love and respect

---

2.   See, for example, Robert John Russell, 'Bodily Resurrection, Eschatology and Scientific Cosmology: The Mutual Interaction of Christian Theology and Science', in *Resurrection: Theological and Scientific Assessments*, edited by Ted Peters, Robert John Russell and Michael Welker (Grand Rapids: Eerdmans, 2002), 3–30.

114   *From Resurrection to Return*

for creatures. Such a view of divine power can be based on the way the power of God is revealed and defined in Jesus of Nazareth, above all in his death and resurrection. In the cross, divine omnipotence is revealed as the transcendent divine capacity to give oneself in love. The cross does not reveal the absence of divine power but its true nature. Only an omnipotent love can give itself away in radical vulnerability.[3] Theology has always taught that God can act only in accord with the divine nature, and that this nature is revealed in the Christ event as radical love. It can be argued that the God revealed in the cross and resurrection is a God whose nature it is to respect the proper autonomy of creatures, to work through them and to bring them to fulfilment. In such a view of divine power, the love that defines the divine nature is understood as a love that *waits upon* creation, living with its processes, accompanying each creature in love, rejoicing in every emergence, suffering with every suffering creature, and promising to bring all to healing and fullness of life.

In what follows I will assume the position on divine power outlined here, which I have discussed in more detail elsewhere.[4] My focus will be the other two requirements, eschatological power and nonintervention, as they apply to the resurrection. Many would think of the resurrection as the hardest case for a noninterventionist theology of divine action. I will ask: Can the resurrection be understood as an act of God that is objective and powerfully transformative but is also noninterventionist? Before addressing this question directly I will situate my own approach to divine action (which I ground in the tradition of Karl Rahner), in the context of the wider discussion of divine action and noninterventionist theology that took place in the 1990s.

1. Noninterventionist theologies of divine action

In September 1987 the Vatican Observatory, at the initiative of Pope John Paul II, held an important international conference on science

---

3.   On this subject see Walter Kasper, *The God of Jesus Christ* (New York: Crossroad, 1984), 195.

4.   See, for example, Denis Edwards, 'Every Sparrow That Falls to the Ground: The Costs of Evolution and the Christ-Event', *Ecotheology*, 11 (2006), 103–23; *Ecology at the Heart of Faith* (Maryknoll: Orbis, 2006), 39–45.

Resurrection and the Costs of Evolution 115

and religion that resulted in the publication *Physics, Philosophy, and Theology*.[5] Building on this work, George Coyne, the director of the Observatory, invited Robert John Russell and the Center for Theology and the Natural Sciences at the Graduate Theological Union, Berkeley, California, to co-sponsor a series of research conferences and publications. These conferences took up the theme of divine action, exploring it first in relation to quantum cosmology, followed by chaos and complexity, evolutionary and molecular biology, neuroscience and the person, and quantum mechanics.[6]

In these discussions, participants agreed that a theology of divine action needed to include not only God's continuous creative act (*creatio continua*), but also special and objective divine acts that would include personal providence and the Christ event. At the same time, they sought to articulate a theology of divine action that sees God acting without violating or overturning the laws of nature. A consensus emerged from the conferences around a form of divine action that was special and objective, but noninterventionist—in the sense of not violating or suspending the laws of nature.[7]

Within this consensus, however, one can discern at least five positions: (1) Ian Barbour, Charles Birch, and John Haught represent the perspective of process theology that understands divine action as the inviting lure of God, which is operative in every actual occasion, but which does not determine the outcome in an exclusive way, (2) other

---

5. Robert J Russell, William R Stoeger and George V Coyne (editors), *Physics, Philosophy, and Theology: A Common Quest for Understanding* (Vatican City State: Vatican Observatory, 1988).

6. The conferences yielded the following publications in the series 'Scientific Perspectives on Divine Action', all from the Vatican Observatory and the Center for Theology and the Natural Sciences: Robert J Russell, Nancey C Murphy and Chris J Isham (editors), *Quantum Cosmology and the Laws of Nature*, Second Edition (1996), Robert J Russell, Nancey C Murphy and Arthur R Peacocke (editors), *Chaos and Complexity* (1995), Robert J Russell, William R Stoeger, and Francisco J Ayala (editors), *Evolutionary and Molecular Biology* (1998), Robert J Russell, Nancey C Murphy, Theo C Meyering and Michael A Arbib (editors), *Neuroscience and the Person* (1999), Robert J Russell *et al* (editors), *Quantum Mechanics* (2001).

7. See Robert J Russell, 'Introduction', in *Chaos and Complexity*, 9–13.

116 *From Resurrection to Return*

scholars, including Robert Russell, Nancey Murphy, George Ellis and Thomas Tracy, explore the idea that God acts in the indeterminacy of quantum events to bring about one of a number of possible outcomes.[8] (3) John Polkinghorne thinks of God as acting in the openness of chaotic and complex systems to bring about outcomes through the top-down imparting of information, (4) Arthur Peacocke sees God as acting in and through and under every aspect of nature, acting on the system as a whole, by way of analogy with a 'top-down' or 'whole-part' cause in nature, and (5) finally, William Stoeger and Stephen Happel understand God as acting in and through secondary causes: Stoeger sees the triune God acting in every aspect of creation, through God's immanent and differentiated presence to all things, including those laws of nature we partially understand and those processes and regularities of nature still unknown to us.

My proposal begins from Stoeger's position, which I see as compatible in many respects with Peacocke's.[9] I am drawn to this posi-

---

8. Murphy sees God as acting in all quantum events, not as the sole determiner of events, but in a mediated action, in the sense that God always acts together with nature at the quantum level. Tracy suggests seeing God as acting in some rather than in all quantum events, in order to bring about the effects of God's providence. Russell proposes that God acts in all quantum events until the appearance of life and consciousness, and then God increasingly refrains from determining outcomes, leaving room for top-down causality in conscious creatures, particularly in humans. For a summary of these views see Russell, 'Divine Action and Quantum Mechanics: A Fresh Assessment', in *Quantum Mechanics*, 293–328.

9. Those who see God as determining one of several possible outcomes, either at the quantum level (Russell and Murphy) or at the macro level (Polkinghorne), intensify the problem of theodicy. Murphy and Ellis respond to the theodicy issue with a kenotic theology: *On the Moral Nature of the Universe: Theology, Cosmology and Ethics* (Minneapolis: Fortress, 1996). Polkinghorne explores the issue in, among other writings, 'Kenotic Creation and Divine Action', in *The Work of Love: Creation as Kenosis*, edited by John Polkinghorne (Grand Rapids: Eerdmans, 2001), 90–106. Russell acknowledges that 'theodicy becomes a particularly intense issue in light of the present thesis regarding a noninterventionist approach to objective, special divine action' and argues that a resolution is to be sought in a trinitarian theology of resurrection and final

Resurrection and the Costs of Evolution 117

tion because it clearly respects the absolute transcendence and radical mystery of God's action, and because I continue to be attracted by Aquinas's idea that God acts through secondary causes 'not from any impotence on his part, but from the abundance of his goodness imparting to creatures also the *dignity of causing*.'[10] Aquinas, of course, allows for miracles, wherein he sees God acting without a secondary cause.[11] I will not take up a theology of miracles in general here, but simply focus on the resurrection and ask: Can God be thought of as working consistently through secondary causes even in the resurrection? Can the resurrection be seen as a noninterventionist divine action in the sense that here too God acts through secondary causes? Can God be understood as working in the resurrection through the laws and constants of nature rather than as violating, suspending or bypassing them?

Rahner's work suggests a theology that can extend this discussion of noninterventionist divine action. Such a theology would stand within the perspective of the Thomist tradition, arguing that God can be seen as consistently working through secondary causes. In a brief discussion in *Foundations of Christian Faith* Rahner argues that we do not experience God as one element in the world, but as the very ground of the world. We find God in the openness to mystery that occurs in our experience of created realities, but, if this is so, then God must be 'embedded' in this world to begin with.[12] What is seen as an 'intervention' of God is really to be understood as the historical expression of God's self-communicating presence that is always

---

transformation: 'Divine Action and Quantum Mechanics', 319, 322–3.

10. *Summa Theologiae* 1, q. 22, a. 3, *Summa Theologiae: Latin Text and English Translation*, volume 5, translated by Thomas Gilby, OP (London: Blackfriars, 1964–1976), 99. Central to this tradition is the idea that God does not act as one cause among creaturely causes, but as the ground of all created causes. It is worth noting that Polkinghorne takes an opposing view: 'I have come to believe that the Creator's kenotic love includes allowing divine special providence to act as a cause among causes.' (Polkinghorne, 'Kenotic Creation and Divine Action' 104).

11. *Summa Theologiae* 1, q. 105, a. 6, 8.

12. Karl Rahner, *Foundations of Christian Faith: An Introduction to the Idea of Christianity* (New York: Seabury, 1978), 87.

intrinsic to the world. Rahner says that every divine 'intervention', although it is a free and unpredictable act of God, actually makes concrete and historical the one intervention by which God has embedded God's self in the world from the beginning as its 'self-communicating ground'.[13]

In Rahner's view there certainly are *special* acts of God, but these are 'objectifications' of God's one self-bestowing action. In these special acts, a created reality mediates and expresses the immanent presence and love of God. Because creatures really do express the divine action, Rahner speaks of *objective*, special divine acts. However, he sees these acts as capable of being recognised as special only within the context of subjective experience of grace.[14] In such divine acts, the one self-bestowing act of God finds objective expression in and through a range of created secondary causes. These include words, persons, and events. To those with eyes to see, these become symbolic mediations of the divine.

Rahner offers a 'modest' example of a special divine action. When a person has a 'good idea' that proves effective and is experienced as a gift from God, there may well be a natural explanation for the good idea. But it can still be seen as an act of God, in the sense that in it a person encounters the God who is present and really mediated in this event of a good idea. When a good idea is experienced as the place of encounter with the ground of all reality, it can be understood as willed by God, as God-given, and hence as inspired. It becomes, in Rahner's view, a genuine experience of God's special providence.

In a later (1980) book, coauthored with Karl-Heinz Weger, Rahner comments explicitly on interventionist and noninterventionist approaches to divine action and speaks of a 'fundamental change' away from an interventionist view of God.[15] Rahner acknowledges that, while traditional theology saw God as the ever-present, immanent, all-embracing and ultimate ground of being, it also assumed that divine interventions could be located at certain points in space and time. In fact, the traditional idea of the history of salvation was 'based main-

---

13. Rahner, *Foundations of Christian Faith*.

14. Rahner, *Foundations of Christian Faith*, 88.

15. Karl Rahner and Karl-Heinz Weger, *Our Christian Faith: Answers for the Future* (New York: Crossroad, 1980), 57.

Resurrection and the Costs of Evolution   119

ly on the model of interventions by God'. This interventionist model coexisted with a more universal view of God as the 'deepest energy of the world'. The two models were never completely reconciled.[16]

While Rahner has no wish to condemn the older approach, and while he too holds for a history of salvation and of particular and special revelation, above all in Jesus Christ, he argues for the emergence of a 'universalist basic model' of divine action. In this universalist model, God in God's free grace, has always and everywhere 'communicated himself to his creation as its innermost energy and works in the world from the inside out'.[17] Rahner wants to show that, without interpreting Christianity in a naturalist way, it is possible 'with all due caution and modesty, to do without a particularist model of external intervention by God into his world at particular points of space and time'.[18]

In this kind of theology, Jesus can be seen as the one who makes God's deepest promise historically accessible and irreversible. Because this promise of God is already the fundamental energy at work in all things in the universe, Rahner believes it is possible to understand the event of Christ without the image of intervention.[19] The resurrection of Jesus gives expression to this promise that is always at work in creation. It is certainly an event of revelation, but not one coming from 'outside'.[20]

Rahner simply states this claim. I will explore it further, asking: Can the resurrection itself be understood in noninterventionist terms

---

16. Rahner and Weger, *Our Christian Faith*, 77.

17. Rahner and Weger, *Our Christian Faith*, 78–9.

18. Rahner and Weger, *Our Christian Faith*, 84.

19. 'The event of God's promise of himself in Jesus makes that deepest promise by God of himself to the world historically accessible and irreversible. It is always and everywhere the fundamental energy and force of the world and its history. It is therefore perfectly possible to understand the event of Jesus without the aid of images of an intervention in the world from outside. In doing without such an image, however, we must let history really be history and clearly realise that this deepest energy and power of the world and its history is God in his sovereign freedom, who, by his free promise of himself, has made himself this deepest energy and force of the world.' (Rahner and Weger, *Our Christian Faith*, 103–4).

20. Rahner and Weger, *Our Christian Faith*, 111.

120 *From Resurrection to Return*

without diminishing its eschatological promise? I will propose that four lines of thought in Rahner's theology suggest an affirmative answer: his theology of resurrection as part of the one divine act of self-bestowal, his evolutionary Christology, his sacramental or symbolic theology of salvation and his understanding of resurrection as ontological transformation.

2. Resurrection within the *one* divine act

Rahner sees divine action in terms of God's self-bestowal to creation. He looks to the heart of Christian revelation and finds that God gives God's self to us in the Word made flesh and in the Spirit poured out in grace. He sees this trinitarian self-giving as involving not just incarnation and grace, but creation and final fulfilment. Because the self-giving of God defines every aspect of God's action, the scientific story of the emergence of the universe and the evolution of life is to be seen as part of a larger story of divine self-bestowal.[21] God creates in order to give God's self to creation as its final fulfilment. This fulfilment will be the salvation not only of human beings but also of the whole creation. God wills to bestow God's very self in love, and creation comes to be as the addressee of this self-bestowal.[22]

In the theological tradition there are two schools of thought on the relationship between creation and the Christ event. One school sees the Christ event as a second act after creation, brought about because of sin and the need for redemption. The other school, that of Duns Scotus (1266–1308), holds that God freely chooses from the beginning to create a world in which the Word would be made flesh. Rahner adopts this theology and sees creation, incarnation and final fulfilment as united in one great act of divine self-bestowal. The incarnation is not thought of as an add-on to creation. It is not simply a remedy for sin,

---

21. Karl Rahner, 'Christology in the Setting of Modern Man's Understanding of Himself and of His World', in *Theological Investigations*, 11:215–29, at 219. I am building here on an earlier article, 'Resurrection of the Body and Transformation of the Universe in the Theology of Karl Rahner', forthcoming in *Philosophy and Theology*.

22. Karl Rahner, 'Resurrection', in *Encyclopedia of Theology: A Concise Sacramentum Mundi*, edited by Karl Rahner (New York: Seabury, 1975), 1430–42, at 1442.

Resurrection and the Costs of Evolution 121

although it is this. The Christ event is the irreversible beginning of God's self-giving to creation that will find its fulfilment only when the whole of creation is transformed in Christ. Divine action is *one* act, one act of self-bestowing love in which there are distinct elements that include creation, incarnation and final fulfilment.[23]

Rahner insists that what is most specific to the Christian view of God is the idea of a God who bestows God's very self to creation.[24] This is a God who creates creatures that are *capax infiniti*, who, without being consumed in the fire of divinity, are able to receive God's life as their own fulfilment. While Christianity insists against pantheism on the distinction between creation and God, there is no distance between God and creatures. God's being is the distinction.[25] But this same transcendent Creator is radically interior to each creature in self-bestowing love. God is the very core of the world's reality and the world is truly the fate of God. Creation is intrinsically directed toward self-bestowal. It is not simply that God creates something other, but that God freely communicates God's own reality to the other. The universe emerges in the process of God's self-bestowal. Rahner sees this self-bestowal of the transcendent God as 'the most immanent factor in the creature'.[26]

In this understanding, creation is intrinsically oriented both to the resurrection of Christ and to final fulfilment. It is eschatological from the ground up. This view of God acting in one act of self-bestowal constitutes a first line of thought that can build toward an inside-out rather than an interventionist theology of resurrection. If God acts in

---

23. Creation and incarnation, therefore, are 'two moments and two phases of the *one* process of God's self-giving and self-expression, although it is an intrinsically differentiated process' (Rahner, *Foundations of Christian Faith*, 197).

24. Karl Rahner, 'The Specific Character of the Christian Concept of God', in *Theological Investigations*, 21:185–95.

25. 'God is not merely the one who as creator establishes a world distant from himself as something different, but rather he is the one who gives himself away to this world and who has his own fate in and with this world. God is not only himself the giver, but he is also the gift' (Rahner, 'The Specific Character', 191). See also Rahner's 'Christology in the Setting', 224.

26. Rahner, 'Immanent and Transcendent Consummation of the World', in *Theological Investigations*, 10:273–89, at 281.

122   *From Resurrection to Return*

one differentiated act, then the resurrection is not an intervention of God from without, but the central dimension of this one act by which God creates, saves, and brings all to fulfilment. This idea of the unity of the divine act leads to a second line of thought that can contribute to a noninterventionist theology of resurrection, that of evolutionary Christology.

3. Resurrection within evolutionary Christology

While divine action can be considered from God's side as divine self-bestowal, it can also be considered from the perspective of its effect in the creature, as enabling creaturely self-transcendence. According to Rahner, the effect of God's immanence is that creation has the capacity to transcend itself. This concept, worked out in Rahner's anthropology and central to his evolutionary Christology, functions in much of his work.[27] With the concept of divine self-bestowal, it provides a way of grasping the radical unity of God's one act. It is God present in self-bestowal who enables creaturely self-transcendence. Divine self-bestowal and creaturely self-transcendence characterise not only creation, grace and incarnation, but also final consummation.[28]

The ancient theological tradition always had a theology of continuous creation. It saw God as sustaining all creatures in being (*conservatio*) and enabling them to act (*concursus*). Rahner transforms this theology of conservation into a theology of becoming. God enables creatures not only to exist, but also to transcend themselves, to become something new. In his evolutionary Christology, Rahner begins from the fundamental *unity* he finds in creation. All of creation is united in its one origin in God, in its self-realisation as one united world, and in its one future in God. Within this unity are transitions to the *new* in the history of the universe, particularly when matter becomes life, and when life becomes self-conscious spirit. Rahner argues for a theology of God's creative act as enabling the active self-transcendence

---

27.   See Karl Rahner, *Hominisation: The Evolutionary Origin of Man as a Theological Problem* (New York: Herder & Herder, 1965), 98–101, 'Christology within an Evolutionary View of the World', in *Theological Investigations*, 5:157–92, *Foundations of Christian Faith*, 178–203.

28.   Rahner, 'Christology in the Setting', 223–6.

Resurrection and the Costs of Evolution   123

of creation. This capacity is truly intrinsic to creation, but it occurs through the creative power of the immanent God. The presence and constant 'pressure' of the divine being enables the creature to become more than it is in itself.[29] This 'pressure' is not something that can be discerned by the natural sciences, but is the interior, dynamic relationship of all things in the evolving universe to their Creator.

The material universe transcends itself in the emergence of life, and life transcends itself in the human. In human beings the universe becomes open to self-consciousness, freedom and a personal relationship with God in grace. Rahner sees the Christ event in this context, as the definitive self-transcendence of the created universe into God.[30] Jesus in his created humanity is a part of evolutionary history, a part that is completely and uniquely open to the divine bestowal. If the Christ event is considered from below, it can be seen as the self-transcendence of the evolving universe into God. If the Christ event is considered from above, it can be seen as God's irreversible self-bestowal to creation. In this one person Jesus is found the irreversible self-communication of God to creatures and the definitive human acceptance of this communication. Because of this definitive acceptance, Jesus Christ is understood as absolute Saviour.[31]

Jesus' creaturely life of self-giving love culminates in his death as a radical act of love for God and for others. In the resurrection, God radically and irreversibly takes creation to God's self. The life, death and resurrection of Jesus are always to be seen together. In this paschal event, part of evolutionary history gives itself completely into God and is taken up and transformed in God, as the beginning of the transformation of all things.

Together, the death and resurrection are to be seen as the culminating moment of the self-transcendence of creation to God, and as the irreversible self-bestowal of God to creation. Within the context of an evolutionary Christology, the resurrection can be seen not as an

---

29. Karl Rahner, 'Natural Science and Christian Faith', in *Theological Investigations*, 21:16–55, at 37.

30. In Jesus, we find the 'initial beginning and definitive triumph of the movement of the world's self-transcendence into absolute closeness to the mystery of God' (Rahner, *Foundations of Christian Faith*, 181).

31. Rahner, *Foundations of Christian Faith*, 193.

124   *From Resurrection to Return*

intervention from without, but as the free and unpredictable breaking forth of that divine self-bestowal to the world that has been immanent in creation from the very beginning in the presence to creation of the Creator Spirit.

4. Resurrection as real symbol of salvation

A third dimension of Rahner's theology that supports a view of resurrection that is both objective and noninterventionist is found in his concept of salvation. The Christian tradition has always claimed that Jesus died and was raised up 'for us'. Rahner asks how this is to be understood. In what sense is the paschal event the cause of our salvation?

Rahner finds that the biblical concept of redemption through the sacrificial blood of Jesus fails to communicate in the cultural contexts of today. It 'smacks of mythology' when an angry God seems to insist on reparation for the offence done and then becomes a forgiving God as a result of a bloody sacrifice.[32] Rahner also rejects Anselm's theory of satisfaction as meaningful for today: it assumes that the sins of the world are an infinite offence against God, because of the dignity of the one offended, it assumes that the satisfaction is of infinite value because it is measured by the dignity of the person making satisfaction. These assumptions are difficult to justify in today's world.[33] Rahner acknowledges that these theologies can be meaningful when properly understood in their historical context, but he sees them as secondary and derivative in relation to the primary experience of salvation in Christ.

Rahner argues that a more contemporary theology of salvation is needed. A fundamental requirement for such a theology would be that it shows clearly that God is the cause of salvation. What needs to be avoided is any suggestion that the cross changes God from being a God of wrath to a God of grace. Jesus' death and resurrection do not cause God to begin to love us sinners. They are the expression and consequence of God's divine love. They give expression to God's eternal will to save. Rahner suggests a theology of salvation in which

---

32.   Rahner and Weger, *Our Christian Faith*, 114.

33.   Rahner and Weger, *Our Christian Faith*, 114–5.

Resurrection and the Costs of Evolution

the Christ event has a causality of a quasi-sacramental and real symbolic nature.[34] Jesus' life, death and resurrection taken together can be seen as the real symbol in which God's saving will reaches its full and irrevocable realisation and manifestation in the world. Rahner's concept of the real symbol is a strong one. It involves not only the revelation of salvation but its accomplishment.

Jesus' life finds its climax in the surrender to God in his death and in God's acceptance of this in the resurrection. The event of Jesus' life, death and resurrection is both the symbol and the radical accomplishment of God's saving love. Jesus, who is one of us, who has given himself in death to God, is raised up by God. This is the irreversible manifestation of God's saving love for our world. In the Christ event, God's salvific will is made present in the world 'historically, really and irrevocably'.[35] The universal experience of the Spirit in grace is always ordered to the Word made flesh, to Jesus' life, death and resurrection. The grace of the Spirit is always the grace of Christ. In this sense Christ is the final cause of the Spirit, and the Spirit is always the Spirit of Jesus Christ.[36]

In this framework, the resurrection is not an event that comes from outside, but the expression in history of God's will to save, which has been operative in creation from the beginning and will find its fulfilment in the transformation of the whole creation. The resurrection is the radical expression of the promise of God and the beginning of the fulfilment of the promise. It is the real symbol, the expression and the reality, of God's saving, self-bestowing love at work in the world. It brings to visibility and initial accomplishment the self-bestowing love that has always been present to every aspect of the universe and its creatures.

The church in essence is to be the visible sign and agent of the resurrection at work in the world.[37] The risen Christ is encountered to-

---

34. Rahner, *Foundations of Christian Faith*, 282–5, 'The Theology of the Symbol', in *Theological Investigations*, 4:221–52, 'Salvation', in *Encyclopedia of Theology*, 1499–530, at 1527.

35. Rahner, *Foundations of Christian Faith*, 284.

36. Rahner, *Foundations of Christian Faith*, 317.

37. See Karl Rahner, *Meditations on the Sacraments* (New York: Seabury, 1977), xv.

126 *From Resurrection to Return*

day in the experience of grace that occurs in the church's mediation, above all in the word of God, in the Eucharist and in the other sacraments. But these sacraments are linked to the mysticism of everyday life. They 'awaken, deepen, strengthen and bring to full expression' the sacramental experiences of everyday life.[38] Christians go out from the Eucharist and encounter the resurrected Christ in words, persons and events in this world. In the light of the word, they meet the risen one in the transcendental experience of grace that occurs in daily life. The experience of the risen one is not the experience of an intervention from without but a meeting with the mystery of God incarnate in Christ that occurs in and through our encounters with fellow creatures in the world. It has a sacramental structure.

5. Resurrection as ontological transformation

A fourth line of thought concerns the objectivity of the resurrection and its impact on creation. It is all too easy to maintain a noninterventionist theology of resurrection in a reductivist model, where the resurrection is understood simply in terms of the subjective experience of the disciples. Such a reductivist theology fails not only to represent the Christian tradition adequately, but also to provide a basis for the eschatological transformation of creation. It has little to offer suffering creation.

Rahner's robust and objective claims about the resurrection and its eschatological impact are developed by working with a theology of salvation in Christ that is strong in the East: divinisation. Rahner asks why the theology of the resurrection, when compared to its New Testament origins, has suffered such an 'astonishing process of shrinkage' in the theology of the West.[39] He thinks that a central reason was the adoption by the West of a purely juridical notion of redemption: Jesus, because of his full divinity and full humanity, is able to make proper satisfaction for human sin. In this kind of theology, the focus is on the cross, rather than on the resurrection.

---

38. Harvey D Egan, *Karl Rahner: Mystic of Everyday Life* (New York: Crossroad, 1998), 163.

39. Karl Rahner, 'Dogmatic Questions on Easter', in *Theological Investigations*, 4:121–33, at 122.

Resurrection and the Costs of Evolution 127

In the East, by contrast, the resurrection plays a central role in the theology of salvation. Salvation occurs because God takes humanity and the whole creation to God's self in the incarnation. The incarnation culminates in the death and resurrection of Jesus, and these events promise final fulfilment. The resurrection transforms humanity and creation from within. This theology of resurrection is more concerned with ontological change than with legal relations. Because God embraces creaturely life in the incarnation, and above all in its culmination in resurrection, creaturely life is changed forever. Human beings and in some way all creation are taken up into God. Rahner takes three interrelated themes from the Eastern model: salvation as ontological rather than juridical, salvation as involving the divinisation of humans and the whole creation and the resurrection of Jesus as the beginning of this divinising transfiguration.

In this ontological model of the redemption, God's adoption of creaturely reality as God's own in the incarnation culminates in the resurrection of the crucified.[40] In the life and death of Jesus, a part of the creaturely reality of this world is fully handed over to God in complete freedom, obedience and love, and in the resurrection this creaturely reality is fully taken up into God. In the resurrection God irrevocably adopts creaturely reality as God's own reality, divinising and transfiguring it. Because of the unity of the world that springs from the Creator, this is an event for the whole creation. What occurs in Jesus, as part of the physical, biological and human world, is *ontologically and not simply juridically* the 'beginning of the glorification and divinisation of the whole of reality'.[41] It is 'the beginning of the transformation of the world as an ontologically interconnected occurrence'.[42] The resurrection of Jesus is understood not only as a unique and radical transformation of the crucified, but also as the beginning of the transformation of all things in God. It is not the resuscitation of

---

40. 'The redemption was felt to be a real ontological process which began in the incarnation and ends not so much in the forgiveness of sins as in the divinisation of the world and first demonstrates its victorious might, not so much in the expiation of sin on the cross as in the resurrection of Christ.' (Rahner, 'Dogmatic Questions on Easter', 126).

41. Rahner, 'Dogmatic Questions on Easter', 129.

42. Rahner, 'Resurrection', 1442.

128   *From Resurrection to Return*

a corpse to live again in the old way, but the 'eschatological victory of God's grace in the world'.[43] Rahner insists that our future participation in resurrection life will be a completely unforeseeable and unimaginable transfiguration of our spiritual, bodily, social selves. He sees continuing identity in resurrection life as provided not by the molecules that make up our bodies before death and that in this life are always subject to metabolic processes, but by the free, spiritual subject that can be called the soul. Finding a corpse in a grave could therefore not be taken as evidence of no resurrection.[44]

Christ in his risen, bodily reality is the hidden presence that gives meaning and direction to the universe. The transfiguration of the world has begun in the risen Christ and is 'ripening and developing' to that point where it will become manifest in the final fulfilment of all things.[45] Clearly this is not a theology with a purely psychological or interior understanding of the resurrection and its effects. It has no interest in a reductivist view of the resurrection. It makes the very large claim that the resurrection is the central event in the history of the universe, that it is the irreversible expression of God's saving love in our world, and that it has already begun transforming the whole of creation from within. But, as I have been attempting to show, this large claim is made about a divine action that springs from the God who is always at work from within creation, rather than being seen as an intervention from without. It is seen as the radical transformation, unpredictable fulfilment, and the real meaning and goal of God's work of creation, rather than as a miracle that overturns the natural world and its laws.

6. Resurrection: transforming but noninterventionist

My proposal is that, to respond to the issue of suffering built into creation, a theology of divine action is needed that is both eschatological

---

43.   Karl Rahner, 'Jesus' Resurrection', in *Theological Investigations*, 17:16–23, at 22.

44.   Karl Rahner, 'The Intermediate State', in *Theological Investigations*, 17:114–34, at 120.

45.   Karl Rahner, 'The Festival of the Future of the World', in *Theological Investigations*, 7:181–5, at 184.

and noninterventionist. This proposal raises the test case of the resurrection. Many have understood the resurrection to be the greatest of divine interventions. Is it to be seen as an intervention from without? Rahner thinks not, but does not argue the case. I have been attempting to show that four lines of thought from within Rahner's theology support a noninterventionist but still objective and powerful theology of resurrection. These lines of thought involve seeing the resurrection as a dimension of God's *one* divine act of self-bestowal, as within the framework of an evolutionary Christology, as real symbol of God's universal saving love, and as an ontological event, the beginning of the divinising transformation of all things. Taken together these theological positions give general plausibility to the claim that the resurrection can be seen as an objective but noninterventionist act of God.

To take this argument further, however, I will consider how the resurrection impinges on human beings and on other creatures. Can these impacts of the resurrection be considered as objective and noninterventionist? I will take up briefly two important ways in which the resurrection impacts creation: first, the experience of the risen Christ by the first disciples and, second, the ontological transformation of creation that the resurrection involves.

Clearly the encounter between the first disciples and the risen Christ had a distinctive character. Many of the disciples who encountered Jesus beyond death had walked with him in Galilee and accompanied him to Jerusalem. Their experience was distinct because they had known him in life and death and now knew him as the risen from the dead. It was distinct from later Christian experience in a second way: it had a church-founding character. For both these reasons their witness is unique and irreplaceable. All later Christian life depends on their experience and their testimony.

But were their experiences of the risen Christ miraculous interventions in the sense that they broke the laws of nature? Or did they take place in and through the laws of nature, and thus in and through secondary causes? Historically, there is no evidence that can tell us exactly what kind of experience was involved in the appearances of the risen Christ to the first disciples. Theologically, however, there is good reason to think that these encounters were not the same as everyday encounters with other persons in our lives, or with Jesus during his lifetime. As Rahner insists, the experience of the risen Christ cannot be

130   *From Resurrection to Return*

thought of as one among other ordinary experiences, but must be seen as an experience that is *sui generis*:

> Such a resurrection, into a human existence finalised and bringing history to fulfilment, is essentially an object of knowledge of an absolutely unique kind. It is essentially other than the return of a dead man to his previous biological life, to space and time which form the dimensions of history unfulfilled. Hence it is not in any way an ordinary object of experience, which could be subsumed under the common condition and possibilities of experience.[46]

Granted this uniqueness, I believe that it is possible and appropriate to understand the appearances of the risen Christ in a noninterventionist way. They might be seen as unique revelatory encounters with the risen Christ that occur in a way that is related to our own experience of God in grace. Rahner suggests that the best analogy for understanding the appearances may be the experience of Christ in the Spirit that Christians have today, rather than imaginative visions or everyday sense experience.[47] Rahner gave much of his theological life to articulating the nature of the experience of God as transcendental experiences that occur in and through the experience of creaturely realities in the world. I have discussed this matter in detail elsewhere and here simply note that this experience is one of grace in which God really does act, but which is experienced by us in a truly human and creaturely way.[48]

The appearances of the risen Christ may have the structure of a transcendental experience that occurs in and through the experience of created realities, where the one encountered is recognised as Jesus

---

46. Rahner, 'Resurrection', 1431.
47. Rahner says: 'So far as the nature of this experience is accessible to us, it is to be explained after the manner of our experience of the powerful Spirit of the living Lord rather than in a way which either likens this experience too closely to mystical visions of an imaginative kind in later times, or understands it as an almost physical sense experience.' (*Foundations of Christian Faith*, 276).
48. Denis Edwards, *Human Experience of God* (New York: Paulist, 1983).

Resurrection and the Costs of Evolution

who had walked with the disciples in Galilee but who is now radically transformed as the power of new creation. The encounters with the risen Christ may have been mediated by the communion of the church, the word of God, the breaking of the bread, the natural world, the love of another human being or the experience of prayer. What matters is that these encounters were experienced as unique revelations of the crucified Jesus, risen from the dead as the power of new life from God. Such experiences can be understood in a noninterventionist way, and yet at the same time be thought of as church-founding encounters with Jesus, in which the risen one reveals himself as alive beyond death with the fullness of bodily life transformed in God and embodying resurrection life.

Now to the question about the ontological change that the resurrection promises and initiates. If the resurrection is the beginning of the transformation of the whole creation in Christ, how does it impact on the laws of nature? Does it overturn the laws of nature or inaugurate new laws of nature? The theology developed above says no, because God has been creatively involved with every aspect of the universe from the beginning precisely as the one who would raise Jesus from the dead and bring all creation to its consummation. This had always been the very meaning of creation, that for which the processes and regularities of the natural world exist. The God of resurrection, the God who will transform all things in Christ, is the God of creation. God is present in the Spirit to every creature in the long history of the universe as the God of self-bestowing resurrection love. God creates a universe that is capable of being transformed from within. As Robert John Russell says, God creates a universe that is transformable by resurrection:

> Our starting point is that the new creation is not a replacement of the old creation, or a second and separate creation *ex nihilo*. Instead, God will transform God's creation, the universe, into the new creation *ex vetere*, to use Polkinghorne's phrase. It follows that God must have created the universe such that it is transformable, that is, that it can be transformed by God's action. Specifically, God must have created it precisely with those conditions and

132 *From Resurrection to Return*

characteristics that it needs as preconditions in order to be transformable by God's new act.[49]

Because God creates a universe capable of being transformed into a new creation, there is no need to understand what Rahner calls the ontological change of resurrection as an intervention. Rather, it can be seen as the instantiation of potentialities that God had placed in the natural world from the beginning, potentialities that have always been directed toward resurrection and new creation. In a series of articles, Stoeger has distinguished between two meanings of 'the laws of nature': on the one hand, the phrase refers to the laws contained in our scientific theories, which are only a partial description of reality, and on the other, it can refer to something far wider: the relationships, processes, and causal connections of the natural world itself, much of which escapes our theories.[50] The laws of nature as we know them are provisional and imperfect and not well suited at this stage to deal with important areas of life, including the mental, the interpersonal, the aesthetic and the religious, all of which are part of the natural world. This view of the laws of nature makes it quite possible to think that the eschatological transformation of creation begun in the resurrection may occur through secondary causes that exist in the natural world but that are either not mapped well or are not mapped at all by our scientific theories.

The impact of the resurrection on the universe might be seen as a new and, to us, unforeseeable instantiation of potentialities of nature that are already built into God's creation from the beginning. This view fits well with Rahner's idea that the eschatological consummation of the universe will take place as the act of God, but that this act works in and through the self-transcendence of creation. God is at work as the

---

49. Russell, 'Bodily Resurrection, Eschatology, and Scientific Cosmology', 21. In this volume, of course, Russell explores the possibility that the resurrection might involve new laws of nature.

50. William R Stoeger, 'Contemporary Physics and the Ontological Status of the Laws of Nature', in *Quantum Cosmology and the Laws of Nature*, 209–34, Stoeger, 'The Mind-Brain Problem, the Laws of Nature and Constitutive Relationships', in *Neuroscience and the Person*, 129–46, Stoeger, 'Epistemological and Ontological Issues Arising from Quantum Theory', in *Quantum Mechanics*, 81–98.

Resurrection and the Costs of Evolution 133

power of the future in every aspect of creation. In God's final act, God will embrace the whole of creation in self-bestowing love, but this love is already 'the most immanent element in every creature'.[51]

At the beginning of this article I proposed that a theology of divine action that can make some kind of response to the suffering of creation might have at least three characteristics: (1) it would offer eschatological hope for the redemption of creation, (2) it would be a noninterventionist theology, and (3) it would understand divine power to be defined by the cross and resurrection as a power that by nature finds expression in love and respect for creatures, that waits upon creation, lives with its processes and accompanies each creature in love.

I have focused on the first two of these characteristics as they apply to the all-important case of the resurrection. I have argued for a theology of resurrection that makes strong objective claims about Christ's resurrection and its liberating eschatological consequences. At the same time, I have proposed that the resurrection can be understood in noninterventionist terms as the central expression in our history of God's one act that embraces creation and redemption, an act that consistently finds expression through secondary causes. I see this combination of objectivity with nonintervention in a theology of resurrection as a partial theological response to the suffering of creation.

The physicist Paul Davies is a learned and helpful contributor to the discussions between science and theology. Many years ago, after expressing openness to the idea of a creator, he was asked, 'What do you think about Christianity?' He replied that Christianity is based on the miracle of the resurrection, and as a scientist he did not hold for exceptions to the laws of nature. My own theological response, framed inwardly at the time and made more explicit here, is that the resurrection is not best thought of as a miracle that overturns the laws of nature. It is far more than this. It is the event that gives meaning and direction to the whole universe and to all of its laws. It does not come from without but from within, from the presence of the creative, saving God who enables creation not only to emerge and unfold, but to come to its final fulfilment.

---

51. Rahner, 'Immanent and Transcendent Consummation', 289.

A Purposeful Creation: Evolution, Convergence and Eschatology

Graham J O'Brien

The notion of purpose within the universe remains one of the central areas of disagreement between theology and science today. Even within theology itself, there is the belief that purpose is a religious inference rather than a biological realty.

Recently however, Simon Conway Morris has gone against current evolutionary opinion and suggested that the biological process of evolution does appear to be purposeful through the process of convergence.

Although this concept is controversial, there is some theological merit because if evolution as a process can now be considered purposeful, a theology of purpose can be developed that emphasises the complementary aspects of theology and science. By using the doctrine of election as outlined by Karl Barth, I believe such a theology can be derived through which the purpose for evolution can be seen in producing the 'inevitable humans'.

Furthermore, a theology of purpose also incorporates an eschatological view where creation can be understood as *creatio continua*, moving towards its eschatological completion and communion with God.

In this view, creation is reorientated to its proper end through the resurrection of Jesus, an end that is realised fully in the 'new creation' of the eschaton. A theology of purpose therefore fits within the bounds of natural theology and acts to support the dialogue between theology and science.

It also provides a basis for an ethic of care where humanity acts as the created co-creator 'to steward our resources and opportunities in light of our vision of the coming new creation'.[1]

---

1. Ted Peters and Martinez Hewlett, *Evolution, from Creation to New Creation: Conflict, Conversation, and Convergence* (Nashville: Abingdon Press, 2003), 176.

A Purposeful Creation: Evolution, Convergence and Eschatology 135

1. Introduction

For theology to be relevant within our society it must be able to dialogue with and integrate the developments of science so that the contribution of theology to the general understanding of human life can be available and acknowledged by our society.[2] Even though theology and science both share the belief that the world is 'characterised by regularity and intelligibility',[3] one of the central differences is their understanding of 'purpose' within the universe. Purpose means the 'realising of value', so that for the universe to be purposeful suggests that it is 'orientated towards the implementation of something intrinsically good'.[4] A religious worldview affirms the purposefulness of the natural world, however this position has been challenged by science—especially evolutionary biology. Since the advent of modern genetics, some scientists have developed a philosophical view that 'life has no direction, that there is no purpose to the universe, and that matter is "all there is" '.[5] In this context, the term 'teleonomy' is used to imply that purpose is only apparent and is the result of chance in natural selection.[6] In contrast, the Christian tradition affirms that God's creative action is purposeful (teleology) leading to communion with God and fully realised in the 'new creation' of the eschaton. Within this view, evolutionary history is placed within the broader story of God's creative and redeeming work, however there are many different interpretations and implications of God's purposes for creation.[7] One such position is that of Ted Peters and Martinez

---

2. Philip Hefner, *The Human Factor: Evolution, Culture, and Religion* (Minneapolis: Fortress Press, 1993), 219–20.

3. Alister E McGrath, *Nature*, volume 1, *A Scientific Theology*, Edinburgh: T&T Clark, 2001), 218.

4. John F Haught, *Deeper than Darwin: The Prospect for Religion in the Age of Evolution* (Oxford: Westview Press, 2003), 186.

5. Haught, *Deeper than Darwin*, 7 and 185. On page 7 John Haught is quoting Stephen Jay Gould.

6. Peters and Hewlett, *Evolution, from Creation to New Creation*, 49. Teleonomy is defined as 'the quality of apparent purposefulness in living organisms that derives from their evolutionary adaption'.

7. Peters and Hewlett, *Evolution, from Creation to New Creation*, 163. This view

136 *From Resurrection to Return*

Hewlett who agree with scientific methodology that 'nature's purpose is not inherent within nature itself . . . its value or direction belongs to the relationship of nature with God'.[8] Recently however, biologist Simon Conway Morris suggested that purpose can be seen within the biological material of creation through 'convergence', resulting in the inevitable evolution of a fully sentient being.[9] Placing this view within theistic evolution would affirm that evolution is purposeful leading to the generation of the creature who can relate not only to creation, but also to the Creator.

The intent of this essay is three-fold. First, this essay seeks to explore the connections between theology and the evolutionary understanding of Conway Morris by proposing a 'theology of purpose' that points forward towards our eschatological fulfilment. Second, in proposing a theology of purpose I have drawn on Karl Barth, one of the most influential theologians of the twentieth century, and whose doctrine of election is a significant contribution to systematic theology.[10] Although Barth himself did not engage in 'natural theology', I am suggesting that by developing the doctrine of election it is possible to infer that one of creation's purposes is to produce the creature whom God has elected, without denigrating the value of creation as a whole.

I believe this insight provides a compatible theological understanding for the suggestion of Conway Morris that the biology of nature shows purposefulness. Finally, a theology of purpose includes an eschatological perspective that has ethical implications as outlined in an 'ethic of care' in which *interconnection/integrity* forms the central understanding.

---

is termed 'Theistic Evolution'. For a survey of 'Theistic Evolutionists' see pages 115–81.

8. Peters and Hewlett, *Evolution, from Creation to New Creation*, 28 and 159.

9. Simon Conway Morris, *Life's Solution: Inevitable Humans in a Lonely Universe* (Cambridge: Cambridge University Press, 2003), 313 and 328. This view contrasts with that of current scientific understanding. I was introduced to the work of Simon Conway Morris during a second year Theology and Science course taught by Dr Nicola Hoggard-Creegan.

10. John Webster, 'Introducing Barth', in *The Cambridge Companion to Karl Barth*, edited by John Webster (Cambridge: Cambridge University Press, 2000), 1.

A Purposeful Creation: Evolution, Convergence and Eschatology 137

2. Creation and purpose

The Christian understanding of creation is centred on the Judeo-Christian belief that God is the 'Creator', and within this view humankind is understood as the climax of God's creative activity, as the only creature made in the image of God.[11] The relationship between God and creation is expressed in covenantal terms, where God in the act of creation 'brought into existence a world other than himself ... [and] will not hold himself apart from it or be known except in relation to the world he has made'.[12] Creation is the outflow of God's love, the result of God's free and sovereign will and as a result, creation is seen as very good.[13] In creating, God freely decided to not exist alone, but rather to exist in fellowship with a reality that is truly distinct from Godself. This distinction between God and creation is expressed in the understanding of creation *ex nihilo*—creation out of nothing, in which God does not rely on anything outside of Godself, and is therefore truly sovereign and free.[14] Within Christian doctrine, God's act of creation is understood as an action of the Trinity as articulated in the Nicene-Constantinople Creed, and is distinguished from other monotheistic religions because of its Christological orientation. As a result, God's creative act is aligned with God's further works in order to provide the 'institution, preservation and execution of the covenant of grace'.[15]

---

11. Karl Barth, *Dogmatics in Outline* (London: SCM Press, 2001), 41. Edward M Curtis, 'Image of God (OT)', in *The Anchor Bible Dictionary*, edited by David N Freeman, *et al*, volume 3 (New York: Doubleday, 1992), 390. Alister E McGrath, *Christian Theology: An Introduction*, third edition (Oxford: Blackwell Publishers, 2001), 440. Quote is taken from Karl Barth.

12. Thomas F Torrance, *The Christian Doctrine of God, One Being, Three Persons* (Edinburgh: T&T Clark Ltd, 2001), 223.

13. Barth, *Dogmatics in Outline*, 49. Colin E Gunton, 'The Doctrine of Creation', in *The Cambridge Companion to Christian Doctrine*, edited by Colin E Gunton, (Cambridge: Cambridge University Press, 1997), 141.

14. Barth, *Dogmatics in Outline*, 43 and 46. Gunton, 'The Doctrine of Creation', 141. Colin E Gunton, *The Christian Faith: An Introduction to Christian Doctrine* (Oxford: Blackwell Publishing, 2002), 17. McGrath, *Nature*, 166.

15. McGrath, *Nature*, 181 and 187. Torrance, *The Christian Doctrine of God*, 203–4.

138   *From Resurrection to Return*

Because the doctrine of creation emphasises that the world was created out of divine intention *ex nihilo*, the entire cosmos owes its existence and purpose to God, with creation existing in the context of God's purposes. The 'supreme end' for which God has acted as Creator is the 'purpose of his Holy love', by which God wills to bring a creaturely realm of heaven and earth into existence that reflects God's glory. Within this realm, God chooses to share with the creature the communion of love which is the Trinity through a covenantal framework of grace. Therefore the purpose and meaning of creation is to make the history of God's covenant with humanity possible in a purposed and unequal coexistence between God and the world in which the world is reliant (contingent) upon God for its existence.[16] In the act of creation God also gives creation freedom—the time and space to become itself—through what Karl Barth describes as 'God's patience'.[17] Therefore, the act of creation can be seen to have two purposes: to create something that is intrinsically of value and to make something valuable in itself because it is created to serve God's glory.[18] For humanity as the *imago Dei*, freedom is a 'relational concept'[19] that is limited by the existence of fellow creatures and the sovereignty of God. As a result, human freedom is 'an imperfect mirroring of the divine freedom', and is ultimately freedom to decide for God in obedience.[20]

Even though creation is understood as a once-only action of God (*ex nihilo*), God's continuing presence is recognised as sustaining creation's existence, and is identified with the incarnation. Here Christ's redeeming action has not only restored the *imago Dei* in humanity, but also includes all of creation and can be understood as the final per-

---

     Quote is taken from McGrath.

16.   McGrath, *Nature*, 179 and 181. Hefner, *The Human Factor*, 46. Torrance, *The Christian Doctrine of God*, 218–9 and 223. Quote is taken from Torrance.

17.   See Karl Barth as quoted in Gunton, *The Christian Faith*, 6. In a similar manner John Haught talks of creation as 'truly other' than God, where nature's contingencies and evolutions randomness shows God's caring and waiting for the 'other' to appear. See Haught, *Deeper than Darwin*, 80.

18.   Gunton, *The Christian Faith*, 19.

19.   Gunton, *The Christian Faith*, 45.

20.   Barth, *Dogmatics in Outline*, 47.

A Purposeful Creation: Evolution, Convergence and Eschatology 139

fection of cosmic history. Creation is therefore re-orientated toward its proper end through the resurrection of Jesus and fully realised in the 'new creation' of the new heaven and the new earth (Revelation 21:1).[21] As a result creation is dependent on God as its source and continues towards completion, a view expressed in the understanding of *creatio continua* (continuing creation) where creation is '[pulled] from the future' towards its eschatological completion and is judged 'very good'.[22]

The notion of a continuing creation does not deny the goodness of God's creative act but identifies that creation is to become something else, so that God's providence denotes God's gracious day-to-day involvement in creation, as the God who is actively concerned for the continuing life of the world which was created.[23] For Rikki Watts, the 'something else' is the reunification of heaven and earth where the renewed earth now becomes Yahweh's throne room.[24] Therefore, as Torrance suggests, God is revealed as personal and has 'graciously bound himself to the creation even in its fallen condition, and has assumed the fearful cost of its redemption, reparation and preservation upon himself'. In doing so, God ensures that the world continues over

---

21. Gunton, *The Christian Faith*, 7. Hefner, *The Human Factor*, 414. Ted Peters, *Science, Theology and Ethics* (Aldershot: Ashgate Publishing Limited, 2002), 282. Peters and Hewlett, *Evolution, from Creation to New Creation*, 161–3. Rikki E Watts, 'On the Edge of the Millennium: Making Sense of Genesis', in *Living in the Lamplight: Christianity and Contemporary Challenges to the Gospel.*, edited by H Boersma (Vancouver: Regent College Publishing, 2001), 149.

22. Peters, *Science, Theology and Ethics*, 85–6. Peters and Hewlett, *Evolution, from Creation to New Creation*, 158–61. Peters and Hewlett do not however see creation as a once-for-all event, but see it as an ongoing process where divine activity provides the world with an 'open future'. Quote is taken from *Theology and Ethics*.

23. Gunton, *The Christian Faith*, 19–21 and 37. Kathryn Tanner, 'Creation and Providence', in *The Cambridge Companion to Karl Barth*, edited by John Webster(Cambridge: Cambridge University Press, 2000), 122.

24. Rikki E Watts, 'The New Exodus/New Creational Restoration of the Image of God: A Biblical-Theological Perspective on Salvation', in *What Does It Mean to Be Saved? Broadening Evangelical Horizons of Salvation*, edited by J Stackhouse (Grand Rapids: Baker Academic, 2002), 36.

140   *From Resurrection to Return*

time, and directs the world for a loving purpose. This highlights the eschatological perspective of providence, which Gunton describes as 'conservation in eschatological perspective', where the purposes of the Creator are realised in advance by creation (including humanity) becoming that which it was made to be.[25]

3. Evolution and purpose

In contrast to the Christian understanding, the scientific-evolutionary position outlines a very different view of purpose, where the process of evolution is 'at its core, directionless and purposeless'.[26] Chance thereby is the antithesis of any notion of God's divine providence and design.[27] This view has its origins in the theories developed by Charles Darwin, in which descent by modification driven by natural selection offered a scientific explanation for the mechanistic theological understanding of the day. Therefore, as a process that maintained adaptation, natural selection gave the appearance of design.[28] To-

---

25. Gunton, *The Christian Faith*, 36. Tanner, 'Creation and Providence', 122. Torrance, *The Christian Doctrine of God*, 211–2.

26. Peters and Hewlett, *Evolution, from Creation to New Creation*, 49. Daniel Dennett calls evolution 'a mindless, purposeless process'. As quoted in Ian G Barbour, *When Science Meets Religion: Enemies, Strangers or Partners?* (San Francisco: HarperSanFrancisco, 2000), 95.

27. John F Haught, 'Does Evolution Rule Out God's Existence?', in *An Evolving Dialogue: Theological and Scientific Perspectives on Evolution*, edited by JB Miller (Harrisburg: Trinity Press International, 2001), 340. This issue has caused considerable debate over the teaching of evolution in American schools. As a result, theologians Huston Smith and Alvin Plantinga managed to persuade the National Association of Biology Teachers to remove 'unsupervised' and 'impersonal' from its official description of evolution, because it implied the non-existence of God. See Religion News Service, 'Evolution Statement Altered', *Christian Century* November 12 (1997), 1029.

28. Francisco J Ayala, 'Biological Evolution: An Introduction', in *An Evolving Dialogue: Theological and Scientific Perspectives on Evolution*, edited by James B Miller (Harrisburg: Trinity Press International, 2001), 13. Peters and Hewlett, *Evolution, from Creation to New Creation*, 42. The mechanistic theology of creation was typified by William Paley. See Alister E McGrath, *Science and*

A Purposeful Creation: Evolution, Convergence and Eschatology 141

day, neo-Darwinism (synthetic theory of evolution) combines natural selection, Mendelian genetics and molecular biology to provide a mechanism of action and an understanding of gradual change within Darwin's original theory.[29]

This view stresses the opportunistic nature of natural selection, whereby 'variations arise by chance and are selected in accordance with the demands of the environment'.[30] Chance (contingency) is needed to produce random variation through mutations, and natural selection (necessity) then selects for those variations that produce adaptations to environmental pressure. This results in the non-random selection of randomly occurring events, where natural selection acts like a filter that retains the useful chance variations. Natural selection therefore creates novelty by increasing the probability of improbable genetic events.[31]

Evolutionary understanding has been taken further in the twentieth century and given a metaphysical status based on the presuppositions of scientism, the belief that truth is only obtainable through science. Assumed within scientism is the principle of 'materialism',

---

Religion: An Introduction (Oxford: Blackwell Publishing, 1998), 99–102, Jacques Roger, 'The Mechanistic Conception of Life', in *God and Nature: Historical Essay on the Encounter between Christianity and Science*, edited by David C Lindberg and Ronald L Numbers (Berkeley: University of California Press, 1986), 283.

29. Ayala, 'Biological Evolution: An Introduction', 15–7. Also see Peters and Hewlett, *Evolution, from Creation to New Creation*, 45–6.

30. G Ledyard Stebbins and Francisco J Ayala, 'The Evolution of Darwinism', in *An Evolving Dialogue: Theological and Scientific Perspectives on Evolution*, edited by James B Miller (Harrisburg: Trinity Press International, 2001), 181.

31. Francisco J Ayala, 'Intelligent Design: The Original Version', *Theology and Science* 1/1 (2003): 19–24. Francisco J Ayala, 'Chance and Necessity: Adaption and Novelty in Evolution', in *An Evolving Dialogue: Theological and Scientific Perspectives on Evolution*, edited by James B Miller (Harrisburg: Trinity Press International, 2001), 231. Mark Ridley, 'The Mechanism of Evolution', in *An Evolving Dialogue: Theological and Scientific Perspectives on Evolution*, edited by James B Mille (Harrisburg: Trinity Press International, 2001), 58. Simon Conway Morris defines contingency as 'historical accident'. See Conway Morris, *Life's Solution*, 297.

142   *From Resurrection to Return*

where matter is the 'fundamental reality of the universe' and 'ontological reductionism', where all phenomena will eventually be explained by the actions of the material components. The result is the perceived conflict between science and theology, where 'evolutionism' denies any transcendent purpose to evolution. [32] Added to this position are the predictions of a cosmological future without hope, where the universe will end either in fire or by freezing which as Peters suggests, highlights the dissonance between theological and cosmological eschatology.[33]

However, as John Greene suggests, 'Science becomes pointless and even destructive unless it takes on significance and direction from a religious affirmation concerning meaning and value of human existence,'[34] so the question remains: Can 'purpose' be reinstated within an evolutionary framework?

3.1. Evolution, a purposeful process: Simon Conway Morris
The discussion so far has highlighted the contrast between the theological and the neo-Darwinian understandings of purpose. which are commonly viewed as conflicting positions. However, even among scientists the view that evolution is purposeless is not shared by all. Although affirming evolution as a process, biologist Simon Conway Morris suggests that evolution shows three features that enable the evolutionary process to be viewed at a deeper level. These levels of 'depth' are congruent with an understanding of creation and thereby provide an opening for an integrated theological and biological view of evolution.[35]

---

32.   Barbour, *When Science Meets Religion*, 11. Graeme Finlay, *Evolving Creation, Faith and Science Series* (Auckland: TELOS Books, 2004), 12–4. Haught, *Deeper than Darwin*, 32 and 48. Quote is taken from Barbour. For an overview of the conflict model, see Barbour pages 10–7 and 90–9.

33.   Arthur Peacocke, *Evolution, the Disguised Friend of Faith* (London: Templeton Foundation Press, 2004), 154. Peters, *Science, Theology and Ethics*, 6–7.

34.   John Greene as quoted in Conway Morris, *Life's Solution*, 325.

35.   Conway Morris, *Life's Solution*, 5 and 329. Conway Morris emphasises these features: the underlying simplicity, navigation towards the biological solutions within a vast number of possibilities, sensitivity, inherency—rearrangement and co-option, biological diversity and convergence, inevitability of sentience.

A Purposeful Creation: Evolution, Convergence and Eschatology   143

First, *evolution is constrained*, so that the physical constraints limit the possible biological outcomes.[36] Rather than relying on novelty *per se*, evolution utilises the 'tried and trusted building blocks of organic architecture' using the principle of 'inherency', where the molecules essential for existence are already in place at an earlier stage in the history of life. The result is that emergence relies on cooption and re-deployment rather than invention.[37] Even though evolutionary adaptation is ubiquitous, the constraints of life lead to the inevitable result—evolutionary convergence, where the same biological solutions are reached in order that life continues. Evolutionary convergence is defined as the 'recurrent tendency of biological organisation to arrive at the same "solution" to a particular need', of which Conway Morris provides many examples. Convergence not only confirms evolutionary adaptation in this view, but also provides the 'motor' for evolution.[38] In contrast to evolutionary orthodoxy, where every evolutionary possibility has an equal chance of being explored, convergence indicates that the number of biological possibilities is dramatically restricted. The bulk of biological 'hyperspace' therefore can never be explored, instead evolution is channelled to 'stable nodes of functionality'. The consequence of ubiquitous convergence and the constraints of life, it is suggested, 'make the emergence of the various biological properties very probable, if not inevitable'.[39]

Second, *evolution shows trends*, and in particular the trend of increasing complexity so that natural selection cannot be a 'random walk through genetic drift'. According to Conway Morris, geological time shows the emergence of more complex worlds, with one such trend being the increase in body size of terrestrial mammals, which he

---

36. Conway Morris, *Life's Solution*, 11, 12, 106 and 298. One example is the specificity of amino acids where life as we know it uses only twenty amino acids, all of the L-isomeric form. See page 40.

37. Conway Morris, *Life's Solution*, 8,166, 234–5 and 238. Co-option is defined as the redeployment of existing structures and putting them together in sometimes unique ways.

38. Conway Morris, *Life's Solution*, xii, 125 and 302–3.

39. Conway Morris, *Life's Solution*, 127–8, 145–6, 283 and 309. 'Hyperspace' refers to the seemingly unlimited number of possible combinations accessible for use in biological solutions.

144   *From Resurrection to Return*

suggests 'sounds like progress'.[40] Increasing complexity has also been noted by Pierre Teilhard de Chardin, who suggested that in proportion to physical complexity, there has been an increase in 'consciousness' giving rise to the 'law of complexity consciousness'. Here the increasing complexity of matter's organisation results in the emergence of consciousness and eventually self-awareness.[41]

Third, an understanding of convergence suggests that *evolution contains deeper patterns*, which Conway Morris identifies as 'genuine creation'. Here the paradox exists between the vast richness of life and the constraints of life, as seen in the growing list of molecules that have undergone convergent evolution.[42] The metaphor of evolutionary 'navigation' provides an informative concept for understanding convergence, where life has the propensity to navigate to rather precise solutions in response to adaptive challenges, thus allowing evolution to move across the 'multidimensional hyperspace' of biological possibility to the specific biological solutions. Evolution is therefore seeded with 'probabilities if not inevitabilities' in which the entire 'foundational economy' of the universe must be just right in order for life to develop.

Therefore as Conway Morris suggests, this is a world underpinned by deeper commonalities.[43] A parallel understanding of 'depth' can be found in the work of theologian π. In his view, the universe may be though of in-depth as a story filled with 'promise', where the promise of life and evolution were present at the 'cosmic dawn'. Haught produces a metaphysics of promise where 'a promising God who opens up the world to the future is the ultimate explanation of evolution'. Evolution therefore is both 'adaptation and anticipation', as God awaits the world in this unfinished universe, with the fundamental

---

40. Conway Morris, *Life's Solution* 21, 132 and 304–7.

41. Pierre Teilhard de Chardin as outline in Haught, *Deeper than Darwin*, 162–3.

42. Conway Morris, *Life's Solution*, 20, 290 and 295.

43. Conway Morris, *Life's Solution*, 298, 303, 308–10 and 327. 'Foundational economy' is a term borrowed from Howard Van Till. It is interesting to note that Alister McGrath is also going to be using a model based on 'a ship at sea' in his development of Christian doctrine. See Alister E McGrath, *The Science of God: An Introduction to Scientific Theology* (Grand Rapids: Eerdmans, 2004), 228–30.

A Purposeful Creation: Evolution, Convergence and Eschatology 145

meaning of the evolving universe being identified in the carrying of a promise.[44]

The unique implication from Simon Conway Morris' work is that because evolution has produced a uniquely sentient species (humanity) with a sense of purpose, we must take the claim of theology seriously—the world does have meaning.[45] This position goes against the neo-Darwinist position where the naturalistic system is devoid of ultimate purpose.[46] The position of Simon Conway Morris is also distinct from that of other theistic evolutionists in that he attempts to provide a biological basis for seeing purpose through contingency. In contrast, Ted Peters and Martinez Hewlett accept that nature is devoid of inherent purpose, but they ascribe God's divine purpose for nature. Purpose therefore is discerned eschatologically, where God's redemptive act defines what the previous creation will have meant.[47] Similarly, Philip Hefner suggests that it is 'certainly not possible to assert a teleology for nature, except as an item of faith'. Here the eschatological perspective suggests that God's purposes include creation acknowledging its creator and freely fulfilling the Creator's will.[48] Peters, Martinez and Hefner emphasise teleonomy not teleology by placing evolutionary history within the context of God's creative and redeeming work, therefore no purpose can be discerned within the bounds of scientific methodology.[49] This position is refuted in the work of Simon Conway Morris, where the principles of inherency, convergence and directionality show that there is a sense of meaning and purpose to the evolutionary process that can be extrapolated from its origins. Another feature of Peters and Hewlett is their belief that all possible

---

44. Haught, *Deeper than Darwin*, 53, 63, 128, 142–4. Here John Haught draws on Moltmann who suggests that waiting is the highest form of interest in the other.

45. Conway Morris, *Life's Solution*, 328.

46. Peters and Hewlett, *Evolution, from Creation to New Creation*, 26 and 48–9.

47. Peters and Hewlett, *Evolution, from Creation to New Creation*, 159–60.

48. Hefner, *The Human Factor*, 39 and 43–4. Hefner uses 'teleology' as referring to 'preprogrammed goals that can be extrapolated from the original programming'. 'The term "eschatological" affirms that God is able to provide new possibilities and new futures without destroying the life giving continuities with our origins'. See page 47.

49. Peters and Hewlett, *Evolution, from Creation to New Creation*, 163 and 167.

146   *From Resurrection to Return*

paths must be available for creation. However, as Conway Morris suggests, 'Not only is the universe strangely fit to purpose, but so too… is life's ability to navigate to its solutions.' All the possible biological paths are not open to be explored, in fact the constraints of life lead to the probable if not the inevitable emergence of various biological properties.[50] So can we identify God's purposes within the biological matrix? I believe we can through a theology of purpose where the eternal intentions of God are brought to actuality within the biological process. Therefore we can move away from teleonomy as 'perceived purposefulness' in the evolutionary process, to teleology as biologically expressed purpose in creation, in which science accepts different levels of nonreductionist evolutionary understanding. This would provide a true sense of an 'evolving creation'[51], where theology and biology co-exist and mutually enhance each other.

4. A theology of purpose

At the start of this essay, the importance of theology's ability to integrate aspects of scientific understanding was highlighted in order for theology to be relevant in our society today. The concept of purpose is one area where theology and science differ, especially in relation to an understanding of evolution. As the previous section suggests, there are deeper levels within the understanding of evolution into which theology can speak. I suggest that one of these 'deeper levels' relates to the notion of purpose.

In seeking to articulate a theology of purpose within the created order, I recognise that I am speaking of 'natural theology'—the framework by which the natural order, including humanity, can be interpreted as God's creation. Karl Barth in particular objected to the notion of natural theology, however as Alister McGrath notes, Barth's objection must be viewed in the context of his objection to Enlightenment theology, and in particular the view of natural theology as asserting human autonomy and undermining the necessity and uniqueness of God's

---

50. Peters and Hewlett, *Evolution, from Creation to New Creation*, 167. Conway Morris, *Life's Solution*, 283 and 327.

51. Howard J Van Till, 'Basil, Augustine, and the Doctrine of Creation's Functional Integrity', *Science and Christian Belief*, 8/1 (1996): 34–6.

A Purposeful Creation: Evolution, Convergence and Eschatology 147

self-revelation. Natural theology was, in Barth's view, functioning as an autonomous discipline through which access to knowledge of God could be gained. According to McGrath, TF Torrance suggested Barth did sanction natural theology as a subordinate aspect of revealed theology. Furthermore, Torrance outlined a methodology for natural theology within a Trinitarian context, linked with both revelation and salvation through Christ.[52] My suggestion is that the doctrine of election provides such a framework through which God's purposes in creation can be understood. In particular, the reading of purpose into evolution as suggested by convergence provides a biological process that I believe is compatible with the biological outworkings of God's eternal purposes in creation, as previously determined by God's eternal election.

4.1. Election and God

The unifying concept of Karl Barth's theology is based on God's salvific action.[53] Within God's saving action, the doctrine of election provides a 'hermeneutical rule' that allows talk about 'what God was doing and who and what God was/is—"before the foundation of the world" '.[54] For this reason I believe the doctrine of election can be a tool in developing an integrated theology of purpose. For Barth, the primary statement about God is that God is 'the electing God', where election is understood as what God does in, with and to Godself, in order that God's grace can be shown to what God is not.[55] It is God's 'primal decision' of 'self-ordination' where God is eternally complete

---

52. McGrath, *Nature*, 136–7, 268–72, 279–83, 285 and 294–5.

53. Colin E Gunton, 'Salvation', in *The Cambridge Companion to Karl Bart* , edited by John Webster (Cambridge: Cambridge University Press, 2000), 143.

54. Bruce McCormack, 'Grace and Being: The Role of God's Gracious Election in Karl Barth's Theological Ontology', in *The Cambridge Companion to Karl Barth*, edited by John Webster (Cambridge: Cambridge University Press, 2000), 92.

55. Colin E Gunton, 'Karl Barth's Doctrine of Election as Part of His Doctrine of God', *Journal of Theological Studies*, 25/October (1974): 383–4 and 390. Karl Barth, *The Doctrine of God*, edited by GW Bromiley and TF Torrance, volume II/2, *Church Dogmatics* (Edinburgh: T&T Clark, 1957), 76. In this definition God is the gracious God, the 'One who is God in the beginning'. See page 93.

148   *From Resurrection to Return*

within the triune life and in an act of divine freedom determines to be the 'covenant-God' in an act of loving grace to humanity.[56] Within this Trinitarian view, Jesus Christ is understood as the electing God and the elected human, both the subject and the object of election. As the subject of election, God's very being is defined by what Godself is revealed to be in Jesus Christ.

As the object of election, God's covenantal relation was established in God's eternal act of self-determination, as a relation with the man Jesus and with others and the world 'in him'.[57] Therefore humanity is chosen as the covenant partner in whom the Son should be one person with the man Jesus, humanity's representative and the reality of our human response to God as the image of real humanity in free obedience to God. The role of the Holy Spirit in this framework is located in God's freedom to love as the bond of fellowship between the Father and the Son and active in the transformation of the world to unite creation with God.[58] It is therefore through Christ and in the power of the Holy Spirit that humanity can participate in the life of God, and salvation becomes the completion of the purpose of election that originates in the eternal being of God.[59]

4.2. Election, creation and purpose

For Barth, all the other actions of God—Creator, Reconciler and Redeemer, are 'grounded and determined in the fact that God is the God of the eternal election of his grace'.[60] Election forms 'the presupposi-

---

56. Barth, *The Doctrine of God*, 11, 89 and 168. Alan Torrance, 'The Trinity', in *The Cambridge Companion to Karl Barth*, edited by John Webster (Cambridge: Cambridge University Press, 2000), 86–8.

57. Barth, *The Doctrine of God*, 3 and 26. Paul S Fiddes, 'The Atonement and the Trinity', in *The Forgotten Trinity: A Selection of Papers Presented on the BCC Study Commission on the Trinitarian Doctrine Today*, edited by AIC Heron (London: Council of Churches for Britain and Ireland and the British Council of Churches, 1991), 110. McCormack, 'Grace and Being', 97 and 105. Barth's view is based on John 3:16 as the active demonstration of God's will for fellowship.

58. Fiddes, 'The Atonement and the Trinity', 110–11.

59. Colin E Gunton, 'Salvation', 145.

60. Barth, *The Doctrine of God*, 14. Gunton, 'Karl Barth's Doctrine of Election', 384.

A Purposeful Creation: Evolution, Convergence and Eschatology 149

tion of all God's works'[61] so that the covenantal relationship is the 'internal basis of creation', and creation is the 'external basis of the covenant' as the arena for God's saving action,[62] the stage for salvation history,[63] and the 'road or means' to grace.[64] Christ therefore is the origin, centre, meaning and goal of creation and history, enabling humanity and the whole of creation to 'participate in the being of God'.[65]

Because election has priority over all of God's acts, the doctrine of election can be used to form the basis of a theology of purpose by placing God's decision for humanity and Jesus as its elected representative, prior to God's action as creator. As Gunton suggests, Barth's doctrine of election identifies that:

> The God who creates, reconciles, and redeems . . . is first and foremost the one who elects: that is, who loves and chooses the other to be his own, before the other knows it, before he shares in it, indeed, when he resists it, before, even, he is created.[66]

Therefore I suggest that God's election of humanity from eternity, an eternal event prior to creation, implies that God's creative act has the purpose to produce the creature that can respond to God in covenantal fellowship—the creature whom God has elected.[67] For elec-

---

61. Gunton, 'Karl Barth's Doctrine of Election', 384.

62. Wolf Krötke, 'The Humanity of the Human Person in Karl Barth's Anthropology', in *The Cambridge Companion to Karl Barth*, edited by John Webster (Cambridge: Cambridge University Press, 2000), 167. Gunton identifies the universe as 'the arena on which [God's] gracious purposes may come to pass'. See Gunton, 'Karl Barth's Doctrine of Election', 384.

63. John C McDowell, 'Learning Where to Place One's Hope: The Eschatological Significance of Election in Barth', *Scottish Journal of Theology*, 53/3 (2000): 323.

64. Tanner, 'Creation and Providence', 118.

65. Tanner, 'Creation and Providence', 114 and 125. McDowell, 'Learning Where to Place One's Hope', 323. Quote is taken from Tanner.

66. Gunton, 'Karl Barth's Doctrine of Election', 391.

67. As Barth suggests, 'the purpose and meaning of the eternal divine election of

150   *From Resurrection to Return*

tion to play out on the stage of creation would necessitate a creative biological process that would show signs of purpose resulting in a being like humanity. It is this biologically purposeful process of 'convergence' as described by Simon Conway Morris that I suggest is compatible with a theological view of God's eternal purposes in election, the arrival of the 'inevitable human'—God's covenant partner. Furthermore, as Conway Morris has suggested, evolutionary constraints and the ubiquity of convergence point to aspects of evolution that fit within a creation theology.[68] Therefore we can glimpse the teleological aspects of evolution in biology, and so evolution can be placed within the framework of a purposeful creation. Also because election supposes a covenantal relationship, I would suggest that God's creative act also presupposes the gifting of a future for creation, thereby providing hope for creation's continued relationship with God.[69] As a result, humanity and the whole of creation is drawn through God's purpose towards its eschatological fulfilment, the point at which creation's full value will be realised.[70]

4.3. Justification for a theology of purpose
This essay proposes a theology of purpose within the scope of natural theology, and so it is first important to identify the connections to the 'foundational insights of the Christian tradition'.[71] In countering Barth's objection to autonomous natural theology, the doctrine of election in my opinion provides a means to a legitimate natural theology in which nature is viewed as God's creation and humanity as the *imago*

---

grace consists in the fact that the one who is elected from all eternity can and does elect God in return'. See Barth, *The Doctrine of God*, 178.

68.   Conway Morris, *Life's Solution*, 5 and 329.

69.   Peters, *Science, Theology and Ethics*, 85–6. Peacocke, *Evolution, the Disguised Friend of Faith*, 156.

70.   In a similar manner, Celia Deane-Drummond has recently linked natural wisdom, natural law, convergence and purpose, while emphasising the connection between natural wisdom and God's Wisdom, and between natural law and Eternal Law. This view is compatible with my use of the doctrine of election. See Celia Deane-Drummond, *Wonder and Wisdom: Conversations in Science, Spirituality, and Theology* (Philadelphia: Templeton Foundation Press, 2006), 66–74.

71.   McGrath, *Nature*, 295.

A Purposeful Creation: Evolution, Convergence and Eschatology 151

Dei. Election also grounds creation's ability to disclose God, by reflecting the rationality of God as a consequence of God's eternal decision for election.[72] Finally, the doctrine of election places natural theology within a Trinitarian framework where election is the primal decision of the Trinitarian God, and humanity can participate in the life of God through Christ in the power of the Holy Spirit, and live in the hope of the life to come.

One possible objection to using a theology of purpose that places humanity in a position of primacy is the perception of diminishing the importance of creation as a whole. Colin Gunton however identifies humanity as the primary object of God's providential care and suggests this does not downgrade nature, but rather affirms that nature was created to be perfected 'with and partly through human agency'.[73] Although some may feel uncomfortable with giving humanity a pre-eminent position in creation, Conway Morris reminds us that humanity is unique. One aspect of this uniqueness is the human's disproportionately large brain, which is seven times the size it should be given our body size.[74] I suggest this fact could relate to the human ability of grasping the orderly nature of the created universe, a feature of the natural world which theologically is understood to result from God's character (rationality) in the act of creation and is explored and described by the natural sciences. As a result, McGrath suggests that the divine rationality is 'embedded in creation and embodied in Christ', and it is this rationality that humanity as the *imago Dei* can perceive.[75] This rationality I suggest underpins the concept of 'convergence' and the arrival of the inevitable human. Therefore, within my view, the being whom God created for relationship can perceive God's ordering of nature, and in doing so turn toward the Creator in praise.[76]

---

72. McGrath, *Nature*, 295–98. Creation and the *imago Dei* are important criteria in the scheme of TF Torrance.

73. Gunton, *The Christian Faith*, 36.

74. Conway Morris, *Life's Solution*, 310 and 246–47. See Figure 9.3.

75. McGrath, *Nature*, 188, 196–97 and 220–33. As McGrath suggests, this could have been another way.

76. McGrath outlines the laws of nature proposed by Paul Davies: Universal, Absolute, Eternal, Omnipotent. See McGrath, *Nature*, 227–28. Given this

152 *From Resurrection to Return*

Another aspect of humanity's uniqueness can be seen in the paradox whereby 'humans have an overwhelming sense of purpose', yet have arisen from a seemingly meaningless process. The arrival of sentience in humans, therefore, is part of the imprinted evolutionary process of terrestrial creation.[77] Humans represent one unique node of biological inevitability and are as such embedded in the natural world, through 'one continuous unfolding'.[78] This fact is made clearer through genetic analysis, which has clearly shown that human beings are an evolved species based on genetic similarities between *Homo sapiens* and other primates, especially the great apes.[79] Even Darwin himself felt unease at the conclusion from his work that humanity was not the goal or apex of evolution, and our uniqueness is also not lost on some neo-Darwinists who admit that of all organisms, 'we alone are able to resist our genes'.[80] Of particular importance however, is the fact that *Homo sapiens* is the only surviving species of the hominid diversification,[81] which I suggest provides a sense of true election. Of all the possibilities only *Homo sapiens* remains, and only in the form of *Homo sapiens* did God make himself fully known in the person of Jesus Christ. Humanity is unique, the truly elect, not in a negative sense (supremacy), but in a humbling way, that as the last surviving hominids, God has chosen us and revealed Godself to us in an act of unlimited grace.[82] Therefore the Christian faith provides an interpre-

---

discussion I would also add 'Inevitable'.

77. Conway Morris, *Life's Solution*, 2, 131, 303 and 327.

78. Conway Morris, *Life's Solution*, 310 and 312. Haught, *Deeper than Darwin*, 155. Quote is taken from Haught.

79. Graeme Finlay, *Gods Books: Genetics and Genesis* (*Science and Faith Series*) (Auckland: TELOS Books, 2004), 13–28. Graeme Finlay, '*Homo Divinus*: The Ape That Bears God's Image', *Science and Christian Belief* 15 (2003): 18–32. Ian Tattersall, 'Human Evolution: An Overview', in *An Evolving Dialogue: Theological and Scientific Perspectives on Evolution*, edited by JB Miller (Harrisburg: Trinity Press International, 2001), 206–09.

80. Alister E McGrath, *Dawkins' God: Genes, Memes, and the Meaning of Life* (Oxford: Blackwell Publishing, 2004), 45–6. The neo-Darwinist position is represented by Richard Dawkins.

81. Conway Morris, *Life's Solution*, 270.

82. The question of the relationship between God and the other hominid species

A Purposeful Creation: Evolution, Convergence and Eschatology 153

tative framework for an evolutionary understanding, by insisting that the evolutionary process and the emergence of human beings within that process is the work of God. Within this framework, God is the one who specifies the purpose of humanity's emergence and that of the whole of creation.[83]

Finally, the distinguishing characteristic of this approach is the utilisation of a 'from above' view, which contrasts to the 'from below' interpretation that I consider other theistic evolutionists to adopt.[84] Philip Hefner places great emphasis on the natural processes through which God has created, and through which grace and redemption occur. Hefner's 'teleonomic axiom' places the conception of meaning and purpose in terms of their placement within, and contribution to natural processes. The notion of purpose is therefore directed to the natural realm where God's will for humanity resides within God's will for the entire natural order.[85] My proposal places God's purposes primarily in the notion of relationship, whereby the purpose for humans is to be able to relate freely to God the Creator. Hence, the being which God elected in eternity, is the being which God's creative process (evolution) created, and who shares in the creative process.[86]

5. The praxis of purpose

The understanding of *creatio continua* emphasises that salvation encompasses all of creation and so, as Colin Gunton suggests, 'If God's

---

remains unanswered.

83. Hefner, *The Human Factor*, 38.

84. My view would also be distinct from that proposed by 'intelligent design' because I affirm evolution as a biological process. For a brief summary of 'intelligent design' see Peters and Hewlett, *Evolution, from Creation to New Creation*, 97–114.

85. Hefner, *The Human Factor*, 40, 57, 60, 62, 237 and 268–69. The 'teleonomic axiom' states that 'integral to *Homo sapiens* and its evolutionary history are certain structures and processes, the requirements for whose functioning may be said to constitute, at least in a tentative way, goals and purpose for human life'

86. I do not however what to suggest that the doctrine of election is inconsistent with human freedom, and would imply predetermination (determinism). A discussion of predetermination is outside the bounds of this current study.

154   *From Resurrection to Return*

purpose is for the redemption and perfection of the creation, all human action will in some way or other involve the human response to God that is ethics.'[87] A theology of purpose would therefore entail ethical praxis that views creation as 'a project in which we are invited to share', and looks forward to the fulfilment of God's purposes in the future. [88] I propose that the praxis of purpose can be envisaged as an *ethic of care* to answer the ethical question: 'Can we in the present generation envision wholesome possibilities, make the right decisions and take the actions that will enhance human health and global wellbeing?'[89] Central to such an ethic is the principle of *interconnection/integrity*, which recognises 'how wonderfully varied our world is, but how underpinned it is by deeper commonalities'[90] and therefore links care for creation and care for humanity. For humanity, these deep commonalities identify us scientifically as a single species, the sole survivors of the hominid diversification, and theologically as beings made in the image of God. Therefore we should care for each other as the bearers of this image.

Both the scientific and theological perspectives identify humanity as relational/communal and not a society of individuals, so that an ethic of care implies a community ethic rather than an individual ethic, which also relates to the future generations to which we have a moral responsibility.[91]

The principle of interconnection/integrity also recognises the commonalities between humanity and the natural world, with both originating in God's creative action. We as humans are a product of an evolutionary process and as such are intimately connected to the whole of the created order as we 'share the terrestrial creation'.[92] Furthermore, as the *imago Dei*, humanity has a representative function to look after creation on God's behalf.[93] This 'caring' function is emphasised in

---

87.   Gunton, 'The Doctrine of Creation', 144. Peters, *Science, Theology and Ethics,* 282.

88.   Gunton, 'The Doctrine of Creation', 155.

89.   Peters and Hewlett, *Evolution, from Creation to New Creation*, 174.

90.   Conway Morris, *Life's Solution*, 303.

91.   Peters and Hewlett, *Evolution, from Creation to New Creation*, 179.

92.   Conway Morris, *Life's Solution*, 303.

93.   David J Bryant, '*Imago Dei*, Imagination, and Ecological Responsibility',

A Purposeful Creation: Evolution, Convergence and Eschatology   155

the metaphor of 'creation-as-temple-place', which pictures creation as God's throne room for which humanity is responsible. Eschatologically, humanity's role then is to work with God in the restoration of humanity and creation, because our ultimate reckoning is with God for the use or abuse of creation, which ultimately belongs to God.[94] Therefore ultimately to not care for creation is to not care for ourselves, so that 'as long as the universe is unfinished, so also is each of us . . . Our personal redemption awaits the salvation of the whole.'[95] As a result, humanity as the created cocreator participates in a much larger creative process directed by God, 'acting in freedom, to birth the future that is most wholesome for the nature that has birthed us', to enhancing both human and global wellbeing.[96]

Finally, the Christian life is about a relationship with God, with creation and with each other. It is a life transformed by Christ to be lived in the power of the Holy Spirit so that we live in the reality of God's kingdom through love, justice and compassion. Within an ethic of care, the hermeneutic of 'sacrifice' provides a Christological foundation for the care of creation as a whole.

Furthermore, as Michael Northcott suggests, Christ's understanding of 'neighbour' in the double love command can be extended to include the whole of creation, because Christ's redemptive work included the whole of creation.[97] Humanity as the *imago Dei* can therefore act in a sacramental way, as a means of God's grace to each other

---

Theology Today 51/1 (2000), 36. Traditionally the word 'stewardship' has been used to describe humanity's role. See Ian G Barbour, *Nature, Human Nature, and God* (Minneapolis: Fortress Press, 2002), 124.

94.   Watts, 'The New Exodus', 19–22, 35–6 and 41.

95.   Haught, *Deeper than Darwin*, 155.

96.   Hefner, *The Human Factor,* 27. Peters and Hewlett, *Evolution, from Creation to New Creation*, 174. Quotes are taken from Hefner.

97.   Hefner, *The Human Factor,* 244–8. Michael S Northcott, 'Ecology and Christian Ethics', in *The Cambridge Companion to Christian Ethics*, edited by Robin Gill, 209–27 (Cambridge: Cambridge University Press, 2001), 224–5. Hefner uses 'sacrifice' as a model because it is the most widely used hermeneutical category in the New Testament for the life, death and resurrection of Jesus Christ. For the double love command, see Matthew 22:35–40, Mark 12:28–34 and Luke 10:25–8.

156   *From Resurrection to Return*

and to the whole of creation, 'in light of our vision of the coming new creation'.[98]

6. Conclusion

Within Christian theology, 'natural theology' provides an arena for dialogue between theology and science, especially since 'the question of how the natural order is to be interpreted is of critical importance'.[99] This essay is an attempt to develop an integrated concept of purpose, utilising the theological understanding of 'nature-as-creation'[100] in partnership with the biological understanding of convergence as outlined by Simon Conway Morris. The approach taken contrasts with the competing, and sometimes conflicting concepts of purposefulness (theology / creation), and purposelessness (science / evolution). Even within theology itself, the tendency has been to interpret any notion of purpose as a religious inference. I would suggest, however, that the recent work of Conway Morris has indicated that purpose can be identified within the biological process of evolution through 'convergence'. In support of this scientific position, I propose that we can understand the biological expression of purpose theologically through the doctrine of election. Since God's election is prior to God's creative act, evolution can be understood as purposeful biologically—to create the inevitable being made in the image of God that God has elected for a covenantal relationship. This theological understanding of purpose also entails an ethic of care so that the inevitable human can live out the life it was created to live, for the benefit of the whole of creation as creation is drawn towards its eschatological completion.

---

98.   Gunton, *The Christian Faith*, 41. Peters and Hewlett, *Evolution, from Creation to New Creation*, 176. Quote is taken from Peters and Hewlett.

99.   McGrath, *Nature*, 303.

100. McGrath, *Nature*, 297.

Resurrection and Cosmic Eschatology

Neil Ormerod

For most of its 2000-year history Christian eschatology has been unable to distinguish between the end of human history and the end of cosmic history. One implied the other. The discoveries of the size and age of the universe mean that we can no longer make such an identification. The universe will continue to unfold long after human history ends. What sense then are we to make of traditional assertions concerning final judgment and resurrection 'at the end of time'? Does a universe devoid of human life have theological significance? Or does resurrection imply on ongoing relationship to the material universe? Just as science has forced theology to radically review our understanding of protology so too it is now forcing us to review our understanding of eschatology. This paper will review some alternative proposals in relation to these issues.

Published at the beginning of the twentieth century, the *Catholic Encyclopaedia* stated the following in relation to hell:

> But the damned are utterly estranged from God; hence their abode is said to be as remote as possible from his dwelling, far from heaven above and its light, and consequently hidden away in the dark abysses of the earth. However, no cogent reason has been advanced for accepting a metaphorical interpretation in preference to the most natural meaning of the words of Scripture. Hence theologians generally accept the opinion that hell is really within the earth.

Reading this text now, close to 100 years later, we might be struck both by the literalism of the reading of scripture and by the naïve cosmology that seems to underlie that reading. What is perhaps more worrying is a student who presented this to me in an essay, taking it as evidence of current theological thinking.

158   *From Resurrection to Return*

Of course it is easy to be glib in light of our current knowledge. We should not forget that we have really only had a good idea of the size and age of the universe for about eighty years, with the discovery of the expansion of the universe by Edwin Hubble. In 1924 Hubble was indeed the first to prove the existence of galaxies beyond our own. We now know that there are around 100 billion galaxies in a universe whose age is around fifteen billion years. In cultural terms these are very recent discoveries, certainly more recent than the proposals for biological evolution put forward by Charles Darwin and others.

We are all well aware of the impact that Darwin's theory of evolution has had, and remarkably continues to have on Christian belief.[1] Most of us have learnt to go with the flow, and accept that questions of biological origins need to be settled on the basis of science, not a literal reading of Genesis. We don't want to make the same mistake that the Catholic Church made in relation to Galileo, of trying to settle scientific issues by theological means. However, there are still the faithful remnant who want to intrude faith into science, either in the form of 'creation science' or its more recent version, 'intelligent design'. It is fair to say that for most of us, modern science has caused us to review our understanding of protology, to read Genesis in a way which does not seek to instil scientific facts, but religious truths about God, humankind and the rest of creation.

However, it is not yet clear that modern discoveries in cosmology have yet had a similar impact on our understanding of eschatology, particularly at the level of popular belief. This is most evident in the popularity in the USA of belief in the so-called 'rapture'.[2] Certainly

---

1. On the positive side of that impact we might think of the writings of Teilhard de Chardin, Karl Rahner and more recently of Denis Edwards, who have brought Christology into an more evolutionary perspective. See for example Denis Edwards, *Jesus and the Cosmos* (Homebush: St Paul's Publications, 1991).

2. 'The belief in rapture—the certainty that the end-time is near—has become widespread in the United States. Consider the current rage on the Christian right, the 'Left Behind' series. The upcoming book in the series is titled *Armageddon*. The publisher's blurb reads, 'No one will escape Armageddon and few will live through the battle to see the Glorious Appearing.' These publications are targeting children. The Left Behind industry has a 'Kids Series'. A blurb from the publisher: 'With over ten million copies sold, Left Behind: The Kids Series is a

Resurrection and Cosmic Eschatology   159

most of our eschatological beliefs have been formed in an era that knew very little about the cosmos, its age and size. They reflect the type of three-level cosmology we find in the *Catholic Encyclopaedia*. In this paper I want to focus on one issue that arises from eschatology that needs revision in light of modern cosmology. The issue concerns Christian belief in the resurrection of the dead and our final judgment.

1. End of history—end of cosmos

In popular Christian imagination the phrase 'end of the world' evokes a number of distinct biblical themes—the final judgment of all humanity (Matthew 25), the 'coming' of the Son of Man, the risen Jesus as judge, the end of the world as we know it and the emergence of a 'new heaven and a new earth', whose relationship to the old heaven and earth remains somewhat vague. Of course, those with a more apocalyptic imagination may fill in this account with a variety of other events, based on increasingly literal readings of the Bible. The issue that concerns us is what we mean by 'end of the world' in such scenarios. Are we talking about the end of our planet, or human history in some time in the future? Or are we talking about a more cosmic conclusion to creation itself, something which encompasses the whole cosmos? And if we in fact make such a distinction when do we locate the final judgment and resurrection of the dead?

Let us begin with an overview of the biblical material. It is often noted that biblical thinking is more historically oriented than cosmologically oriented. It rejects the more cyclic view of the world (often a feature of more cosmologically oriented cultures[3]), which it tends

---

favorite for all ages. Following a group of teens that were "left behind", and are determined to stand up for God no matter what the costs, they are tested at every turn.' At the Left Behind website (http://www.leftbehind.com/), they have a video promotion for *Armageddon* replete with footage of American troops in Kuwait." From http://www.publiceye.org/apocalyptic/bush-2003/austin-providence.html, accessed 09.02.06.

3.   I use the term 'cosmological culture' drawing on the work of Robert Doran who speaks of such cultures in following terms: 'Cosmological symbolisations of the experience of life as a movement with a direction that can be found or

160 *From Resurrection to Return*

to identify with paganism, to embrace a more linear view, one with a beginning, a middle and an end. The beginning is evident in the material of Genesis 1–11, which moves from paradisal origins to a period of increasing violence and despair over human activities. The middle is the history of God's chosen people beginning with the story of Abraham (Genesis 12), chosen as God's instrument to turn around human history, moving through the gift of the Torah, the prophetic critique of Israel's failures, and a messianic longing for God to fulfil the divine promises and bring the redemptive process initiated in Abraham to its completion. From a Christian perspective this history is proleptically completed in the ministry, death and resurrection of Jesus and continued in the history of the church (particularly in Acts). Increasingly this history is viewed biblically in conflictual apocalyptic terms, a conflict between powerful forces of evil (in Christian literature captured in the symbol of the anti-Christ, 1 John 2:18, 22, 4:3) and God's faithful remnant who suffer persecution at the hands of these evil forces. In the apocalyptic imagination this conflict takes on a cosmic dimension, a conflict between the angels and demons battling over the fate of the entire creation (Daniel, Book of Revelation). History is not just 'secular history' but ultimately has theological significance. In the end victory is gained, not through human achievement, which proves inadequate to the task, but through divine intervention, which snatches victory or at least vindication from the jaws of defeat. God's enemies are punished in the fires of hell, while the righteous enjoy the rewards of new life. History as we know it is brought to an end with the coming of the Son of Man as judge of all humanity. God's kingdom will come, peace and justice will reign, every tear will be wiped away, every sadness removed. Not only has human history come to an end, but the whole cosmos is implicated, leading to a 'new heaven and a new earth', a new Jerusalem where God *is* the temple in which we worship (Revelation 21:22).

---

missed find the paradigm of order in the cosmic rhythms . . . Cosmological constitutive meaning has its roots in the affective biologically based sympathy of the organism with the rhythms and process of non-human nature.' Robert M Doran, 'The Analogy of Dialectic and the Systematics of History', in *Religion in Context*, edited by T Fallon and P Riley (Lanham: University Press of America, 1988), 54–5.

Resurrection and Cosmic Eschatology

With the warnings of NT Wright ringing in our ears, we should be slow to read these apocalyptic statements as literal accounts of future events.

They are primarily statements seeking to provide a theological significance to historical events and processes.[4] Nonetheless the New Testament does seem to imply a sense of a final judgment of humanity, linked to resurrection of the dead, and that these events take on a cosmic significance, just as the resurrection of Jesus himself has cosmic significance (Ephesians 1:10, Philippians 2:10, Colossians 1:19–20). Certainly, within the history of Christian thought the linkages between these events and their cosmic significance is firmly established, finding expression in the Middle Ages in the theology of Thomas Aquinas. When Aquinas speaks of the final judgment coming at the 'end of the world', the cosmic significance is to the fore:

> As Augustine states (De Trin. iii, 4) 'Divine providence decreed that the grosser and lower bodies should be ruled in a certain order by the more subtle and powerful bodies': wherefore the entire matter of the lower bodies is subject to variation according to the movement of the heavenly bodies. Hence it would be contrary to the order established in things by Divine providence if the matter of lower bodies were brought to the state of incorruption, so long as there remains movement in the higher bodies. And since, according to the teaching of faith, the resurrection will bring men to immortal life conformably to Christ Who 'rising again from the dead dieth now no more' (Romans 6:9), the resurrection of human bodies will be delayed until the end of the world when the heavenly movement will cease.[5]

---

4. 'Apocalyptic language was . . . an elaborate metaphor system for investing historical events with theological significance.' NT Wright, *Jesus and the Victory of God*, volume 2, *Christian Origins and the Question of God* (Minneapolis: Fortress Press, 1996), 96.

5. St Thomas Aquinas, *Summa Theologiae Supplement*, Question 77, Article 1.

162   *From Resurrection to Return*

The notion of the cessation of the heavenly movement indicates an end to cosmic process, within the limits of the cosmological vision of the day. For Aquinas this initiates the resurrection and the final judgment of humanity, by the risen Christ.

It was relatively easy to maintain this linkage between the end of human history and the end of cosmos while ever our cosmos remained relatively small. The biblical world consisted of the earth, the waters above and below, and lights in the sky to mark the seasons and time of day. The Ptolemaic universe, in which Aquinas operated, was a bit bigger, placing the earth at the centre with the sun, the moon and a few planets circling around within the heavenly spheres. Copernicus may have placed the sun at the centre, but still the cosmos remained a small affair. Newton's universe was marginally bigger, as people discovered more planets within our solar system and realised that the stars were much further away than previously recognised. Growing observation displaced the sun from the centre to take its place in the outer reaches of the galaxy we call the Milky Way. All this time, it remained at least partially plausible that the end of human history might be linked in some way with the end of the cosmos. However, at the turn of the twentieth century, science began to reveal just how big, and how old, the universe really is. According to present calculations, our galaxy, with its 100 billion stars, is just one of another 100 billion galaxies. The size of the universe is staggering, in comparison with the very limited imaginations of the early biblical writers. It becomes increasingly unlikely that the end of human history would be of any consequence to the rest of the cosmos, which would continue on its merry path with barely a hiccup to note our passing.

On the other hand, the problem of even speaking about the temporal end of the cosmos is made more difficult if we attempt to absorb the insights of Einstein's theory of relativity. Einstein's theory of special relativity argues that certain features of space and time are relative to observers. Distance and time shift as observers move relative to one another. The truth of Einstein's theory has been verified to remarkable accuracy in experiments with subatomic particles whose rate of decay varies precisely as predicted with their motion relative to laboratory observer. One of the many consequences of Einstein's theory is that the simultaneity of spatially removed events is also relative to observers. Two observers moving relative to one another will not be

Resurrection and Cosmic Eschatology 163

able to agree that spatially removed events are simultaneous with one another. There is no universal measure of time on which all observers will agree.

This observation is important when we ask questions about the relationship between the end of the cosmos and the end of history. The end of human history, when it does come either through our own stupidity (ecological disaster) or violence (nuclear weapons), or through cosmic events (asteroids impacting, or the sun going supernova), will be a relatively distinct temporal event. The end of the cosmos, on the other hand, cannot be a distinct temporal event in the same way. The universe cannot 'blink out of existence' because this would imply a common, non-relative measure of simultaneity, in violation of special relativity. The effect of any temporal event can only spread out at the speed of light. It would seem then that the notion that the end of human history would be identical to the end of the cosmos is simply incoherent. Indeed there are two major cosmic scenarios relating to the future fate of the cosmos. The universe could continue expanding 'forever' with matter eventually decaying into energy in some unimaginable time in the future. If so the universe would never strictly speaking 'end'. Or the universe could collapse back into itself into a 'Big Crunch'. In this case the universe could come to an end at a specific time, but only because it had shrunk into a single point. Given that the universe is still expanding, and has been doing so for 14 billion years, any Big Crunch must be at least as far ahead in the future, at the least according to various estimates some 24 billion years away.[6]

It is fair to say that our Christian imaginations have simply not caught up with these scientific perspectives. Joseph Ratzinger, in his work, *Eschatology*, appears quite dismissive of ' "physicist" conceptual games'[7], and speaks of the individual's salvation as being 'whole and entire' (presumably this implies general resurrection) only 'when the salvation of the cosmos and all the elect has come to fruition'[8] thus eliding the distinction between the end of history and the completion

---

6. http://www.answers.com/topic/big-crunch, accessed 26 February 2006.

7. Joseph Ratzinger, *Eschatology, Death and Eternal Life*, edited by Aidan Nichols, translated by Michael Waldstein (Washington: Catholic University of America Press, 1988), 192.

8. Ratzinger, *Eschatology*, 238.

164   *From Resurrection to Return*

of the cosmos. The Catholic International Theological Commission even warns against the notion of a 'certain kind of "eschaton" [which] is brought within historical time', fearful that it will produce a type of 'temporal messianism'.[9] One theologian who clearly distinguishes between the two is Wolfhart Pannenberg. He notes that 'the cosmic eschatology of the Bible that expects an imminent end of the world ... is not congruent with scientific extrapolations regarding a possible end to the universe that look to a remote future. We cannot readily argue, then, that they relate to the same event'.[10] However most of us, theologians included, still live imaginatively in a three-dimensional Newtonian universe of almost Ptolemaic dimensions rather than the four-dimensional space-time universe uncovered by Einstein.[11] In general the differences this might make to our theology are minimal, however there is one question that does need exploration—whenever we distinguish between the end of human history and the end of cosmos, it may make a big difference in how we think of the timing of the resurrection of the dead. When we speak of resurrection at the end of the world, what exactly is our reference point? Finally we have to realise how completely new this question is. It can only seriously arise in the modern era when we are capable of distinguishing between the end of human history and the end of the cosmos.

2. The timing of the resurrection

Given this distinction between the end of human history and the end of the cosmos, when then do we locate the resurrection of the dead?

---

9. International Theological Commission, 'Some Current Questions in Eschatology', *Irish Theological Quarterly*, 58 (1992), 211. Given the previously noted influence in the USA of belief in the 'rapture' such a concern is not groundless.

10. Wolfhart Pannenberg, *Systematic Theology*, translated by Geoffrey W Bromiley, volume 3 (Grand Rapids: Eerdmans, 1991), 589.

11. Of course more recent theories of the physical universe speak of ten or eleven dimensional space-time configurations, for example the attempts at theories to unify electromagnetic, weak and strong nuclear forces and gravity as found in string theory. See B Greene, *The Elegant Universe: Superstrings, Hidden Dimensions, and the Quest for the Ultimate Theory* (London: Jonathan Cape, 1999).

Resurrection and Cosmic Eschatology   165

In particular is the notion of Aquinas that resurrection occurs with the cessation of cosmic process at all plausible?

If we consider the cosmic alternatives open to us then one is likely to conclude that resurrection at the end of cosmic process is not a favoured option. Either there is no clearly distinct cosmic ending, as with the possibility of an open cosmos, extending indefinitely into an unbounded future, or there is a definitive end to the cosmos, but in some unimaginable time in the future, stretching into the billions of years. One would be inclined to ask what the theological significance of this gap between a plausible end of human history and any future cosmic ending might be. If one holds to the notion of an 'interim state', life after death prior to the resurrection, then it would seem an interminable delay. And would our belief in resurrection at the cessation of cosmic process necessitate us holding to a closed cosmos coming to a Big Crunch? Indeed this could render Christian faith scientifically falsifiable because it would link an element of Christian faith with one particular scientific possibility.

Of course there are two solutions to the problems so posed. If one assumes a form of timelessness in the interim state then an interminable delay is of no consequence, and the resurrection would be instantaneous upon death. This is a 'resurrection in death' position that has grown in popularity among Catholic theologians despite its rejection by the International Theological Commission. The Commission asserted the continued existence of a spiritual 'soul' after death, capable of conscious acts of intellect and will, with some sense of temporality, and hence an interim state prior to resurrection.[12] Remove these beliefs and the resurrection of the dead would then be in a truly 'new heaven and new earth'. Such a new creation would no longer be in strict continuity with the present cosmos. About it we could say nothing, or anything we like, since it is no longer related to our present experience in any way.[13]

---

12. International Theological Commission, 'Some Current Questions in Eschatology'.

13. In this regard the Commission speaks of a conception of resurrection as an 'ethereal body, which would be a new kind of creation, [and] would not correspond to the reality of the resurrection of Christ and consequently would pertain to the realm of fables.' International Theological Commission, 'Some Current Questions in

166 *From Resurrection to Return*

A second solution is simply to evoke divine intervention, which brings the cosmos to an end 'ahead of schedule'. This position would be in some respects the eschatological equivalent to those who promote 'intelligent design' as a *deus ex machina* solution to the problem of evolution. Of course divine intervention cannot be completely ruled out—after all, what is the resurrection of Jesus if not a divine act in human history—but it leaves us again being able to say nothing or anything we like. Nonetheless, given the nature of our present creation with its relativistic structures, the universe could still not simply 'end' while ever it is spatially extended.

The alternative then is to consider the timing of the resurrection of the dead in relation to the end of human history. Firstly we may consider the connection between final judgment and the end of human history. In his work of the theology of death Rahner asks whether the connection between death and personal judgment is intrinsic or extrinsic, that is, is death simply a convenient time for personal judgment to occur, or is there something intrinsic to the nature of death, conceived as a personal event, that links it to judgment?[14] The same question can be asked about the final judgment. Does judgment and the 'second coming' of Christ bring about the end of human history as some sort of external determination, or does the end of human history bring about judgment and the second coming?

Just as Rahner argues for an intrinsic connection between death and personal judgment, I would argue for an intrinsic connection between the final judgment and the end of human history. As noted above, the end of human history could come about from a variety of reasons. It is not unlikely that we will be the arbiters of our own fate, as the means of mass destruction become easier to create, and the sources of conflict take on an increasingly global reach. Alternatively our present inability to tackle our growing ecological problems could be the deciding issue.[15]

Eschatology', 214.

14. Karl Rahner, *On the Theology of Death* (New York: Herder and Herder, 1961).

15. Pannenberg describes 'apocalyptic ideas of a destruction of our earthly environment by the misuse of technology' as 'more compelling' possibilities for the end of history than biblical scenarios taken literally. See Pannenberg, *Systematic Theology*, volume 3, 590.

Such an end to human history would itself be a form of judgment, a judgment on the deep-seated nature of the problem of evil, both in the individual and in human history as a whole. It would also be a time of testing, of trial, with a corresponding temptation to despair and hopelessness. Indeed we might well pray, 'Save us from the time of trial.' (Luke 11:4)

Secondly, we must consider the divine response to such a human calamity. Would this apparent triumph of evil in human history be the last word, a final whimper with no-one left to hear it? Or would it be the occasion for the coming of God's definitive Word to pronounce a judgment that redeems all that was good and true in our difficult troublesome history, even while casting aside those very destructive elements that brought human history to its end? If God is indeed the creator God and Lord of history then it is fitting that the end of history be intrinsically linked to judgment and the second coming of Christ.

Thirdly, if all that is true and good in human history is to be redeemed at the end of history, can this mean anything less than the resurrection of the dead? The pattern of suffering, death and final vindication through resurrection is after all the pattern of Jesus himself. Should we expect anything less for the totality of human history itself? None of this implies of course that the end of human history would be a good thing, or an end to be sought after. Indeed it would be nothing less than an appalling evil and indictment on human history. The resurrection is not about justifying the evil that brings it about, but about redeeming and vindicating the good that evil seeks to destroy. It is the divine response of drawing good out of evil, a *creatio ex nihilo*.[16] And it clearly indicates that the hope of human history does not lie in human hands, as in the liberal myth of progress or a communist dream of a workers' paradise, or in Frank Tipler's notion of resurrection through cybernetic reconstruction.[17] Our hope lies in God alone.

---

16. I adopt the Augustinian notion of evil as privation. To draw good out of evil is to draw good 'from nothing', from the absence of good that constitutes evil as evil.

17. Frank J Tipler, *The Physics of Immortality: Modern Cosmology, God, and the Resurrection of the Dead* (New York: Anchor Books, 1994). A preliminary form of the argument is worked out in conjunction with Barrow in John D Barrow and Frank J Tipler, *The Anthropic Cosmological Principle* (Oxford: Oxford University Press, 1988).

3. The nature of the resurrection

The argument so far has been that it would seem fitting that the notions of final judgment and resurrection coincide with an end to human history, realistically brought about by human stupidity and/or evil and malice. This is the model of Jesus' resurrection, of suffering, death and vindication. To locate the resurrection 'at the end of time' creates a variety of problems: does time actually 'end'? Given the length of time involved what happens in the 'interim period'? However, the notion of resurrection at the end of human history involves its own set of distinct problems. It locates resurrection in this cosmos, in a universe we understand to some extent and about whose future we can reasonably speculate. The scenarios of endless expansion of the universe versus a big crunch can be just as problematic for either position.

Here one might express some sympathy for the speculative work of Tipler on the 'physics of immortality'. Tipler has put his finger on the problem. As Polkinghorne suggests, though resurrection cannot be reduced to Tipler's imaginative notion of cybernetic reconstruction, there is a certain sense in which it cannot mean something completely 'less than' what Tipler envisages.[18] If resurrection is about this cosmos then there are questions about energy and matter and their organisation that we cannot afford to ignore. However, I think Tipler's basic argument is around the wrong way. He argues for the continuance of intelligent life as an organising principle of the material universe leading to resurrection through cybernetic reconstruction of personal identity.

On the other hand, a position that argues, perhaps realistically, that human history and with it intelligent life may end, may well view resurrection as a creative act of God. In this way the divine source of all life enables intelligent life to exercise a continuing role as an organising principle of the material universe. This avoids the implicitly 'Pelagian' aspects of Tipler's approach (salvation through human, or at least cybernetic, effort), but maintains the concern he identifies, that

---

18. Polkinghorne notes that a capacity for information storage and processing 'is surely a necessary condition for life, even if one may doubt its sufficiency'. John Polkinghorne, *Science and Providence: God's Interaction with the World* (Boston: New Science Library, 1989), 95.

Resurrection and Cosmic Eschatology

is the need to think concretely about energy, matter and its organisation.

What I am suggesting coheres with Aquinas's classical theological account of the relationship between body and soul and the nature of resurrection. Following Aristotle, Aquinas considers the soul as the form of a living thing. In more modern language the soul is the principle of organisation, the intelligibility of the process of living. When speaking of the human being, the claim that the soul is spiritual means that the principle of organisation of a human being is intelligent, reasonable, and responsible. Thus we are oriented in our living to meaning, truth and goodness.[19] But what is being organised is the underlying reality of instinct, organs, biochemistry and so on. In the classical phrase, a human being is a rational animal. However, because the soul is spiritual in its orientation to meaning, truth and goodness (that is, it has a certain independence of materiality), it also has properties of being a thing in itself, or as Aquinas would say, the soul subsists. It can exist apart from the body, but in doing so it is deprived of its proper role as an organising principle. It is incomplete and in an unnatural state.[20] There is no hint of Platonism in his account of the separated soul. For Aquinas, as for Jewish and New Testament thought, resurrection is the restoration of wholeness to human existence. Resurrection is in some sense 'natural' in that it restores the natural relationship between the subsisting soul as organising principle, and materiality as something to be organised. Nonetheless the event of resurrection remains a supernatural act of divine freedom, that is it is not something

---

19. Cultural anthropologist Clifford Geertz argues that 'the extreme generality, diffuseness, and variability of man's innate (that is, genetically programmed) response capacities mean that without the assistance of cultural patterns [as carriers of meaning, truth and goodness], he would be functionally incomplete, not merely a taleneted ape who had, like some underprivileged child, unfortunately been prevented from realizing his full potentialities, but a kind of formless monster with neither sense of direction nor power of self-control, a chaos of spasmodic impulses and vague emotions'. Clifford Geertz, *The Interpretation of Cultures: Selected Essays* (New York: Basic Books, 1973), 99. Such is the central importance of our orientation to meaning, truth and goodness.

20. See St Thomas Aquinas, *Summa Theologiae*, First Part, Question 89, for his analysis of the state of the separated soul.

170 *From Resurrection to Return*

the soul can achieve by itself.[21] For Aquinas then resurrection remains a question of energy, matter and its organisation. The soul is restored to its proper role as an organising principle within the material order.

The problem Tipler consistently identifies is one of the availability of the required energy needed in order to sustain material organisation. He develops a number of very sophisticated theoretical arguments to support the claim that in various scenarios of 'cosmic eschatology' such surplus energy will remain available, through more and more exotic forms of cosmic manipulation by cybernetic intelligence. Fascinating though these are they shed little light on resurrection in a Christian understanding in that they clearly do not shed much light on the resurrection of Jesus, who is the source and type of all Christian understanding of resurrection. And one could argue that the scriptures themselves point in a different direction from that of Tipler.

It is well known that Jewish belief in resurrection is relatively late in Jewish thought, and can be found explicitly in Daniel and 2 Maccabees. However, this is also the same time that we find the first explicit understanding of *creatio ex nihilo*. Thus in 2 Maccabees 7:28 we find: 'I beg you my child, to look at the heaven and the earth and see everything that is in them, and recognise that God did not make them out of things that existed.'

This same linking between belief in resurrection and *creatio ex nihilo* is also found in the New Testament. There Paul speaks of God, 'who brings the dead to life and calls into existence what does not yet exist' (Romans 4:17). These texts point to a strong connection between a more metaphysically sophisticated account of *creatio ex nihilo* and belief in the possibility of resurrection.

Now *creatio ex nihilo* cannot be equated with, nor reduced to, the notion of a Big Bang cosmology. But a major issue concerning the Big Bang is its relationship to principles such as the conservation of matter / energy.

In that first instance of creation we seem to get 'something for nothing'. It may be, as some have speculated, that the positive energy of the universe is matched by an equal and opposite 'gravitational potential energy' so that 'the energy cost of inflating our universe could

---

21. This is the position developed at length by Montague Brown, 'Aquinas and the Resurrection of the Body', *Thomist*, 56 (1992).

actually be zero'.[22] Nonetheless there must be a process of 'creating' energy simply in the very fact that the universe exists. How such a process might work we may never know, but to deny the possibility is to deny the possibility of the existence of the universe itself. It simply cannot be scientifically denied. If so then there is no real need for concern about sources of energy for the required organisation of matter and energy needed for resurrection, since the one Lord who created the universe *ex nihilo* is also the agent of the resurrection and so can ensure that what is needed will be available.

4. Conclusion

These are difficult and speculative areas for theology. It is often tempting, I find, to escape into a spiritualism that effectively neuters any concern for the ongoing existence of the cosmos by declaring the whole matter irrelevant. 'Resurrection in death' is, I think, a similar strategy for eliminating such problems. However, as a believer, I remain convinced in faith of the goodness of creation, this creation. It is in and for this creation and its completion that we are both created and re-created in Christ. Some theologians have worked mightily to bring our Christian understanding of creation into some dialogue and congruence with scientific accounts of our evolving cosmos. The same struggle needs to be undertaken in relation to our eschatological beliefs and issues of physical eschatology. The alternative is to drive a deeper wedge between faith and reason, theology and science. Faith then becomes truly 'incredible'.

---

22. Martin J Rees, *Just Six Numbers: The Deep Forces That Shape the Universe* (New York: Basic Books, 2000), 131.

The Invasion of Memory:
A Psychological Perspective on Trauma in the Experience of God

Bruce Stevens

The sciences can help us to 'do theology' in different ways. Eschatology is a core theological theme and this book explores resurrection to return from an interdisciplinary perspective. Psychology is the science of the psyche. There has been considerable discussion about integration of the two disciplines, especially among Christian psychologists in the USA, but I think a better way forward is to apply psychological research and clinical insights to theological questions.

In this paper I will consider something familiar to all Christians: the passion of Jesus Christ. The psychological language that describes such human experience is trauma and survivors almost always report intrusive memories. This dimension of human suffering can be transformed through the resurrection of Christ. It also raises the theological question of how the human experience of Christ affects the life of God. The most vivid way this can be expressed is to consider the effect of violence, experienced by Jesus in his passion, on the divine memory. The purpose of this paper is to frame the question in psychological terms and suggest points for further theological reflection.

1. Beyond trauma

Trauma means wounding.[1] The body can be injured, so too the mind. There has been a recent explosion in understanding trauma, how it affects the brain and what works in psychological treatment.[2] People

---

1. In medical pathology trauma means a bodily injury by an external force or violence. See 'trauma' in *The Macquarie Dictionary*, second revision (Macquarie University: The Macquarie Library, 1987).

2. The literature on trauma is now extensive. A good overview is Bessel van der Kolk, Alexander McFarlane and Lars Weisaeth (editors), *Traumatic Stress: The*

The Invasion of Memory   173

commonly survive even extreme trauma—at worst torture. Some will present as patients and this provides clinical grounds for better understanding human experience *in extremis*.

Psychoanalysis has provided one of the most influential 'explanations' of trauma in the twentieth century. Freud developed a theory to understand hysteria (1895).[3] Initially he proposed the cause to be sexual assault, 'a precocious experience of sexual relations with actual excitement of the genitals, resulting from sexual abuse committed by another person',[4] but soon changed to an 'internal seduction' derived from fantasy associated with the oedipal crisis at about age five (1900).[5] In some ways the shift, from reality to fantasy, sent trauma research and treatment down the wrong track for many decades. Essentially Freud continued to understand the traumatic origin of neuroses to be largely internal, a 'stimulus too powerful to be dealt with or worked off in the normal way',[6] with the result being psychic helplessness in the infant (*Hilflosigkeit*). Trauma was also related to a deficiency in the protective shield (*Reizschutz*) against stimuli (1920).[7] He developed a new theory of anxiety in *Inhibitions, Symptoms and Anxiety* (1925),[8] which emphasised the relationship between trauma and the loss of the object (an internal representation of a significant person). And finally in *Moses and Monotheism* (1934–1938), trauma was the result of narcis-

---

Effects of Overwhelming Experience on Mind, Body and Society (New York: The Guilford Press, 1996).

3. Sigmund Freud and J Breuer, *Studies in Hysteria*, in *The Standard Edition of the Complete Psychological Works of Sigmund Freud*, volume 2, translated by James Strachey (Vintage, The Hogarth Press, 2001).

4. Sigmund Freud, 'Heredity and the Aetiology of the Neuroses', in *Standard Edition*, volume 3, 152.

5. Sigmund Freud, *The Interpretation of Dreams*, in *Standard Edition*, volumes 4 and 5. Also 'An Autobiographical Study', *Standard Edition*, volume 20, 1–74, especially 34.

6. Sigmund Freud, *Introductory Lectures on Psycho-analysis*, in *Standard Edition*, volumes 15 and 16, 275.

7. Sigmund Feud, *Beyond the Pleasure Principle*, in *Standard Edition*, volume 18, 7–64.

8. Sigmund Freud, *Inhibitions, Symptoms and Anxiety*, in *Standard Edition*, volume 20, 75–174.

174   *From Resurrection to Return*

sistic injury.[9] The role of memory was at times highlighted, but his perspective was generally intra-psychic.[10] Gradually psychoanalytic theory began to incorporate more of a relational perspective on trauma that naturally has included some recognition of external causes.[11]

In recent years trauma has been high on the research agenda. Much of it is empirical and draws on the hard biological sciences, just how trauma impacts the brain and makes physiological changes. There have been advances in psychiatric diagnosis. Post-traumatic stress disorder (PTSD) has been used to describe the effect of trauma on war veterans.[12] There has also been a growing awareness that this diagnosis is equally applicable to survivors of domestic violence and sexual abuse. Almost inevitably survivors of torture would have such symptoms but usually in the severe range of the spectrum.[13]

Victims of violence commonly present for clinical treatment. Mental health professionals commonly feel the horror that one person can do to another. What results is a kind of psychological vandalism: inevitably hidden and unknown except to a few—usually limited to family, close friends and sometimes a therapist.

The psychological effect of torture is brutal. The perpetrator has complete power, perhaps arrogant, certainly dominating. The victim

---

9.   Sigmund Freud, *Moses and Monotheism*, in *Standard Edition*, volume 23, 72.

10. T Bokanowski gave a historical review of this concept in psychoanalysis, in 'Variations on the Concept of Trauma: Traumatism, Traumatic and Trauma', *The International Journal of Psychoanalysis*, 86 (2005): 251–65.

11. Raul Hartke, 'The Basic Traumatic Situation in the Analytic Relationship', *The International Journal of Psychoanalysis*, 86 (2005): 267–90. A relatively early example of this was S Ferenczi, 'Confusion of Tongues between the Adults and the Child (The Language of Tenderness and Compassion)', *The International Journal of Psychoanalysis*, 30 (1949): 225–30. He accepted the reality of sexual abuse and rape of children to be far more common than was generally supposed, a fact that he derived from the perpetrators in analysis.

12. In general terms it is one of the anxiety disorders. PTSD was officially recognised by the American Psychiatric Association in 1980 with DSM III. The diagnostic classification was considerably refined in 1987 in DSM III-R and more recently in *Diagnostic and Statistical Manual of Mental Disorder IV-TR* (Washington, American Psychiatric Association, 2000).

13. It has been estimated that PTSD symptoms affect 8 per cent of our population.

The Invasion of Memory 175

is reduced to a frightened caged animal, tormented by the prospect of unending pain and unable to resist. It is to be awake in a nightmare. There is a frightening intimacy in torture: a dark secret place becomes besieged and invaded. If we take a developmental perspective: it is a return to the original state of helplessness, extreme dependency and usually only surmountable by the loving care of parents and family. Of course this dependency is betrayed in the link with the perpetrator, substituting torment for care.

The victim is helpless in agony. As Vinar commented, 'The triumph of the executioner is to create this psychic space where only terror resides and where the invocation and activation of this place becomes impossible, the resulting representation of this anguish making this process unbearable. Does this rupture between experience and its representation, between real-life experience and the relating of that same experience not constitute a traumatic experience?'[14] It is a transformation to *something unrecognisable as me*. This is illustrated by the surrender to Big Brother in Orwell's *1984*. Only extreme experiences such as in war or torture have the power to shake up and reconfigure the existing organisation of the psyche.

There are effects in the deeper layers of personality. It can evoke powerful splitting mechanisms (the most extreme form is multiple personality).[15] But more commonly it will lead to regression (becoming more 'child-like') and this can undermine the coherence of personality. In this state even symbolism, which includes a capacity for language, may be disrupted. The analyst Bokanowski (2005) noted, 'The patient's basic sense of self-identity has been disrupted; the mind's experiential content has suddenly disappeared and, with it, all meaningful links.'[16]

It is hard to fully appreciate the depth of the injury, 'There are two aspects of the psychological wound, that which is indecipherable and the scar of something dead and destroyed in the nucleus of psychic life.

---

14. Marcelon Vinar, 'The Specificity of Torture as Trauma: The Human Wilderness When Words Fail', *The International Journal of Psychoanalysis*, 86 (2005): 315.

15. The diagnostic label is now Dissociative Identity Disorder. See *Diagnostic and Statistical Manual of Mental Disorder IV-TR*, 526–9.

16. Bokanowski, 'Variations on the Concept of Trauma', 262–3.

176   *From Resurrection to Return*

The feeling of having crossed the limit of what is human, of breaking a narcissistic contract which binds us to humanity.'[17] The resulting fear is like a black hole that absorbs all mental life. It is a terror that is ever present.[18] But perhaps most disturbing is the abiding memory of the trauma: intrusive, emotionally chaotic and characterised by a reliving of the original psychological torment. It never ends. The victory of the perpetrator is to transform memory into something unbearable.

This dark and abiding reality of humanity's capacity for sin, which can create 'a hell on earth', is of course what Christ experienced.

2. Jesus: the humanity of God

The doctrine of the incarnation means that God became vulnerable in Christ. God does not become less-than-God, the Son is God but with human limitations (Philippians 2:5–8). The gospels portray Jesus' suffering. He had psychological and spiritual struggles, exemplified at Gethsemane (Matthew 26:36–46), being denied and forsaken by his disciples and later isolation: 'My God, My God, why have you forsaken me?' (Matthew 27:46) Jesus was possibly the only truly God-forsaken person who has ever lived.[19] He was also the victim of violence. The brutal fact is that he was tortured to death.[20] He suffered far beyond common human experience (1 Peter 2:24).

Jesus Christ, according to Chalcedon, was *vere Deus et vere homo*. If we are to think of his passion in psychological terms, then extreme trauma has psychological results. This is something that every mental health professional knows from clinical experience. If, for example, a

---

17. Vinar, 'The Specifity of Torture', 321.

18. There is some hope in analytic treatment, 'It is not just the carving of terror and pain on the psyche, a black hole which is unrepresentable and unthinkable; it is about considering a sublimatory destiny and opening up new creative pathways.' Vinar, 'The Specifity of Torture', 321.

19. See David Lauber, *Barth on the Descent into Hell: God, Atonement and the Christian Life* (Burlington: Ashgate, 2004), 31ff, and more generally for an insightful discussion of the implications of Christ's descent into hell.

20. In the first century AD torture could be either judicial or punitive. Jennifer Glancy, 'Torture: Flesh, Truth and the Fourth Gospel', *Biblical Interpretation*, 13/2 (2005): 107–36.

The Invasion of Memory 177

woman is raped and enters psychological or psychiatric treatment, it is common experience that most of the time in sessions will be spent talking about nightmares, reactions to cues and memories about the event that intrude in daily life. This leads to being guarded, or hyper-vigilant, in a way that can be psychologically crippling. It is not so much the event but the aftermath. In this way trauma is an injury to memory. In his humanity Jesus would not have been able to control the images and associated emotional pain from events of that terrible Good Friday. For example on the cross he may have had intrusive im-ages of being crowned with thorns, lashed, falling while carrying the cross and pierced by the nails. It is hard to know what went through his mind while dying, but this much would have been natural follow-ing the extremity of what he experienced. It is part of his suffering, at least until his death, that to some extent has been neglected in the theological tradition.[21]

It is natural to ask if such psychological vulnerability ended at death. 'It is finished'? Maybe not (John 19:30). There are two positions from which traumatic memory can be considered. The first is depend-ent upon a questionable anthropology. There have been theologies of 'the second day', which maintain that Jesus was conscious after death and through until his resurrection. This, in my view, is problematic since it rests upon a dualistic assumption of humanity as body and soul—two distinct substances.

There appear to be traces of dualism in the New Testament. This may be an assumption behind that difficult text in 1 Peter that appears to portray an activity of Jesus in the in-between state before the resur-rection: 'He was put to death in the flesh, but made alive in the spirit, in which he also he went and made a proclamation to the spirits in prison, who in former times did not obey.' (1 Peter 3:18–20) The gospel was 'proclaimed even to the dead' (1 Peter 4: 6).[22] The background

---

21. Irenaeus had the theme of recapitulation, in which the divine plan of salvation is to gather up everything in Christ to renew in the incarnate Son. It was Gregory Nazianzen who had the formula 'that which has not been assumed [by Christ] has not been healed, but that which is united to the divinity is also saved'. B Ramsey, *Beginning to Read the Fathers* (London: Darton, Longman and Todd, 1985), 77.

22. Balthasar did not understand this as Jesus preaching, more of an announcement being made. HU von Balthasar, *Mysterium Paschale: The Mystery of Easter*,

178   *From Resurrection to Return*

may have been an early tradition seen in Enoch, an inter-testamental book (12:5, 13:1, 16:4).[23] Paul asserted that Christ not only ascended but 'descended into the lower parts of the earth' (Ephesians 4:9). This seems Platonic with the inference of Jesus having a disembodied spiritual existence prior to a resurrection body on the third day (1 Corinthians 15:51–7).

The Apostles Creed eventually made the descent into hell, *descendit ad inferna*, an article of faith and while this was a later addition it reflected Christian teaching from the earliest times.[24] Not all theologians have accepted this with any degree of literalness. Some have rejected the idea,[25] while others have maintained that Christ suffered after death—the passion of Holy Saturday. An example is the medieval mystic Nicholas of Cusa, who wrote that God raised Christ 'delivering him from the torture of the underworld . . . Christ's suffering, the greatest one could conceive, was like that of the damned who cannot be damned any more. That is, his suffering went to the length of infernal punishment.'[26] The reformers developed this theme in different ways. Luther emphasised a state of God-abandonment.[27] Calvin

---

translated by A Nichols (Edinburgh: T&T Clark, 1990), 159.

23. See George Nickelsburg, *1 Enoch 1: A Commentary on the Book of 1 Enoch*, (Mineapolis: Fortress Press, 2001).

24. Inserted into the creed sometime between the fifth and seventh centuries. JND Kelly, *Early Christian Creeds*, Second Edition (London: Longmans, Green and Co., 1960), 378–83. Kelly mentions that it was explicitly mentioned by writers such as Ignatius, Polycarp, Irenaeus, Tertullian etc. Later two broad streams of interpretation can be distinguished, one in which Christ preached (Gospel of Peter, Justin, Irenaeus and Origen) and the other in which he performed an act of liberation on behalf of the spirits of the Old Testament saints. He also noted that the exegesis of the church fathers was that he went into the underworld with his divinity and human soul (*anima tantum* or soul alone), with his body still in the grave.

25. John Wesley dropped the line from the creed altogether! Edward Oates, SJ, 'A Review Essay on "Alan Lewis, Between Cross and Resurrection: A Theology of Holy Saturday" ', *Pro Ecclesia*, 12/1 (2003): 99–105, especially 100.

26. Nicholas of Cusa, *Excitationes*, 10 (Basle, 1565), 659, quoted in Balthasar, *Mysterium Paschale*, 170.

27. See his comments on Ephesians 4:8–10, in *Luther's Works*, volume 22, edited by

The Invasion of Memory

portrayed intense spiritual suffering, 'It was expedient at the same time for him to undergo the severity of God's vengeance, to appease his wrath and satisfy his last judgment. For this reason he must also grapple hand to hand with the armies of hell and dread of everlasting life.'[28] In this way Christ both suffered in the sight of men and then 'that invisible and incomprehensible judgment which we know he underwent in the sight of God'.[29]

Karl Barth followed the Lutheran tradition and saw hell as 'exclusion from God'. In the descent 'God Himself, in Jesus Christ His Son, at once true God and true man, takes the place of condemned man. God's judgment is executed.'[30] Leading theologians of the twentieth century have been understandably cautious about the imagery implied in the descent but found elements of truth. Pannenberg has written, 'There is some truth in the Lutheran understanding of the descent into hell as victory over Satan and hell: precisely by suffering vicariously the torments of hell and exclusion from the clearly perceived nearness of God, Jesus overcame this torment, the depth of the fate of death, for all men who are bound up with him.'[31]

Over the centuries the descent has been variously interpreted from the low point of Christ's humiliation to a symbol of his triumphant exaltation, as a victory over hell and death.[32] Some articulated a *Christus Victor* theme with his victory beginning in the defeat of demonic powers in hell, a theme expressed in Orthodox liturgies.[33] This has

---

     J Pelikan (St Louis: Concordia Publishing House, 1957), 322–31.

28.   John Calvin, *Institutes of the Christian Religion*, in *Library of the Christian Classics*, volume 20, edited by J McNeill, translated by FL Battles (London: SCM Press, 1960), book 2, chapter 15, 10:515.

29.   Also this was a greater and more terrible price in suffering in his soul the torments of the condemned and forsaken man. Calvin, *Institutes*, 516.

30.   Karl Barth, *Dogmatics in Outline*, translated by G Thomson (London: SCM Press, 1966), 118.

31.   W Pannenberg, *Jesus—God and Man*, translated by LL Wilkins and DA Priebe (London: SCM Press, 1968), 274.

32.   It can of course be where these two meet, the *status exinanitionis* and the *status exaltationis*. In this way a unity is formed (Philippians 2:8–11).

33.   The Orthodox have a triumphant liturgy where the focus is on Christ storming the gates of hell, breaking the bars and liberating the captives. Pickard noted that

180   *From Resurrection to Return*

been linked to universal themes such as his salvation reaching all.[34] Thielicke asserted what might be considered a safer conclusion, 'Since we know nothing about the inner dimension of Christ's death and passion, nor about the state between Good Friday and Easter Day, from this angle the dogma of the descent becomes the stage for wild speculations which are not subject to any theological control.'[35]

The consciousness of Jesus after death is, however, an interesting 'wild speculation'. There is an opportunity to take seriously the dimension of intrusive memory and include this unexplored dimension in the in-between of the Easter event. However, it is hard to avoid metaphysical problems of body-soul dualism in this account—both on biblical[36] and theological-philosophical grounds[37]. Was Jesus somehow conscious but still in the body in the tomb? Did he imagine himself 'preaching in hell'? If he was conscious before the transformation of the resurrection, then it is possible that intrusive memories became

---

'implied in Christ's active descent is a notion of a struggle of cosmic proportions'. S Pickard, 'He Descended to the Dead', *Ministry*, 6/3 (1996): 5. The gates of hell are broken (Matthew 16:18) and this is symbolised with the graves being opened with corpses raised (Matthew 27:52–3). The drama of the underworld struggle became an important feature of the medieval mystery plays. For atonement as victory see Gustaf Aulen, *Christus Victor: An Historical Study of the Three Main Types of the Idea of Atonement*, translated by AG Herbert (London: SPCK, 1937).

34.   J Moltmann asserted, 'Christ is ascribed saving potentiality for the dead. So the dead are not lost. Like the living they can draw hope from the gospel. That is to say, the dead too can arrive at faith, for Christ does not proclaim the gospel inefficaciously.' J Moltmann, *The Way of Jesus Christ: Christology in Messianic Dimensions* (London: SCM, 1990), 190. This brings the lordship of Jesus over the dead (Romans 14:9).

35.   H Thielicke, *The Evangelical Faith*, volume 2 (Grand Rapids: Eerdmans, 1977), 416.

36.   Joel B Green, ' "Bodies—That Is, Human Lives": A Re-examination of Human Nature in the Bible', in WS Brown, N Murphy and HN Malony (editors), *What Ever Happened to the Soul? Scientific and Theological Portraits of Human Nature* (Minneapolis: Fortress Press, 1998), 149.

37.   This is explored and I think convincingly argued in Nancey Murphy, *Bodies and Souls, or Spirited Bodies?* (Cambridge: Cambridge University Press, 2006).

The Invasion of Memory 181

part of the atonement and what he suffered 'for us and for our salvation'.

3. Death is death

The other position is that 'death is death' and Jesus tasted this fully in the in-between state. This is consistent with the idea that in the resurrection he was 'awakened' from the dead (cf. Daniel 12:2, Ephesians 5:14). Balthasar (1990) argued that death affects the whole person 'a situation which signifies in the first place the abandonment of all spontaneous activity and so a passivity'.[38] He understood being in the tomb to exclude communication with others.[39] Lewis argued for the paradox of 'God in the grave'.[40] In this view such a death was integral to Jesus' humanity. Perhaps when 'raised from the dead' (1 Corinthians 15:15) it was, in the words of Stephen Pickard, to 'reconstituted consciousness'.[41]

It is not easy to walk a fine line. I think it is important to maintain the enduring nature of traumatic memory in the human and possibly divine experience. Clearly human experience is to some extent transformed in the resurrection. For example on purely intuitive grounds it would make not sense for Polycarp, who was burnt at the stake as a martyr (about 155), to continually suffer the undiluted effects of trauma with intrusive memories. So resurrection seems to imply a healing or transformation of trauma. Indeed this holds out an eschatological promise for those who have suffered the effects of trauma in this life. It is a hope between resurrection and return.[42]

---

38. Balthasar, *Mysterium Paschale*, 148.

39. Balthasar, *Mysterium Paschale*, 149.

40. AE Lewis, *Between Cross and Resurrection: A Theology of Holy Saturday* (Grand Rapids: Eerdmans, 2001).

41. This was in a recent conversation with Associate Professor Stephen Pickard, School of Theology, Charles Sturt University.

42. See: 'Jesus was the last Adam, who represented the human race in his life journey. He was not the solitary victim of this crucifixion. He lived, died and rose vicariously on our behalf . . . in his death we have all died (2 Corinthians 5:14).' Clark Pinnock, *Flame of Love: A Theology of the Holy Spirit* (Downers Grove, Intervarsity Press, 1996), 108.

182   *From Resurrection to Return*

All this touches complex theological issues. There has been considerable discussion about whether God changed through the incarnation. The possibility of divine change has been maintained by leading theologians. Moltmann changed the metaphysically determined attribute of *immutabilitas* into the biblical notion of faithfulness of God in *Theology of Hope* (1967) and the *impassibitas Dei* into the possibility of love in *The Crucified God* (1974). I think of the Son becoming 'fully human' as a functional kenosis, which can avoid problems associated with the ontological assertions associated with classic kenotic Christology.[43]

In light of the passion it makes devotional sense to worship a God who has been touched by our suffering, identified with it and had a firsthand experience of the desolation of being human.[44] This recaptures a biblical idea of being-with or a relational ontology.[45] Moltmann went so far as to assert that the death of Christ introduced death into the trinity.[46] While this does might not make sense in metaphysical terms, it does in terms of adding human firsthand experience into life of the trinity.

I am on 'thin ice' with all this speculation, but there is an important question that remains. In what sense is the memory of God shaped by Christ's human experience? I think that there is a hint in the scars of the resurrected Jesus. He challenged Thomas in his unbelief, 'Put your finger here, and see my hands; and put out your hand, and place it in my side.' (John 20:27) The evidence of violation remained. There is a rough edge inherent in traumatic memory, and it is possible that

---

43. In the last century process theology moved to jettison the doctrine of divine immutability. K Ward, 'Cosmos and Creation', in John Polkinghorne (editor), *The Work of Love: Creation as Kenosis* (Grand Rapids, Eerdmans, 2001), 152–66.

44. Ward, 'Cosmos and Creation', 125.

45. See: 'It presupposes the genuine prospect of not being-with, of being against, and being-alone, in short, of discontinuity.' Lucien Richard, *What Are They Saying about the Theology of Suffering?* (New York: Paulist Press, 1992), 125.

46. Since the Son died, death is in God. J Moltmann, *The Crucified God*, translated by R Wilson (Minneapolis: Fortress Press, 1993), 200ff. See also 'Only the Trinity can both experience the rupture of that Saturday and accomplish the resumption which is Easter Day.' Lewis, *Between Cross and Resurrection*, 222.

The Invasion of Memory   183

such memory abides like scar tissue in the resurrected body.[47] Surely it remains as a painful memory, to be anything else would not be to truly remember. This is potentially a human contribution to all that which God remembers. It can add something, even to that which was already infinite, the knowledge of God.

The scars are suggestive of a greater reality: that of the humanity of Christ taken up into divinity. Not in this age abolished, certainly transformed, but maybe a source of 'new experience' for God! This suggests a different more dynamic, open ended teleological perfection, than the usual static perfection understood in traditional metaphysics—but I can not as yet suggest a satisfactory form.[48]

4. Conclusion

The people of Verona were fearful of Dante because they thought that he had visited hell. So too our fears are awakened by those who have been there in the experience of extreme suffering at the hands of others, and the few who return to tell the story.

The last hundred years has been a century of genocide and unspeakable trauma for millions. Sadly, with only notable exceptions, it has left survivors largely inarticulate and mostly forgotten. The four horses of the apocalypse have come and their names are bitterness, resentment, envy and revenge. It is almost inevitable when we are defined by our experiences in an age devoid of eschatological hope.[49]

---

47. The physicality of the resurrection is defended in M Harris, *From Grave to Glory: Resurrection in the New Testament* (Grand Rapids: Academie Books, 1990).

48. One way forward is Daniel Hardy's Trinitarian thought in which God's self-structuring occurs in an ongoing relationship with human life. Daniel Hardy, *God's Ways with the World: Thinking and Practising Christian Faith* (Edinburgh, T&T Clark, 1996), 16.

49. In our age we need to find a new interpretation of the descent. S Pickard, 'He Descended to the Dead', *Ministry Journal for Continuing Education*, 6/3 (Autumn 1996): 4–6. 'By thrusting God into such questionableness the narrative of Holy Saturday demands to be interpreted as "the end of all things", when history is ruptured and the world delivered up to godlessness and negativity.' Alan E Lewis, 'The Burial of God: Rupture and Resumption as the Story of Salvation', *Scottish Journal of Theology*, 40/3 (1987): 347.

184 *From Resurrection to Return*

The passion of Christ is of course trauma. This is a word from the discourse of psychology, but it can call theology back to its substance in the human life in dialogue with God. But my task is essentially theological. I have tried to follow Moltmann's challenge to see God through 'the passion of Christ, and to discover the passion of Christ in God.'[50] If we can better understand the passion, then we can better understand God. Perhaps it follows that if we can better appreciate the psychological dimension of Christ's suffering through the science of theology then we can glimpse something of the way this added to the experience of God, which ultimately reflects the love of God expressed to us most fully in Christ.

There was a third day. We live by faith at least partially in the third day initiated by the resurrected Christ. His was a 'memory invaded', but he came back speaking peace not revenge. This speaks of a reconciliation with self, others and God that is evident when trauma is no longer definitive. It is about transformation. The third day is ultimately about eschatological hope. This is a hope that does not abolish, nor does it forget, but remembers with ever increasing richness into the 'age to come'.

---

50. J Moltmann, *The Trinity and the Kingdom of God*, translated by M Kohl (London: SCM Press, 1981), 22.

Index

A

Actium 23
Adam and Eve 19
analogy 65, 97
analogy, heuristic of 60
analogy, principle of 56, 60, 61, 63, 72, 84, 89, 110
analogy in historical research 54
Anselm of Canterbury 124
apartheid 11
apocalyptic vision of resurrection 100
Apostles Creed 178
Aquinas, Thomas 117, 161, 162, 165, 169, 170
Aramaic 42
Arctic tundra 16
Aristotle 169
Armageddon 42
Ascension 34, 45, 51, 52
Athens 47
Augustine 72, 161
Augustus 23
Auschwitz 11
Ayala, Francisco 79

B

Balthasar, HU von 181
Barbour, Ian 75, 115
Barrow, John 80
Barth, Karl 11, 134, 136, 138, 146, 147, 149, 150, 179
beatitudinal thinking 95
Big Bang 12, 75, 77, 80, 90, 109, 170
Big Brother 175
Big Crunch 12, 163, 165
biology 78
Birch, Charles 115
Blake, William 15

bodily resurrection 68, 72
Bokanowski, T 175
Brown, Raymond 68
Buddha 13, 14
Buddhism 15
Bultmann, Rudolf 55, 72, 73, 97

C

Calvin, John 178
Catholic Church 158
Catholic International Theological Commission 164, 165
Center for Theology and the Natural Sciences 115
chance 140
chemistry 77
Chia, Roland 107
Christ-Omega 10
Christian worldview 51
Christology, evolutionary 129
church 125
citizens of heaven 24
Clayton, Philip 74
coming of Jesus 33, 34
complexity 143
contextual theology 1
contingency 109, 145
continuity 105
continuity and discontinuity 92
continuous creation 122, 139
convergence 136, 143, 144, 145, 150
Conway Morris, Simon 134, 136, 142, 143, 144, 145, 146, 150, 151, 156
Copernicus, Nicolaus 162
Corinth 38
cosmic Christ 10, 29, 51
cosmic Christology 20
cosmic eschatology 170
cosmology 54, 75, 79, 80, 82, 93, 113, 157, 158, 162, 163

186   *From Resurrection to Return*

costs of evolution 112
Coyne, George 115
Craig, William 68
creatio continua 115, 134
creation 21
creation, goodness of 17
creation, meaning of 131
creation, theology of 112
creation *ex nihilo* 137, 167, 170
Crosson, John Dominic 55, 62
crucifixion 4
cybernetics 170

D

Dante 183
Darwin, Charles 8, 9, 140, 152, 158
Davies, Paul 133
Da Vinci Code 15
Day of the Lord 38
death 181
design 140
directionality 145
discontinuity 92
divine action 3, 113, 120, 128
divine intervention 73
divine power 114
divine self-bestowal 120, 122, 123
doctrine of election 134, 147, 149, 150
dualism 17, 27, 177
Duns Scotus, John 120

E

ecological disaster 16
Edwards, Denis vii, 3, 95, 112
Einstein, Albert 162, 164
El Dorado 8
election, creation and purpose 148
election, doctrine of 134, 147, 149, 150
Ellis, George 74, 116
empty tomb 69, 70, 96
Enlightenment 8, 52, 53
Enoch   178

entropy 22
environment 86
epistemic reductionism 64, 65, 66
epistemic unpredictability 73
epistemology, holistic 62
eschatological consummation of the
    universe 132
eschatological future 87
eschatological hope 133
eschatological power 114
eschatological transformation of the
    universe 71
eschatology 1, 71, 103, 105, 112
eschaton 164
ethical praxis 154
ethics 154
Eucharist 50, 126
evil 12, 21
evil, nature of 18
evolution 3, 9, 74, 105, 112, 113, 140,
    142, 143, 158
evolution, costs of 112
evolutionary adaptation 143
evolutionary biology 79
evolutionary Christology 122, 129
evolutionary convergence 143
evolutionary optimism 7, 11, 22
evolving creation 146
existentialist interpreters 97
existentialist philosophy 64

F

faith 5, 100
final judgment 161
FINLON 109
firstfruits 21
first instantiation contingency 110
freeze or fry 80, 85, 89, 90
Freud, Sigmund 173

G

Galileo Galilei 158
general providence 74

Index 187

genocide 183
Gethsemane 176
Gnosticism 14, 15, 16, 20, 22, 26, 27, 42
God's kingdom 27
God's love 125
God's patience 138
God's saving action 147
Goethe, Johann 15
goodness of creation 17
Greek philosophy 5
Greene, John 142
Gulag 11
Gunton, Colin 140, 149, 151, 153

H

Haire, James vii
Happel, Stephen 116
Harnack, Adolf 102
Haught, John 115
Hefner, Philip 145, 153
Hegel, Georg 8
heuristic of analogy 60
Hewlett, Martinez 135, 145
Hezekiah, King 37
Hiroshima 11
historical explanation of resurrection 60, 63, 96
historicity of the resurrection 63
history 160
history, end of 163
holistic epistemology 62
Holroyd, Stuart 15
Homo sapiens 152
hope 5, 6, 7, 13, 17, 30
Hubble, Edwin 158
human suffering 172

I

idolatry 18
imago Dei 138, 150, 154
incarnation 176
inherency 145

integrated concept of purpose 156
intelligent design 73, 74, 90, 158
interconnection 154
interdisciplinary reductionism 66
interventionist God 73, 113, 117, 118, 119

J

Jesus as judge 45
Jesus Seminar 73
John Paul II 61, 114
judge 45
judgment 45, 46, 47, 49
Jung, Carl 15
justification by faith 47, 48, 50

L

Lakoff, George 65
Laplacian determinism 72
laws of nature 84, 89, 90, 109, 131, 132
laws of physics 78
Ledger, Christine vii
Lewis, AE 181
literalism 157
Lord's Prayer 27
love, omnipotent 114

M

Manichaeanism 26
marriage of heaven and earth 27
Marx, Karl 9, 11
material body 107
materialism 141
matter matters 71
McGrath, Alister 146, 151
meaningless process 152
Melville, Herman 15
memories 177
Messiah 22, 23, 39, 40, 46, 47
metaphysical naturalism 79, 90
methodological naturalism 75, 79, 90

188 *From Resurrection to Return*

methodological reductionism 65
Middle East 11
Milky Way 162
miracle 74
Mitchell, Joni 14
Moltmann, Jürgen 25, 57, 61, 68,
   182, 184
Moses 41, 50
Murphy, Nancey 74, 116

N

Nag Hammadi scrolls 15
natural theology 147, 150, 156
nature of evil 18
neo-Darwinism 141
neuroses 173
New Age spirituality 10
Newbigin, Lesslie 30
new birth 26
new creation 2, 22, 86, 91, 98, 102,
   104, 105, 110, 111, 131, 132, 156
new heaven and a new earth 28,
   29, 159
New Jerusalem 27
new law of nature 109, 110
Newton, Isaac 162
Newtonian determinism 72
Newtonian universe 164
Nicholas of Cusa 178
Nineteen Eighty-four 175
NIODA 73
nomological universality 64, 67, 85,
   90, 110
noninterventionist divine action 114,
   115, 117, 118, 119
noninterventionist resrrection 128
noninterventionist theologies 114,
   122, 126, 129, 133
nonreductionist evolution 146
Northcott, Michael 155

O

O'Brien, Graham vii, 3, 134

O'Collins, Gerald 68
omnipotent love 114
once-only action of God 138
ontological change 131
ontological change of resurrection
   132
ontological indeterminism 73, 74
ontological model of redemption 127
ontological naturalism 79
ontological reductionism 142
ontological salvation 127
ontological transformation 126
optimism, evolutionary 22
order 18
Ormerod, Neil viii, 4, 157
Orwell, George 175

P

Pannenberg, Wolfhart 57, 58, 59, 68,
   70, 71, 81, 88, 95, 100, 101, 102,
   104, 109, 164, 179
pantheism 10, 14, 20, 26
parousia 37, 38, 39, 40, 43, 45
Passover 21
Paul 11, 17, 20, 21, 22, 23, 24, 26, 27,
   36, 38, 39, 40, 41, 42, 43, 44, 47, 48,
   52, 68, 69, 70, 96, 97, 99, 106, 170
Peacocke, Arthur 62, 74, 116
Pentecost 21
Peters, Ted viii, 2, 3, 68, 71, 81, 87, 88,
   95, 135, 142, 145
Philippi 23, 38
philosophy 12
physics 75, 76, 78
Pickard, Stephen viii, 181
Planck, Max 78
plan of redemption 19, 21
Plato 5, 13, 14, 15, 20, 51, 169, 178
Polkinghorne, John 30, 74, 88, 91,
   96, 103, 104, 105, 106, 107, 108,
   116, 168
Polycarp 181
Pope John Paul II 61, 114
praxis of purpose 153

Index

presence of Jesus 32
principle of analogy 54, 56, 57, 60, 61, 63, 72, 84, 89
progress 7, 8, 11, 12, 13, 17
prolepsis 95, 98, 110
proleptic events 102
proleptic significance of resurrection 100
Prometheus 8
prosperity 8
protology 158
psychoanalysis 173
psychology 4, 62, 64, 172–184
Ptolemaic universe 162
public theology 1
purpose 3, 134, 145, 153, 156
purpose, theology of 134, 146, 149, 150, 151, 154
purposeful process 142

Q

quantum mechanics 76, 78
quantum physics 93

R

Rahner, Karl 114, 117, 118, 119, 120, 121, 122, 123, 124, 127, 128, 129, 130, 132, 166
rain forests 16
rapture 37, 41, 42, 158
Ratzinger, Joseph 163
rebellion 20
redemption 2, 19, 32
redemption, ontological model of 127
redemption, plan of 19, 21
reductionism 65, 66
reductionism, epistemic 66
reductionism, interdisciplinary 66
reductionism, temporal 66
reductive materialism 90
reductivist theology 126

referent 99, 101
relationships 153
relationship with God 155
relativity 93, 162
Renaissance 8
resurrection 3, 5, 16, 34, 55, 57, 59, 62, 63, 67, 70, 71, 74, 81, 82, 85, 95, 97, 98, 111, 123, 125, 164, 165, 168
resurrection, bodily 6, 68
resurrection, theology of 42, 127
resurrection of the dead 167
revelation 79
Ricoeur, Paul 65
Romantic movement 15
Rome 23
Russell, Robert viii, 2, 3, 54, 96, 108, 109, 110, 111, 112, 115, 116, 131

S

sacraments 126
salvation 124
salvation, theology of 124, 127
salvific action 147
Schneiders, Sandra 68
scientific explanation of events 72
scientific laws 84
scientism 141
secondary causes 117
second coming 2, 6, 33, 34, 35, 36, 50
secular history 64
sin 176
Sistine Chapel 50
social Darwinism 9
social gospel 9
special divine acts 118
special providence 74
special relativity 78
Stevens, Bruce ix, 4
Stoeger, William 84, 89, 116, 132
subjectivist explanation 98
suffering 112, 172, 178
suffering of Christ 177, 178

T

Teilhard de Chardin, Pierre 9, 10, 11, 12, 24, 30, 144
teleology 135, 145, 146, 150
teleonomy 135, 145, 146
temporal reductionism 66
theistic evolution 74
theistic evolutionists 145, 153
theology, natural 147, 150, 156
theology of creation 112
theology of divine action 128, 133
theology of purpose 134, 146, 149, 150, 151, 154
theology of resurrection 42, 113, 127, 128
theology of salvation 124, 126, 127
theory of evolution 158
theory of special relativity 162
Thessalonica 38
Thomas 182
time 87, 88
Tipler, Frank 80, 167, 168, 170
Tom Tracy 74
Torah 21, 160
Torrance, Thomas 139, 147
torture 173, 174, 175
transcendental argument 91
transcendental experiences 130
transformation 3, 40, 71, 85, 86, 96, 104, 105, 109, 127
trauma 4, 172–184
Troeltsch, Ernst 55, 56, 57, 58, 59, 60, 84, 97

U

uniqueness of humans 151, 152
universe 158, 162
universe, expansion of 163
Utopia 8, 12, 52

V

Vatican Observatory 114
Vinar, Marcelon 175
violence 4, 172, 174

W

Watts, Rikki 139
Weger, Karl-Heinz 118
Welch, Claude 56
William Stoeger 116
Worthing, Mark 108
Wright, NT ix, 2, 5, 32, 54, 55, 59, 60, 61, 68, 69, 81, 95, 96, 97, 98, 99, 101, 161

Y

Yeats, WB 15

Z

zimzum 25
Zion 35

Index 191

Biblical References

Genesis 1	18, 28	1 Corinthians 15:42–4	106
Genesis 1, 2	46	1 Corinthians 15:51–7	178
Genesis 1–11	160	1 Corinthians 16:22	42
Genesis 12	160	1 Corinthians 3:10–7	52
Psalm 2	47	1 Corinthians 51–4	40
Psalm 8	23	2 Corinthians 5:10	47
Isaiah 11	46	Ephesians 1:10	27, 113, 161
Isaiah 11, 65, 66	25	Ephesians 1:15–23	29
Daniel	160	Ephesians 1:19–20	24
Daniel 12:2	181	Ephesians 4:9	178
Daniel 7	34, 41, 46	Ephesians 5:14	181
Haggai 2:6–	19	Philippians 2:10	161
2 Maccabees 7:28	170	Philippians 2:10–1	51
Matthew 25	159	Philippians 2:5–8	176
Matthew 26:36–46	176	Philippians 2:6–8	51
Matthew 27:46	176	Philippians 3	24, 27
Mark 5:22	68	Philippians 3:20	41
John 11:1	68	Philippians 3:20–	16
John 16	50	Philippians 3:20–1	23, 40
John 19:30	177	Philippians 3:21	40
John 2:28, 3:2	43	Colossians 1	29
John 20:27	182	Colossians1:15–20	11, 20
John 5:22–30	49	Colossians 1:19–20	161
Romans 14:9–10	47	Colossians 1:20	113
Romans 2:16	47	Colossians 3:1–4	42
Romans 4:17	170	1 Thessalonians 4	40, 41
Romans 6:9	161	1 Thessalonians 4:15	37
Romans 8	26	1 Thessalonians 4:16–7	37, 39
Romans 8:1	48	1 Thessalonians 5	40
Romans 8:18–25	16	Hebrews 11, 12	29
Romans 8:18–26	19	1 Peter 1	16
Romans 8:19	26	1 Peter 1:3	67
Romans 8:19–23	113	1 Peter 2:24	176
Romans 8:22–23	27	1 Peter 3:18–20	177
1 Corinthians	22, 44	1 Peter 4: 6	177
1 Corinthians 11:27–34	50	2 Peter	29
1 Corinthians 15	21, 23, 24, 96	2 Peter 3	44
1 Corinthians15:12–20, 22	69	1 John 2:18, 22, 4:3	160
1 Corinthians 15:15	181	Revelation	27, 44, 160
1 Corinthians 15:19	26	Revelation 21:1	139
1 Corinthians 15:20	111	Revelation 21:5	113
1 Corinthians 15:23	37	Revelation 21:22	28, 160
1 Corinthians 15:23–7	40	Revelation 21–2	16, 27